How to Swing Trade

A BEGINNER'S GUIDE TO TRADING TOOLS, MONEY MANAGEMENT, RULES, STRATEGIES AND ROUTINES OF A SWING TRADER

© **Brian Pezim, BSc, MBA**
Preface by Andrew Aziz, Ph.D.

Traders at Bear Bull Traders
www.bearbulltraders.com

Published in Vancouver, BC, Canada

Email: brian@bearbulltraders.com
Website: www.BearBullTraders.com

First published in 2018
Copyright © Brian Pezim 2018

All rights reserved. No part of this publication may be reproduced, stored in a retrieval system, or transmitted, in any form or by any means without the prior written permission of the publisher, nor be otherwise circulated in any form of binding or cover other than that in which it is published and without a similar condition being imposed on the subsequent purchaser.

Pezim, Brian

How to Swing Trade: A Beginner's Guide to Trading Tools, Money Management, Rules, Strategies and Routines of a Swing Trader

Book typesetting by Nelly Murariu at pixbeedesign.com

Printed by Createspace

DISCLAIMER

The author and www.BearBullTraders.com ("the Company"), including its employees, contractors, shareholders and affiliates, are NOT an investment advisory service, registered investment advisors or broker-dealers and does not undertake to advise clients on which securities they should buy or sell for themselves. It must be understood that a very high degree of risk is involved in trading securities. The Company, the author, the publisher and the affiliates of the Company assume no responsibility or liability for trading and investment results. Statements on the Company's website and in its publications are made as of the date stated and are subject to change without notice. It should not be assumed that the methods, techniques or indicators presented in these products will be profitable nor that they will not result in losses. In addition, the indicators, strategies, rules and all other features of the Company's products (collectively, "the Information") are provided for informational and educational purposes only and should not be construed as investment advice. Examples presented are for educational purposes only. Accordingly, readers should not rely solely on the Information in making any trades or investments. Rather, they should use the Information only as a starting point for doing additional independent research in order to allow them to form their own opinions regarding trading and investments. Investors and traders must always consult with their licensed financial advisors and tax advisors to determine the suitability of any investment.

Preface

The current bull market rally which started March 9, 2009 is known to be the longest one on record since World War II. By 2018, the market has risen more than 300 percent since its low just 9 years ago. Everyone is talking about the markets these days, from coffee shop customers and baristas to nurses and grandmothers. The technology boom, along with widespread high speed Internet use, social media and new gadgets and apps has made everyone with even just a passing interest an armchair expert in the world of investing and trading. While the financial markets once only belonged to the elites of Wall Street, today teenagers are now doubling their parents' accounts by trading complex financial instruments like options or futures.

Millennials are connected 24/7 to the well of knowledge, the Internet, searching for every answer and not accepting unknowns. They do not want to leave their money in the hands of advisors, bankers and mutual fund managers who charge extremely high fees and offer very low returns. They are in control of their lives, and as a result, more savvy toward their investments and assets. Because of these new changes, we now have entered an interesting period for trading. Hot sector mania is not a new thing, but we see them much more often these days. In the past, hot sector mania used to be rare and happen only once every decade or so. They corresponded to technological revolutions such as the birth of the Internet or advancements in IT such as the dot.com bubble of the late 1990s. But today, trading has changed. We see a mania almost every few months. People rush to buy into a sector: the bitcoin and cryptocurrency mania of 2017, the FAANG mania of early 2018 (Facebook, Apple, Amazon, Netflix and Alphabet's Google), and the marijuana and pot mania of the summer of 2018. For traders, everything is different.

Who would have thought that a photo-sharing app like Snapchat with a 27-year-old CEO would be worth more on its IPO than American Airlines, Hilton, Best Buy or Ferrari. The stock opened at $17 per share and closed the day at $24.51, with the market cap as high as $34 billion. Or who would have imagined ordinary people rushing to buy bitcoin and cryptocurrencies in 2017. The blockchain stocks were the hot new thing that year. As Brian Pezim details in his book, the value of companies who simply mentioned the word "blockchain" in a press release would skyrocket. For example, a company called "Long Island Iced Tea Corp." (ticker: LTEA) changed their name to "Long Blockchain Corp." (ticker: LBCC) and decided to shift their focus from beverages to blockchain technology. The stock ran over 200% in a single day. Or who would have thought a company like New Age Beverages Corporation (ticker: NBEV), which sells beverages like tea, coffee and kombucha, would see its stock skyrocket 62.5% following an announcement that they would launch a beverage infused with cannabidiol.

As I sit at my desk writing this preface in September of 2018, the markets are incredible. Successful trading in these markets requires a new perspective and new strategies that complement this new era of trading. It's a whole new world out there! Old school trading textbooks and strategies developed by analysts decades ago need updating. Although those systems have their place, a considerable fortune can be made by adapting to the new market conditions. That is why I think this book is important and different.

I used to work with Brian at a company while I was doing research in clean tech. I traveled with him for work a few times and we became friends. He is older than me, he was semi-retired, and had literally tons of knowledge and experience to transfer to me. I soon learned about trading from him, and he in fact was the person who first introduced me to the world of trading. Although Brian is an engineer by training, he has developed exceptional skills when it comes to trading in the financial markets. He is now a friend as well as a colleague in our community of traders, Bear Bull Traders (www.BearBullTraders.com). We focus mostly on day trading in the stock market, but from time to time Brian will share his swing trades with us. Everyone in the community has been wanting to know how he swing trades. We encouraged him to write a book about his strategies, and he did.

As a person who has known Brian for a long time, I was excited to read his book, *How to Swing Trade*. In his book, Brian explains 3 strategies for swing trading: the conventional method of scanning stocks based on technical analysis, overnight gaps, and hot sector manias. I found these 3 strategies to be effective and easy to understand and execute. In his book, in addition to his swing trading strategies, he also writes about other aspects of swing trading that are just as important, such as proper tools, a sound psychology and effective risk and trade management.

Brian's book, in my opinion, is the quickest way for new traders to get up to speed with how to swing trade in the markets. I hope you enjoy reading this book as much as I did.

ANDREW AZIZ
Author,

1. *How to Day Trade for a Living: A Beginner's Guide to Trading Tools and Tactics, Money Management, Discipline and Trading Psychology*

2. *Advanced Techniques in Day Trading: A Practical Guide to High Probability Strategies and Methods*

www.BearBullTraders.com

Contents

Chapter 1: Introduction — 1

Chapter 2: How Swing Trading Works — 11

Swing Trading vs. Day Trading — 12
    Temperament — 14
    Availability — 15
    Lifestyle Balance — 16
    Financial Demands — 16
    Less Idle Time — 17
    Summary — 18
Swing Trading vs. Position Trading — 18
Market Participants: Retail vs. Institutional Traders — 19
High-Frequency Trades — 23
How to Start Trading — 24
Buying Long or Selling Short — 25
How to Enter a Trade — 32
Investment and Margin Accounts — 33
Chapter Summary — 37

Chapter 3: Tools and Platforms for Swing Trading — 39

Type of Account — 40
Commissions and Fees — 41
Platforms and Tools — 41
Tools Available Online — 44
Chapter Summary — 46

Chapter 4: Financial Instruments for Swing Trading — 49

Exchange-Traded Funds	50
Individual Stocks	57
Currencies	59
Cryptocurrencies	60
Options	61
Chapter Summary	63

Chapter 5: Risk and Account Management — 65

Assessing the Risk and the Reward	66
Setting Stops and Targets	68
Managing the Trade Size	73
Maintaining a Trading Journal	75
Trading Psychology	77
Chapter Summary	80

Chapter 6: Fundamental Analysis — 83

Total Revenue	85
Earnings per Share	86
Price to Earnings Ratio	87
Debt to Equity	88
Return on Equity	89
Short Interest	89
Hot Sector Manias	91
Bitcoin and Blockchain Mania	92
Chapter Summary	96

Chapter 7: Technical Analysis – Charting Basics — 99

Candlesticks	100
Bar Charts	103

Price Action and Psychology	105
Candlestick Patterns	107
Basic Bullish and Bearish Candlesticks	107
Reversal Candles	110
Engulfing Pattern	110
How to Trade Engulfing Candles or Bars	114
Doji – Harami Cross	115
Doji – Gravestone and Dragonfly	117
How to Trade a Doji	119
Gaps	119
Gap and Go	121
Gap and Consolidate	121
Gap and Fill	122
How to Trade Gaps	123
Chapter Summary	124

Chapter 8: Technical Analysis – Indicator Tools   127

Support and Resistance Levels	130
Diagonal Lines	135
How to Use Support and Resistance Levels	137
Moving Averages	139
Simple vs. Exponential Moving Averages	139
Moving Average Time Periods	144
The Golden Cross and the Death Cross	145
Moving Averages in Range-Bound Stocks and Markets	147
How to Use Moving Averages	147
Relative Strength Index	148
How to Use the RSI Indicator	151
MACD: Convergence and Divergence	151
How to Use the MACD	155
Average True Range	155
How to Use the ATR Indicator	157
Chapter Summary	158

Chapter 9: Technical Analysis – Patterns — 163

Double Bottoms and Double Tops — 164
   How to Trade Double Bottoms and Double Tops — 167
Bear and Bull Flags — 168
   Bull Flag — 168
   Bear Flag — 170
How to Trade Flag Patterns — 171
   Target Price Levels — 174
Bear and Bull Pennants — 174
   How to Trade Pennant Patterns — 176
ABCD Patterns — 178
   How to Trade ABCD Patterns — 182
Head and Shoulders Patterns — 183
   How to Trade Head and Shoulders Patterns — 185
Chapter Summary — 186

Chapter 10: Swing Trading Guiding Principles — 189

Keep it Simple — 190
Treat your Swing Trading Activity Like a Serious Business — 191
Develop a Work Plan — 191
Actively Manage your Risk to Reward Ratio; Focus on the Entry — 192
Measure your Results and Adjust Accordingly — 193
Chapter Summary — 194

Chapter 11: Swing Trading Rules — 197

Risks of Holding a Security — 197
   Earnings Reports — 198
   Announcements about a Product or Service — 199
   Secondary Offerings — 200
   Downgrades, Upgrades and Short Sellers Reports — 201

Other Announcements	202
Changes in Market Sentiment	202
Over-the-Counter or Penny Stocks	204
Chapter Summary	205

Chapter 12: Swing Trading Strategies — 207

Regularly Scanning for Trades	208
Review Overall Market Conditions	209
Review Performance of Market Sectors	212
Screen for Opportunities	215
Descriptive Tab	216
Fundamental Tab	218
Technical Tab	219
Review the Short List of Opportunities	224
Short-term Gap Trades	227
Trading for an Overnight Gap Up or Down	232
Hot Sector Manias	237
The 1990s Gold Rush	237
Dot-com Bubble	239
Marijuana Mania	241
Bitcoin and Blockchain Revolution	245
Strategies for Trading Hot Sector Mania Stories	245
Chapter Summary	248

Chapter 13: The Entry and the Exit — 251

The Entry	251
Limit Order or Immediate Fill	253
The Exit	254
Exiting for a Profit	255
Selling for a Loss	260
Chapter Summary	261

Chapter 14: The Routine of a Swing Trader — 263

Setting Goals, Objectives and Strategies — 264
Defining and Building a Routine — 267
    Time Schedule — 268
    Record and Review Process — 269
Chapter Summary — 275

Chapter 15: Final Thoughts — 279

Glossary — *283*

CHAPTER 1

Introduction

Swing trading is a type of trading in which you hold positions in stocks or other investments over a period of time that can range from 1 day to a few weeks or more. In this book, I will explain the fundamentals of swing trading and how it is different from other styles of trading and investing such as day trading or position trading. I will also describe some swing trading strategies that many traders use each day. These strategies, and others that you may decide to develop on your own, could provide you with an opportunity to over time make a good return on your capital.

If you are a beginner trader, this book will equip you with an understanding of where to start, how to start, what to expect from swing trading, and how you can develop your own strategy based on your personal goals. Simply reading this book will not necessarily make you a profitable swing trader though. Profits in trading do not come from reading

1 or 2 books. They will come with education, the right tools, practice and ongoing market research.

If you are a trader with some existing experience, this book will give you some insights on the author's approach to swing trading, rules that I follow and some strategies that I have used over the years to make profitable trades.

When I was a preteen, I would watch my father pour over the stocks in the newspaper and occasionally hear him on the phone with his broker, placing orders to buy and sell shares. One day I asked my father if he could buy some stock and he said sure. He opened an account and bought 1 (one), yes, 1 share of "The Bell Telephone Company of Canada". I still have that 1 share today and it has multiplied into a couple of dozen shares through splits and a dividend reinvestment program.

That was the starting point for my stock ownership/trading career. Ever since, I have been interested in stocks and the stock market and I have subsequently traded throughout most of my adult life.

The one thing we can all count on is change and this holds true for trading the stock market. When I started actively purchasing stocks, the Internet did not exist. If you wanted to research a particular company, you went to the library and asked for a file that would consist of newspaper clippings and maybe annual reports. Charts. What charts?

The advent of the Internet and online trading changed the financial industry dramatically. I tried my hand at day trading during the dot-com era. I made a lot of money and then lost a lot of money. It was a humbling lesson but I learned much and thankfully did not suffer the fate of many who lost more than they started with.

One of the many lessons I learned during that era was that it is easy to make money when prices are increasing (what's called a bull market). The key to keeping your money is managing risk and always being vigilant on the mood or psychology of the market.

I learned trading the hard way but hopefully I can make it easier for you. That is why I have written this book and actively participate on website for a community of traders called BearBullTraders.com.

In this book, "How to Swing Trade", I share how you too can take control over your life and have success managing your trades and investments in the stock market. You will need the right tools and you will need to be motivated, to work hard, and to actively manage your positions and risk. If you can learn and master these techniques, you have the potential to successfully manage some or all of your financial assets.

In this book, I start by describing what makes the market "tick" and the basics of charting. Understanding charting techniques is critical for a trader because it helps them to get a read on the psychology of the market at any particular time. I have written the first part of this book with the novice in mind and have attempted to make it concise, practical and easy to understand. It is written for everyone because I both share a passion to help others better understand the stock markets and to assist them in taking control of their financial situation.

Intermediate traders will benefit from this book's overview of some of the classic strategies that many professional and other Retail traders (they're the ones like us who trade for themselves and not for a firm) use effectively to swing trade. Traders who are already active in the market may decide to skim the first several chapters of this book that deal with how to set yourself up to trade securities.

For your convenience, at the end of each chapter I have provided a short summary in point form of what was covered in that chapter. More experienced traders can use this summary to ensure they already have an understanding of the skills contained in the content of the chapter. Novice traders can use this summary as both a review exercise and for future reference when they want to remind themselves of what was presented in each chapter.

The techniques that you will learn should allow you to see opportunities when they arise, and that will allow you to grow your portfolio over time. One important aspect of swing trading that you must understand and always keep in mind is that this is not a way to "get rich quick". It is a very common misconception that it is easy to make money trading stocks or other securities. Novice traders believe it is as simple as buying low and selling high. It sounds deceptively easy, but it is not. If it were that simple, everyone would be trading and making money.

You need to be prepared to work at this investment activity and treat it like a serious business. If you consider this to be a "get-rich-quick scheme", or you are not prepared to put the time and effort into managing your assets, then I recommend you take your savings to a registered and qualified investment advisor. Working with a professional would be a much better option compared to losing your money to some other traders in the stock market.

Having emphasized this point, trading can be a profitable way to add to your income and take charge of all or part of your own financial future. Keep in mind that it does require time and work to learn the techniques, to stay abreast of the market conditions and to monitor your positions. Traders who are consistently profitable always have a plan and they follow that plan while making adjustments as required.

In the first several chapters, I will discuss how swing trading works, how it differs from other types of trading and how this type of trading may be a good fit with your preferences and lifestyle. I will also discuss what a swing trader needs in terms of tools to do this type of trading as well as the different securities that you can trade. A swing trader has a number of different options that they can trade including individual stocks, Exchange-Traded Funds and currencies, to name but a few.

In Chapter 5, I discuss the very important topic of risk and account management. Your capital (money) is one of the most important assets that a swing trader holds. Without capital, you cannot trade, so you must actively manage your risk and capital at all times. This means you must trade with a plan that takes into account how much you are risking on a trade versus how much you hope to make. This is referred to as a risk to reward ratio and a good trader will only enter trades that are expected to give them at least 2 times the reward for the risk they are taking.

Another account management strategy discussed in the book is related to how much you will risk on each trade. A disciplined trader will not risk more than about 2% of their total account on any one trade. If you risk a significant amount of your capital on one trade and it does not go the way you hoped, it could result in a large loss of one of the things you value most as a trader: your money. Limiting how much you risk on every trade ensures that you will survive to trade another day even if you have a few bad trades in a row.

A good trader realizes that they will have losing trades and they will accept those losses and move on to finding the next good setup. I will discuss how you need to avoid taking losses emotionally or personally because the markets do not care how you feel or whether you win or lose. The best thing you as a trader can do is record the details of the trade and then review them, to both reinforce what you did right and to learn from any mistakes that you made.

In Chapters 6 through 9 you will learn some basics on fundamental and technical analyses that will be helpful in finding and entering swing trades with the best possibilities for success. I will discuss chart basics and conclude with some familiar patterns that repeat and often provide predictable outcomes that you can use and trade. The patterns work because they are, in a sense, a self-fulfilling prophecy. Many traders look for these patterns and technical indicators and will trade based on certain events happening. When you have a large number of traders all responding to a certain event in a predictable manner, then the outcome unfolds as almost everyone expected.

I will follow these chapters with a set of guiding principles and rules that I like to use when swing trading. My basic rules are ones that I have developed over years of trading and you are free to adapt them or change them as you see fit for your own swing trading style. For example, I do not like to hold stocks through an event such as an earnings report. These reports can cause a stock price to move significantly up or down. The problem you encounter is that there is no way of knowing which direction the price will move. This kind of event can give you a nice profit if you are right but it can also result in a significant loss if you are wrong. I view this more like gambling where you are at a roulette wheel betting on red or black. I do not like to gamble with my capital.

Chapter 12 covers several different swing trade strategies that you can use in your business. Two of these strategies do not work all of the time while one strategy can be employed regularly. That specific strategy involves finding and getting involved in what I call "hot sector plays". This strategy requires patience and diligence because these types of plays do not happen often, but when they do, they offer one of the best opportunities for a swing trader to profit and make excellent returns on their capital.

Another strategy of regularly scanning the market for tradable entries can be done in any market condition. Everything you require in order to do these scans is readily available for free on the Internet. You can change scanning parameters to search based on certain criteria that you decide appropriate for the market conditions and your own personal trading style preferences.

In Chapter 14, I discuss your routine as a swing trader. Swing trading is a profession, very much like engineering or accounting. Swing trading, similar to any business, requires the right tools, education and practice. You will have to spend a lot of time researching, practicing and managing your money. This means that you should develop a routine that you regularly follow. By following this routine, you will be able to actively and continuously monitor your trading business and measure your results accordingly. You can adjust and adapt your trading approach as market conditions change and you become a more experienced and skilled trader.

Your routine will also include starting and maintaining a trading journal where you will document your trades. This process will be very important to your trading business because it will allow you to methodically plan out each trade with as little emotion as possible. Making emotional and spur of the moment trading decisions can be a trader's worst enemy. Emotional trades tend to be irrational and certainly not well-thought-out.

By maintaining a trade journal, you will plan each trade you intend to enter, including the entry price and the price that you will exit the trade. There are 2 possible outcomes on the exit. You will either take a loss because the trade did not work the way you planned or you will book a profit. Knowing the exit prices before you enter the trade is critical to your risk and account management and, as mentioned, I will thoroughly discuss that topic in the coming chapters.

A trade journal also provides a document that you can reference to see where you were successful and where your trades did not work as planned. You cannot make improvements to your trading business unless you start by measuring your performance. The journal allows you to review trades and make adjustments to your style as needed.

I wrap up with some final thoughts for you to consider regarding a swing trading business. As a swing trader, you have the advantage of time. Compared to day trading, everything is slowed down, and that is a big help, especially for new traders. You do not get caught up in a process where you need to make a decision in seconds. This type of pressure situation is where many day traders lose out and let their emotions get the better of them. Swing traders have the luxury of time to make their decisions and are less likely to make an impulsive losing trade in the heat of the moment.

Lastly, at the very back of this book, I have included a handy Glossary of the most common terms you will come across in swing trading. If, as you are reading this book, you come across a term or phrase that you don't recognize or recall the meaning of, please go and have a look at its definition in the Glossary. I've used easy to understand language to explain the "lingo" of swing traders.

If you decide you would like to try swing trading, it will be a relatively easy process to start

1. **Start with a Business Plan:** think about why you are trading and what goals you want to achieve. Do you want to supplement an existing income, manage some of your assets to get better returns, become a full-time trader, etc.?

2. **Develop a plan and routine:** when will you do your swing trading work, what will your routine look like and how will it fit into your schedule with your other responsibilities such as work or family?

3. **Next step:** you do not need any capital to start. I suggest new traders start by "paper trading". This is the process of going through all of the research and work you would normally do to find trades and then pretend to trade them. Journal the process as you would with a real trade. By paper trading, you can determine if swing trading is something you would like to do and whether you can be profitable if you were to switch to trading with real money.

4. **Startup capital (cash):** determine how much you can afford to put into your business to start with. Everyone's financial situation is different and I recommend discussing your situation with a qualified investment advisor.

I hope that there is much useful information in this book that will benefit everyone from the novice trader looking to try swing trading to the more experienced and seasoned trader hoping to learn some new strategies or a new trading style.

CHAPTER 2

How Swing Trading Works

In this chapter, I will review many of the basics of swing trading and how it differs from other types of trading such as day trading and position trading. This chapter will also introduce you to some different types of participants in the market. At the end of the chapter, I will discuss the different types of accounts you can open as well as the process of buying and selling stocks.

What do you look for as a swing trader? You're looking for stocks that you expect to move in a relatively predictable manner for a period as short as overnight to as long as several weeks or more. Holding on to securities for periods of time longer than 1 day comes with risks, but it also comes with rewards. Investing in a security that is making a multiday run higher allows the swing trader to take advantage of and profit from those moves.

Let's look now at what differentiates a swing trader from other types of traders and their approach to investing.

In the following sections, I will look at a swing trader's approach to trading and compare that approach to the ones used by a day trader and position trader.

Swing Trading vs. Day Trading

Swing trading is a type of trading in which you hold positions in stocks or other investments over a period of time that can range from 1 day to a few weeks or more. In comparison, day traders hold positions ranging in time from several seconds to the close of the trading day. Day traders do not hold positions overnight – their trading positions are all cashed out when they finish trading for the day.

I do both day trading and swing trading. However, I am aware that I am operating 2 different businesses, and I understand that while these 2 types of trading methods have similarities, they also have some very key differences.

One of the key differences between day trading and swing trading is the approach to stock picking. If you are part of the community of traders at BearBullTraders.com, you will be familiar with the process we go through to find stocks at the beginning of each trading day. One of the key tools we use in the morning pre-market session and throughout the day is a screening system provided by a company called Trade Ideas. This is not a strategy you would use for picking a swing trade position. However, if you are alerted to a trending security in the morning, you might watch it throughout the day and then decide to hold it overnight, hoping to make additional profits on the following trading day.

While there are numerous strategies to identify swing trade opportunities, stocks that make for a good day trade can also be candidates for a swing trade in the short term. Veterans of Wall Street often talk about the 3-day rule, which refers to the period of time you should wait after a significant event happens to a company before taking a position. This is because it often takes a couple of days to shake out weaker stockholders and for the price volatility to subside. However, this volatility offers a swing trader an opportunity to capitalize on further follow through moves in a subsequent day of trading. I will discuss this strategy at greater length in Chapter 12, Swing Trading Strategies. To be clear, you do NOT need to be involved in day trading activities to do swing trading.

There are a number of other stock-picking strategies that you could employ for swing trading other than this momentum type trade from a stock that is trending daily. Many swing traders will also use strategies that identify stocks in solid companies that they hope will not lose a significant amount of their value overnight. Holding overnight or longer can provide for good returns but can also result in significant losses; therefore a swing trader should do more research to minimize their risk when holding securities for extended periods of time. I will deep dive into these strategies in Chapter 5, Risk and Account Management, where I discuss mitigating risk.

As a swing trader, you have a number of advantages over a day trader and you may find this type of trading more suitable to your lifestyle and personality. These advantages include the following:

1. **Temperament:** swing trading may be a better fit for your personality.

2. **Availability:** when is the best time for you to do your research and trading?

3. **Lifestyle balance:** finding time in your busy day to balance your work and leisure activities.

4. **Financial demands:** swing trading can be less financially demanding, especially if you are just getting started.

5. **Less idle time:** no sitting around waiting for an alert or a trade to set up.

Let's discuss each of these in a little more depth.

Temperament

If you are the type of person who typically does not like to make snap decisions, then swing trading could be a better option for you over day trading. One advantage swing traders have is the luxury of time. A swing trader has more time to consider their trades before taking a position in a security. They have time to analyze their trade with the tools that they choose to use with their strategy. In addition, they also have time to determine their risk and reward, which is critical to becoming a successful trader. In comparison, a day trader must make those decisions in as little as a matter of seconds.

Swing trading is good for a methodical thinker who likes to have time to plan their trade out in advance – to determine their entry point, analyze the upside and downside, and then settle on their exit strategy – and all before pushing their buy or sell button.

In summary, you are the one who is best able to determine if this trading style is a better approach for you and your particular personality. It is possible that you may be comfortable doing both types of trading, like myself. People who are comfortable day trading are often comfortable doing swing trading as well, but traders using swing trading strategies may not feel the same way about day trading.

Availability

The opening bell rings on all exchanges in North America at 9:30 AM Eastern Time (ET) and normal trading continues until 4:00 PM ET. The opportunities to trade outside of these normal hours are referred to as the pre-market and after-market, however I rarely trade during these periods due to the higher volatility and reduced predictability of price movements. That said, some traders do trade outside of normal hours and it is up to the individual to decide if that is right for them.

Your opportunity to trade the markets at certain times during the day is going to depend on where you live and, specifically, what time zone you are in. For example, I live on the West Coast, which puts me in the Pacific Time Zone (PT). This means that for myself, the markets open at 6:30 AM PT and close down at 1:00 PM PT. If you have a regular job in the PT Zone that requires you to be at work at 8:30 in the morning, then it is possible you could day trade for perhaps an hour before you need to get ready for your other job.

However, if you live in Chicago for example, and are expected to be at your office desk or on the shop floor at 9:30 AM ET, day trading at the market open is not going to work for you. In this case, swing trading would be a much better suited trading strategy given your availability. You have the luxury in the evening or maybe even on your lunch break to review the market action, check in on the stocks you are watching as well as set appropriate entry and exit orders. Hopefully the price movements of the securities will come to you and fill your orders during the day while you are busy with your other commitments.

Lifestyle Balance

As I discussed above, you must work around the markets based on the style of trading you chose to do and the time zone that you live in. You must also decide how you want to balance your life between work and play. Everyone is different – some enjoy their work so much, that is all they want to do. Others work hard and then on occasion they like to play hard. The bottom line is you need to figure out how to best balance your life and what works best for you and your personal situation. You may also have family responsibilities and other regular commitments that need to be taken into consideration.

Again, the advantage of swing trading is the flexibility it offers the trader. You are not tied to a specific time that you need to be in front of your computer. Almost every day you will need to take some time to review your positions, research and look for new opportunities, and just stay in touch with what the market is doing, e.g., going up, down or churning sideways. However, as a swing trader, the time that you do that review and research is more up to you and can be based around the other demands you have during your day and evening.

Financial Demands

In order to start swing trading, ideally you will have at least $5,000.00 to put into a trading account. More is better but you can start with less. However, the less money you have to start with, the more limited number of choices you will have in tradable stocks. To open a margin account, you must deposit at least $2,000.00 according to government regulations. The deposit can be in cash or in other negotiable securities such as stocks or bonds that you may already hold. More information on using margin and margin accounts will be set forth below.

In comparison, day trading accounts in the US require that a minimum deposit of $25,000.00 be put into your account before you can start trading. This amount may be out of reach for some people, so you can see the advantage of beginning your trading career with swing trading.

Consider a stock like Net Element, Inc. (NETE), a US-based Internet company that at the time of writing currently trades at around $10.00/share. If you have $5,000.00 in your account plus available margin, you will be able to purchase up to almost $10,000.00 in stock. Using NETE as an example, you would be able to buy 100 shares and have lots of room left to take positions in other opportunities.

In summary, swing traders can start with much less capital than day traders can.

Less Idle Time

I do not enjoy sitting around and waiting for something to happen. Most people usually have other things to do during the day such as chores, work, recreational activities, family responsibilities, etc. For a day trader, that initial hour of market action often provides the best trading opportunities from a risk to reward perspective. So many traders continue to trade throughout the day and get chopped out of trades – eventually giving back all of their profits from the open. Others do make additional profitable trades but there is considerable sitting, watching and waiting involved in-between tradable opportunities.

Swing trading allows the investor to take and/or monitor positions and then continue on with their other duties and responsibilities for the day. They are not tied to a computer screen waiting for an alert from a scanning software program or for a market event to take place that will move securities decidedly in one direction or the other.

In comparison, day trading requires a lot of sitting, which some will find tedious.

Summary

Given all of the factors listed above, swing trading may be a better option for you compared to day trading. However, as I previously mentioned, it is also possible to be a swing trader and a day trader. If you have the time, temperament and financial ability to do both, then that is an option you should consider. Many of the skills required to do swing trading, such as recognizing chart patterns, are equally applicable to day trading.

Swing Trading vs. Position Trading

There is another type of stock trader who is commonly referred to as a position trader. Position traders are usually large institutions such as mutual funds, but individuals can be position traders as well. Position traders make investments in a company's stock for the long run. They may feel that a particular company or sector is undervalued and they are willing to take a position in the hope that eventually things will turn around and the market will value their company in line with where they see it going in the future.

Warren Buffett would be a good example of a position trader. He invests for the long term and takes positions in companies he considers to be undervalued, either because of market conditions or because he expects the companies' fundamentals to improve in the future.

The one reason investors like Warren Buffett take positions is because they are managing billions of dollars. They cannot use their massive wealth effectively to buy and sell large quantities of stocks in a small capital company in a short period of time without moving the stock and distorting the market price. They will often make deals with other large security holders and trade shares using a block order (where a large number of shares are traded between 2 parties, usually hedge funds or institutions). The other option they have is to accumulate their positions over weeks or months. This is where the relatively small-sized swing trader such as yourself has the advantage over the position traders – you can jump in and out of positions without impacting the market price of a stock you are trading.

At the time this book is being written, Warren Buffett has just announced that Berkshire Hathaway has bought another 75 million shares of Apple Inc. stock in the first quarter of 2018. This is added to his existing position that is reported to be over 165 million shares. While a swing trader would never be able to take that size of a position, they can still benefit by buying based on the news of Warren Buffett's purchase, which is an event that moved the price of Apple stock.

Market Participants: Retail vs. Institutional Traders

Now that I have discussed the different trading styles that can be used in the markets, let's look at the different types of traders who are employing these trading styles. Retail traders are independent people who are likely trading from a home office. Retail traders can be part-time traders or full-time traders, but they are not working for a firm and they are not managing other people's money. Although it is much higher than compared to even 5 years ago, Retail traders still make up a relatively small percentage of the total daily trading volume in the market.

More and more people are striking out on their own and doing their own self-directed investing. The Internet, with its plethora of information and tools, has primarily driven this trend, along with the opportunity to trade online without the use of a professional broker. Many investors have discovered that with a little work they can match or better the performance of many of the mutual fund managers, especially when taking into account the at times exorbitant management fees being charged by these money managers.

The larger category of traders in the market are the *Institutional traders*, which include the Wall Street investment banks, proprietary trading firms (called prop traders), mutual funds and hedge funds. A lot of their trading is based on complicated computer programs (also called algorithms). In many cases, there are no humans directly involved in the trading operations of these large accounts. These Institutional traders have considerable money behind them and they are very sophisticated. These guys are pros and, as a Retail trader, you need to keep that in mind. These are the people and machines that you are competing against. Retail traders can compete with them, but you need the appropriate tools and a well-thought-out plan.

Individual Retail traders do have some advantages over Institutional traders. These Institutional traders are motivated to trade often and in large volumes. In comparison, Retail traders can wait for a good setup and trade when they see a good risk to reward opportunity. Institutional traders also have large accounts and cannot move their money in and out of a position as readily as a Retail trader. An Institutional trader is not going to take a 1,000 share position in the stock of a small company that trades 250,000 shares in a day. It is just too small for them to bother.

Mutual funds and similar Institutional traders may also have internal fund restrictions that prevent them from buying stocks that trade below a certain price or have a market capitalization below a certain level (market capitalization is the total value of all of the shares of a company, for example, if a company has 1,000,000 shares, and they are trading at $10.00 each, then their market capitalization is $10,000,000.00). This leaves some stock opportunities for the Retail trader that larger institutions cannot participate in.

Ironically, large numbers of individual Retail traders will not use this advantage to their benefit and for various reasons they will instead overtrade. They succumb to greed and fear and that causes them to trade unwisely. Instead of being patient and exercising the self-discipline of winners, they become losers by overtrading. Retail traders who want to be successful in trading with the professionals must be patient. They must also recognize and manage the psychology of fear and greed and how it affects a trader's actions.

With swing trading, you are waiting for an opportunity to move in and out of the market in a relatively short period of time in order to generate profits while keeping your risk to a minimum. That period of time can be as short as overnight (from the market close on one day to the opening of the market on the following trading day) to as long as several weeks or more. You don't necessarily want to outsmart or beat these Institutional traders. In fact, you may be trading with them and taking the same positions that they are building or already holding. It never hurts to hitch a ride on their cruise ship, but your advantage is that you can jump on and off of the ship very quickly, whereas it takes them a lot longer to stop or change direction. As a Retail trader, you are simply waiting for an opportunity to reach your profit target and either sell or start to scale out of your position.

Managing your risk is also easier as a Retail trader. You can follow your trading plan and exit your losing positions quickly if the stock you are holding does not move as you expected. This is much more difficult if a trader is holding several hundred thousand shares or more in an Institutional account. I will discuss determining your risk to reward and exit plan in Chapter 5, Risk and Account Management.

As a Retail trader, you can also play stocks that other Retail investors are playing. Checking in on social media sites like StockTwits and Twitter will give you a good sense of where Retail investors are investing their money, however, do not get caught up in the specifics of all of the posts. There are lots of twits on StockTwits making wild predictions and touting how they just made $7,000.00 on a trade in XYZ Company. Take everything you read with a large grain of salt.

A Retail trader can use these social media sites to their advantage in several ways. First, use these sites to find out where other traders are playing. I like to use the playground analogy – if you are in a playground at the far corner of the field and a bunch of people are playing soccer on the other side of the field, you're obviously not in the game. Hot stocks and sectors will show up as trending in social media – a swing trader should always be going with the flow, especially if they're playing momentum type trades.

Another way to use social media is to follow a handful of credible traders and posters. These traders make meaningful posts like, *"MU is bouncing off the 50-day moving average and may go higher,"* versus a meaningless post like, *"I just made $6,000.00 buying and selling Micron."* There is a huge advantage to being in a community of smart traders for harvesting ideas and getting other "intelligent" opinions and thoughts on individual stocks and the market.

Summarizing, as a swing trader, you must be careful that you are not on the wrong side of the trade against either Institutional or other Retail traders. Institutional traders can move markets, but they try to buy in or sell out of positions without distorting prices through aggressive buying or selling. As a Retail investor, you will never know for sure what these institutions are doing, so you need to rely on the charts and your own technical analysis in order to help you read the market sentiment. You can often see where Retail investors are playing by watching social media and using various technical tools. These technical tools will be explained in Chapters 7, 8 and 9 where I discuss technical analysis.

High-Frequency Trades

There are a number of investment banks, funds and other companies that base their trading on sophisticated computer algorithms. They trade frequently and at lightning speed. To illustrate how important speed is to these firms, some have located close to the exchanges while others install dedicated fiber optic cables to gain a tiny fraction of a microsecond execution on a trade. These types of trades are referred to as High-Frequency Trades (HFT) due to how often they happen during a normal trading day.

There is much debate about whether HFT are good for the market. Some say they add liquidity, while others say the machines are getting their trades in ahead of individual traders, which creates an unfair advantage for the machines and their operators. As a swing trader, you should not be overly concerned about these types of trades. These programs are often designed to make a profit by trading multiple times on very small moves in the price of the stock, hence the term HFT. As a swing trader, you are looking for larger trends or reasons to hold the stock longer than a few seconds.

These HFT can be annoying to some traders, specifically day traders. As a swing trader, you realize that all stocks will move in waves, climbing and falling as the day traders enter and exit positions or as funds try to take or exit larger positions in a stock. Swing traders are looking to capture moves that go on for days or weeks and are therefore not concerned with the minute-by-minute movements in a stock's price during a trading day.

In summary, you should be aware that there are many types of traders in the market, but as a swing trader, this should not affect your overall trading strategies.

How to Start Trading

Now let's look at how I trade in the market. Some readers of this book may already be well-versed in these concepts, but others who are completely new to trading will need to understand these fundamentals. In this section, I will discuss the following concepts:

- the types of positions you can take: going long or going short
- how to enter a trade and take a position
- I will look at each topic separately as follows.

Buying Long or Selling Short

A stock price will do 1 of 3 things over time: it will go up, go down or move sideways. As a swing trader, if you take a position in a stock, you are expecting it to either go up or down. If a swing trader expects a stock will go up in price, they will buy the stock. This is referred to as *going long* or having a *long position* in a stock. Being long 100 shares of Facebook, Inc. (FB) means that you have bought 100 shares of FB and are expecting to sell them later at a higher price for a profit. Obviously, going long is what you do when you expect the price to go higher.

This also means you are "bullish" on FB stock. Bulls expect prices to rise.

What if you believe that the price of a stock is about to go lower? In this situation, you can borrow shares and sell them with the expectation that you will buy them back at a lower price and make a profit. But how is it possible to sell shares that you do not own or hold in your account? Simple – brokerages have a mechanism that allows traders to "borrow" shares. Selling shares that you do not actually own is referred to as *going short*, or *being short* a stock. When traders say, *"I am short IBM"*, it means they have borrowed shares from their broker and sold them with the expectation that the price of IBM will drop and they will be able to replace those shares by purchasing them later at a lower price. It is still the same old adage of "buy low and sell high"; you're just doing it in reverse. You are selling high and buying low.

An investor who shorts IBM is "bearish" on that stock. Bears expect prices to fall.

When you set up your account to trade, you will likely need to fill out additional forms with your broker that will allow you to take a short position in a stock. You should understand that shorting a stock could be riskier compared to purchasing or going long on a stock, so you need to actively manage your position. Simply put, when you go long on a stock, the absolute worst thing that could happen is the company goes bankrupt and you lose all of your original investment. If you go short on a stock and the price starts to rise, your losses can be much higher than your original investment because there is no limit to how high in price it can go.

Let's look at an example from a company called Longfin Corp. (LFIN). Imagine you think the stock is overvalued at

$5.00, so you decide to short 500 shares and then go about your other daily duties without monitoring the position or setting up a stop (I will discuss stops later). The next day, you check your position and see that LFIN is now trading at $20.00. The 500 shares you sold for $2,500.00 now will cost you $10,000.00 to replace. If you decided to hold, thinking it could not go any higher, things got a lot worse, with the stock heading to a high of $140.00 per share. Replacing the 500 shares that you borrowed at that price would have cost you $70,000.00. This example is illustrated in Figure 2.1 below, the chart of LFIN.

Obviously, this is an extreme example and most smart traders would not have let this trade go so wrong. However, the example does illustrate an important concept about shorting stocks and the need to manage your position, especially when going short. You can lose a lot more than your original investment.

How Swing Trading Works 27

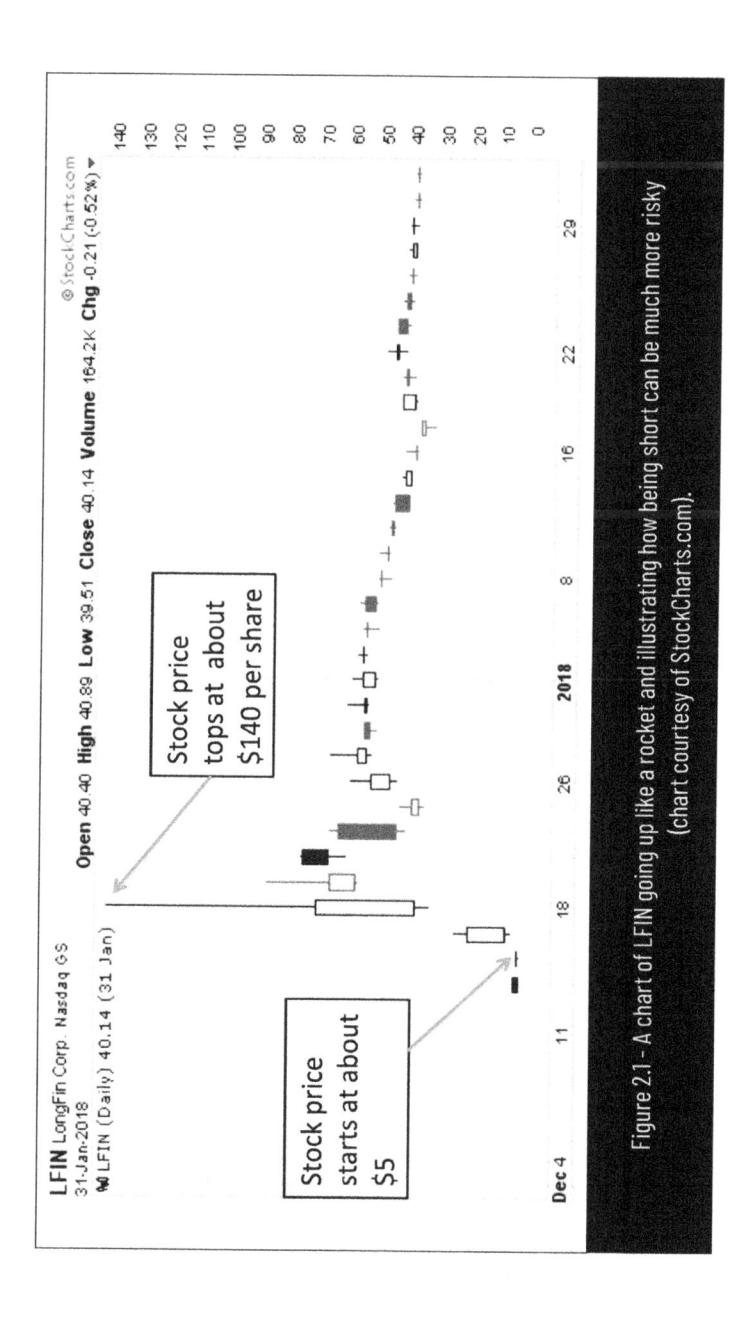

Figure 2.1 - A chart of LFIN going up like a rocket and illustrating how being short can be much more risky (chart courtesy of StockCharts.com).

Short selling is an important tool for a swing trader because stock prices usually drop much more quickly than they go up. It is a commonly held rule of thumb that stocks fall 3 times faster than they rise. The explanation for this lies in the human psyche – the fear of loss is much more powerful than the desire for gain. When a stock starts to move lower, shareholders fear they will give up their profits or gains and they quickly sell. This selling activity feeds into more selling as shareholders continue to take profits and traders start shorting. The additional shorting activity adds to the downward pressure on price. The stock price goes into a strong decline, which means short sellers can make very good profits while other long traders and investors go into panic mode and dump their shares on the decline.

The following is an old stock market adage with the Bull-Bear terminology:

**BULLS TAKE THE STAIRS UP;
BEARS TAKE THE WINDOW DOWN.**

As an illustration of this adage, look at the chart of SPY in Figure 2.2 below. This chart shows how SPY stair steps higher from November 2017 through January 2018. After 2 months of a gradual rise in price, SPY subsequently drops and loses all of those gains in about 8 trading days.

How Swing Trading Works

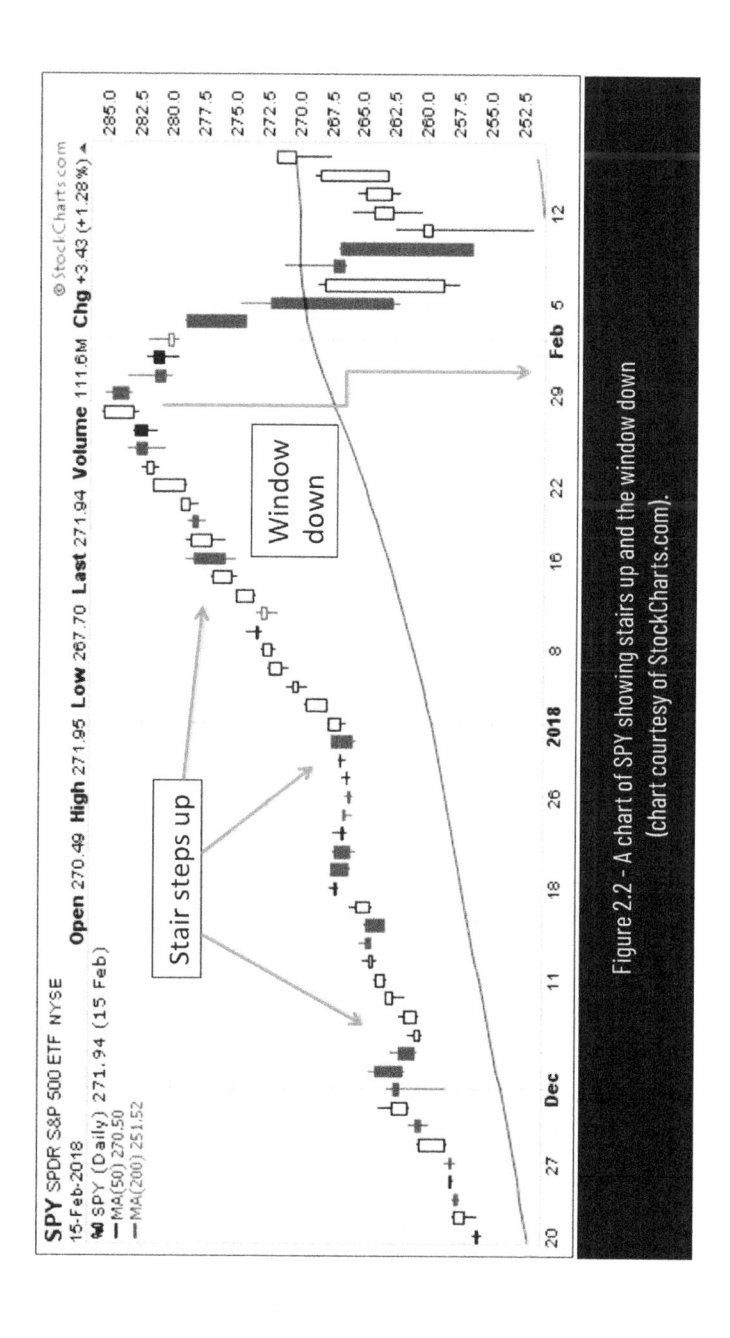

Figure 2.2 - A chart of SPY showing stairs up and the window down (chart courtesy of StockCharts.com).

One other thing to note in this chart is the gradual rise in the price with small waves of selling as SPY trends higher. This price action offers some insight into how it is relatively easy to make money in a bull market. There are very few violent moves that would shake a long-term stockholder out of their long position.

However, when SPY does roll over and the selling starts to kick in, notice how much more volatile the moves become. There are a few significant bounces that occur on the way down as traders try to pick the bottom of the sell-off. Traders who are short also cover their positions for fear of giving up their gains, which adds to the more volatile bounces. With each bounce up, eventually the buying runs out of steam and the sell-off continues with the trend continuing lower.

Let's discuss short selling a little more since it offers a good way to make a profit for a swing trader. Short selling was made legal in the US in 1937 and referred to as the uptick rule because you could only short a stock on a price move at or above the previous trade. This rule has been relaxed since then and now you can short on down moves in stocks. However, if a stock price is dropping significantly, exchanges can impose what is referred to as a *"short selling restriction (SSR)"*. Short selling restrictions impose an uptick rule temporarily to prevent an unwarranted precipitous drop due to relentless selling by traders taking short positions.

Shorting stocks as a legitimate trading activity is still hotly debated today. Some feel that short sellers unnecessarily punish investors by causing stocks to drop faster and in larger moves than otherwise would have occurred. In addition, short sellers can use social media and other methods to spread inaccurate information to cause a stock price to drop.

Traders who are active supporters of short selling argue that it brings more liquidity and healthy price discovery to the market. Short sellers often perform a large amount of due diligence to discover facts and flaws that support their belief that a company may be overvalued. Without short sellers, the price of stocks could unreasonably move higher.

Citron is an investment firm that specializes in attempting to find "overvalued" stocks. This firm is quite powerful. An announcement by Citron that indicates they feel a stock is overvalued often sends the price of that stock plummeting. For example, look at Figure 2.3 below, the chart of SHOP. On October 4th, 2017, Citron came out with research indicating they felt the stock was extremely overvalued based on their business model. SHOP's share price fell precipitously on this announcement.

Figure 2.3 - A chart of SHOP after a negative report from Citron (chart courtesy of StockCharts.com).

This news release provided a great opportunity for a swing trader to join the party by shorting SHOP. Knowing the power that a Citron opinion holds, it was obvious that this sell-off was going to be more than a 1-day selling event, as SHOP stockholders scrambled to get out of their long positions. It was like yelling fire in a crowded room; it takes time for everyone to get out.

In summary, there are 2 ways to make a profit trading a stock. You can be bullish and go long on a stock, meaning you will buy and hope to sell at a higher price. Alternatively, you can be bearish on a stock and, as a swing trader, you would borrow and sell the shares. This means you are going short and hope to buy the shares back at a lower price.

How to Enter a Trade

If you are a new trader, you are likely wondering how you buy or sell a security. Whenever the market is open, there are always at least 2 prices listed for any stock or other financial instrument being traded. There is a *"bid"* and an *"ask"*. A bid is what buying traders are offering to pay for that stock at that particular moment. The ask is the price that traders are wanting in order to sell. A bid is always lower because buyers want to pay less. The ask is always higher because sellers want more for their holding. The difference between the bidding price and the asking price is called the *"spread"*.

These spreads in the bid and ask can vary for each stock and even for the same stock at different times of the day. If the stock does not have a lot of buyers and sellers, then the spread could be quite large (up to $0.50 or more per share). If there are lots of buyers and sellers then the spread between the bid and ask could be as low as $0.01 per share.

When a swing trader wants to enter a position, they have 2 choices. They can pay what the seller is asking immediately or they can place a bid at or below the current bid price. Paying the ask immediately ensures that the order is filled (filled means the purchase transaction is completed).

When a trader places a bid at or below the current bid price, they may get a purchase at a lower price. The disadvantage of this purchase option is that the trader may not get their order filled. For example, if a trader puts in a bid to buy an uptrending stock, the bid may never get filled, leaving the trader without an entry in a profitable trade.

I will discuss more about entering a trade in Chapter 12, Swing Trading Strategies. An important factor to remember is managing the risk you are taking in each trade and making sure you are not chasing a security price past your planned entry. Managing your risk will be discussed in Chapter 5, Risk and Account Management.

Investment and Margin Accounts

Let's look at 2 types of accounts you can open to trade stocks. One is generally referred to as an *investment account* and the other is called a *margin account*. The margin account allows you to borrow against the capital that is in your account. The investment account allows you to buy up to the dollar value you hold in that account. A straight investment account is like a debit card; you cannot spend more than is in your account.

When you open a margin account, you may be able to borrow money from your investment firm to pay for part of your investments. This is commonly referred to as buying on margin. Buying on margin offers you the advantage of being able to buy more shares than you would be able to afford compared to having a basic investment account. It's a way of using leverage to get greater returns from your money. However, as with anything that offers greater returns, it also comes with greater risks. When you borrow money to make investments, at some point you need to pay back that loan. Making investments with leverage can magnify the percentage losses on your money.

Here are 9 things you should know about buying on margin:

1. You have to open a margin account to buy on margin.

2. Investing on margin is generally not allowed in "government registered accounts".

3. The brokerage firm sets the minimum amount you must deposit in a margin account. This is sometimes called the minimum margin.

4. How much margin you will have access to partially depends on the price of the stocks you're buying (usually stocks that trade under $5.00 are not eligible as margin security).

5. Your investment firm will dictate how much margin they are willing to offer you. This is called your maximum loan value.

6. Like all loans, there are interest charges applied to any funds you borrow to buy or sell on margin. Those interest costs may be a deduction from your taxable income.

7. The stocks you buy are used as collateral for the loan (unless they do not qualify as per point #4) and therefore must remain in your account in order for you to have access to the loan value of those securities.

8. If you are at your loan value maximum limit and your stocks drop in value (assuming you are long), your investment firm will likely ask you to put more money into your account to maintain

your margin. This is referred to as a margin call – more on that below.

9. Shorting stocks on margin have different funding requirements versus holding long positions on margin. Check with your broker on their specific funding requirements.

Different brokerages will offer different levels of margin. Some might offer to lend up to 100% of the value of your existing assets in your account. For example, if you hold 100 shares of a security that has a value of $50.00 per share, you have $5,000.00 worth of assets in your account. Therefore, the brokerage firm will allow you access to another $5,000.00 to invest in other securities. Sounds great, but as I mentioned, there is a downside.

If your $50.00 security suddenly drops to $45.00 per share, your broker is going to revise down to $4,500.00 how much they are willing to lend you. If you have already used that $5,000.00 margin to buy another security, you are going to get a call from your broker. This is referred to as a *"margin call"* and depending on the broker, they may expect you to sell some of the holding immediately to get you back inside of their borrowing requirements.

Alternatively, they could just ask that you immediately put more money into your account to meet their requirements. They also have the right to sell your positions to get your account back in line and they may do this without your approval.

Let's look at an example of shorting on margin. When you short a stock, a broker will want you to maintain a certain amount of excess capital in your account to make sure they do not end up with costs if you do not have enough money to buy back the shares you have borrowed. The usual amount is 150% of the original short value, so if you short shares and get $5,000.00 in your account from selling those shares, the broker will want you to have another $2,500.00 of other shares or dollars in your account as margin.

Imagine that you have the bare minimum when you enter a short. You have $2,500.00 cash and you went short 500 shares at $10.00/share so you have $5,000.00 from the short trade. Your account now holds $7,500.00 of cash and an obligation to replace those shares at a future date. But what if you are wrong and the stock moves against you with the price jumping to $11.00/share – now you immediately need $8,250.00 to maintain that 150% margin requirement (500 shares x $11.00/share = $5,500.00 **plus** the 50% of $5,500.00 = $2,750.00).

This is when you get the call from the broker to say you need to come up with the extra capital immediately or all or part of the position will be closed. Don't be surprised if the brokerage sells your shares without notice to ensure they do not incur any liability for your short position. It is their right to do so, but with proper risk management and an understanding of this aspect of margin trading, you should not ever get into this situation.

Going long and short selling on margin offers an active trader another tool for making money and getting a better return on their investment and can be very effective when combined with some of the strategies in trading that will be discussed later in this book.

Chapter Summary

In this chapter, I provided an overview of swing trading, participants in the market, trading basics and some swing trading rules. The following is a summary of the chapter for your review.

- Swing trading differs from other types of trading such as day trading and position trading, however, some of the basic principles of trading are the same.

- Swing traders look for stocks that are expected to move in a predictable manner over a relatively short period of time. That period of time can be as short as overnight (from the market close on one day to the opening of the market on the following trading day) to as long as several weeks or more.

- Swing trading may be a better fit as a trading style for some people due to their personality, time schedule and availability, lifestyle balance with other responsibilities, financial restraints that limit how much they are able to invest, and the less idle time that must be spent sitting in front of one's monitors waiting and watching for trading opportunities.

- I discussed how the Retail investor is a relatively small player in the overall market that is dominated with Institutional traders, which can give the Retail trader an advantage. They are easily able to enter and exit positions with small trades compared to Institutional traders with larger positions.

- High-frequency trading was discussed along with the fact that these participants in the market have little to no impact on swing traders.

- The term "going long" was discussed. Going long means a trader buys a security with the expectation that the price will go higher and they will be able to sell for a profit. When a trader goes long they are considered "bullish" on the security.

- The term "going short" was discussed. Going short means a trader borrows and sells a security with the expectation that the price will go lower and they will be able to buy the security later for a profit. It is the same principle as "buy low and sell high", but it is done in reverse. When a trader goes short they are considered "bearish" on the security.

- The basics of "the bid" and "the ask" were discussed when buying and selling a security. The bid is what traders are willing to pay for a security at a certain time and the ask is what the traders are willing to sell the security for. The bid is always lower than the ask and the distance between the bid and ask is called the spread.

- Different types of accounts were discussed including margin accounts. A margin account allows the trader to buy more securities than the value in their account. The broker essentially is loaning the trader funds that are secured by what is already in the account (cash or securities).

- A margin call will occur if the trader does not meet the loan requirements of the broker. In this case, the trader must provide more cash, more security or sell some positions to meet the requirements.

CHAPTER 3

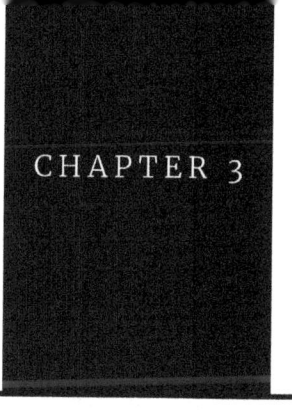

Tools and Platforms for Swing Trading

Like starting any other business and profession, be it part time or full time, you require a few important tools to trade. First, you will need to open an account with a broker if you do not already have one. Your broker will supply an online order execution platform. It will be up to you to learn how to use it, but all of the platforms are pretty straightforward and easy to use.

Fortunately, there are numerous brokers and stock trading platform options available today that allow you to trade online. The brokerage choices available to you will depend on the country you are currently residing in.

If you do not have an active trading account, I suggest you do a Google search to find current reviews on brokers in your area that come recommended. The following is a list of factors you will want to consider when choosing a broker:

1. type of account
2. commissions and fees
3. platforms and tools

Let us examine these factors in more detail below.

Type of Account

The first decision you need to make is whether to open an investment account or a margin account. I covered this topic extensively in Chapter 2 and discussed the pros and cons of these 2 types of accounts. Margin accounts allow you to borrow against equity that you hold in the account. This allows you to make bigger investments with your money, which can result in better returns but can also result in higher percentage losses. There are also minimum funding requirements for margin accounts.

You will also need to complete additional paperwork that will allow you to short securities. I discussed going short in the previous chapter as well and mentioned it can be a little riskier unless you manage your risk actively. From my perspective, not being able to short a security would be like buying a car that only has forward gears. I like to be able to play both sides of a security's move – remember, as a general rule, stocks go down a lot faster than they go up.

In summary, you will need to decide which type of account makes the most sense for you and your personal financial situation and whether you want to go short as well as go long. These are things you can always change or add later, so if you are not sure, start with the basics.

Commissions and Fees

Trading costs are usually on an investor's mind when it comes to buying and selling stocks. If you do several trades a day, these trading costs can add up. For a frequent trader, getting the best deal on commissions is somewhat important. However, as a swing trader, you may do several trades a day and there may be days when you will not trade at all.

Comparing broker commissions can be a little confusing. Many offer a flat fee that will typically range between $5.00 to as high as $25.00 per trade. These flat fees can change depending on how many trades you do in a month. Many brokers will give discounted trading commissions based on making a minimum number of trades each month.

Other brokers will charge a fee based on how many shares you purchase or sell (with a minimum charge). An example of this type of fee would be $0.005 per share with a $1.00 minimum. Therefore, if you purchased 1,000 shares of a stock, it would cost you $5.00 in commission.

Some also charge an activity fee or other fees depending on the level of services and tools that they provide; more about that topic in the next section. Regardless, if you are considering swing trading or position trading only, I suggest getting a broker with a commission rate of $5.00 to $7.00 per trade. This commission fee will not impact your account significantly even if you do a couple of trades every single day.

Platforms and Tools

Trading platforms can vary significantly from brokerage to brokerage. Some brokerage firms offer different levels of services for various costs. To do swing or position trades, you will want a platform that offers real-time quotes and a straightforward order process that executes immediately so you can confirm your trades.

It would also be ideal to have a platform that can do real-time charting, provide at least a basic level of technical analysis (moving averages, etc.) as well as provide research reports, financial data and analysts' ratings. These features are not absolutely critical though since you can get much of this information from sites like Finviz and ChartMill.

Some of the more powerful broker platforms will also have tools that do technical analysis and studies that will find the price and volume patterns that I look for as swing or position traders. These tools will identify and flag them for your consideration. While these can be helpful in making a trading decision, I never blindly trade off of these tools without further research.

In summary, if you do not have an account, I recommend that you do some research on a site like StockBrokers.com and find a platform that offers the following:

- Research: some platforms will provide exclusive research reports to subscribers. Much of the research you need is available online so I do not put much value on this factor.

- Investment offerings: some brokers will differ on what stocks, mutual funds and Exchange-Traded Funds they will allow you to trade. Most offer a relatively good range of financial instruments to trade, so again, I think most brokerages will be suitable.

- Education: there are brokers that will offer some tutorials on how to use their platform and maybe even some basics regarding stocks and trading.

These are nice to have but are not critical since the platform should be designed for ease of use and there are many resources available to better understand swing trading (such as this book you are reading!).

- Mobile access: having mobile access is "nice to have" but, as a swing trader, generally speaking, you should not be making trades on the fly. With that said, mobile access to your trading platform can be an asset on occasion.

- Scanning tools: you will also need a way to scan for buying opportunities. Fortunately, you do not necessarily need a real-time scanner like Trade Ideas, which is a tool that a day trader would utilize. Some excellent scanning tools are available for free online, which I will discuss in the following section.

- Alerts: the brokerage should provide an alert service that sends a text or email to a client when a certain event occurs. For example, if you are watching a stock for a good entry price, you can set an alert and then quickly act if needed, without letting an opportunity pass you by.

Let's discuss now some free services available to swing traders.

Tools Available Online

Fortunately for the swing trader, a number of excellent free resources and online tools are readily available. Below are several I have used in the past with some details on the kinds of information they provide.

- **Finviz (finviz.com):** the website name is short for Financial Visualizations. This site provides a massive amount of information on the stock market, different sectors, currencies, etc. It further provides financial analysis, research and data visualization, as well as excellent scanning tools. The website does a good job of summarizing a large volume of information into charts and maps. This is a go-to site for a swing trader and I will discuss using this site in Chapter 12, Swing Trading Strategies.

- **ChartMill (chartmill.com):** this site offers much of the same information provided by Finviz (discussed above). The site also has a proprietary rating feature that gives a grade on a stock's situation and rates the quality of the setup if a trader is considering entering a position. This is another excellent site to find investment opportunities.

- **StockCharts.com (stockcharts.com):** this is another excellent website that contains information similar to that offered by Finviz including charting tools, research data, commentary, and education. I have found that the ability to visualize data, such as through the services offered by StockCharts.com and similar companies, helps us to make informed decisions.

- **Estimize (estimize.com):** Estimize is an open financial estimates platform designed to collect forward-looking financial estimates from independent, buy-side, and sell-side analysts, along with those of private investors. The site also has an excellent calendar which can be used to see the upcoming company, government and industry announcements that might move individual stocks, market sectors or the market overall.

- **StockTwits (stocktwits.com):** StockTwits is a social media platform designed for sharing ideas between investors, traders, and entrepreneurs. Anyone can join and share their thoughts and ideas related to different securities. There are many worthless posts but the site does offer a way to see what is trending and actively trading.

- **CNBC (CNBC.com):** CNBC is a provider of business news and real-time market coverage.

- **Yahoo Finance (finance.yahoo.com):** a quick go-to website for business news, commentary and real-time quotes.

The websites listed above are only a few of the sites that a swing trader can utilize to find trading opportunities. These are primarily the ones that I utilize and I suggest you visit each one and become familiar with the information, research and scanning tools they offer. The scanning tools that are offered for free online will likely be as good as anything that your broker offers.

The services and information presented here were available as of the writing of this book. Be aware that the owners of these websites may change the service levels and information they provide at any time.

Chapter Summary

In this chapter, I discussed the tools that you will need to run a successful swing trading business. I also presented some free online resources that a trader can use for research and scanning tools. The main points of the chapter are outlined below.

- Different account types are available for swing trading. A normal investment account allows a trader to buy shares up to the limit of the cash deposited in the account. In comparison, a margin account allows the trader to borrow money against security that they have in their account. The additional borrowing gives the trader more buying power.

- Commissions and fees can vary between brokers. For a swing trader, the commissions are not as important because of the limited number of trades that are done with this type of trading. Most brokers offer competitive rates of under $10.00 per trade.

- Other services such as research reports, scanning tools, charting tools, etc. are offered by many brokers. They are nice to have but many of these resources are also available for free on the Internet.

- A large number of excellent resources are available on the Internet including, but not limited to, the following:
    - Finviz (finviz.com)
    - ChartMill (chartmill.com)
    - StockCharts.com (stockcharts.com)
    - Estimize (estimize.com)

- StockTwits (stocktwits.com)
- CNBC (CNBC.com)
- Yahoo Finance (finance.yahoo.com)

CHAPTER 4

Financial Instruments for Swing Trading

There are numerous types of financial instruments that you can swing trade with and each one of them has its own advantages and disadvantages. As I have discussed previously, each trader is different, so there may very well be one particular instrument you prefer over others based on your personal risk profile, your level of experience in the market, the current market conditions, your personal temperament, etc.

Below I will discuss a number of different instruments that you can consider for swing trading. The list is not all-inclusive but does cover the most popular vehicles for this type of trading. This list includes:

- Exchange-Traded Funds (ETFs)
- individual stocks

- currencies
- cryptocurrencies
- options

While I will discuss each in more detail below, I will focus my discussions on the first 3 in the list.

Exchange-Traded Funds

You can trade ETFs on the market through your brokerage account similar to how you would trade a regular company's stock such as Microsoft Corporation (MSFT) or Apple Inc. (AAPL). You can buy them and sell them as a day trade or hold them longer for a swing trade. In the United States, most ETFs are set up as "open-ended" investment companies. This type of investment structure allows the funds to have greater flexibility in utilizing futures and options as well as being able to participate in security lending programs.

ETFs have been available to trade in the US for about 25 years now. In 2008, the US Securities and Exchange Commission proposed changes that essentially loosened the rules on the requirements for ETFs. Since then, these funds have grown dramatically in numbers and according to the "2017 Investment Company Fact Book", ETFs now make up about $2.5 trillion dollars in value.

These funds have changed significantly since the first broad-based index fund appeared in 1993. This first fund was set up to track the S&P 500 Index. You can think of an ETF as a pool of investments that the owners each own a piece of. The manager of the ETF will have a set of objectives and policies that will dictate the focus of the fund.

Today you can find ETFs that track virtually everything from indexes and bonds to stock sectors, commodities, currencies, and even the volatility of the market. Most recently, several firms have tried to create an ETF based on holding a basket of cryptocurrencies. ETFs can also be used to play both the long and short side of the market. If you suspect a sector like gold mining companies is dropping in price, then you can in effect go short on gold mining stocks by going long on DUST – an ETF that goes up in price when the prices of stock in gold mining companies drop.

To make things a little more interesting, some ETF managers have also created what is referred to as *"beta"* funds. These funds use derivatives like *"options"* and *"futures"* to magnify the movements of the underlying asset in the fund. For example, UNG is an ETF that moves with the price of natural gas, which can be quite volatile on its own. If that is not enough excitement for you, try UGAZ, which is another ETF that moves in sync with the price of natural gas except, through the use of these derivatives, it will move 3x in whatever direction the underlying natural gas asset does.

For example, let's say the price of natural gas jumps up 3% on an inventory report. If you hold the ETF UNG, the price will be up about the same 3%, but if you owned UGAZ, the price of that ETF would be up 9% (3 beta times 3%). You can easily see that owning UGAZ is great as long as the price of natural gas is going up, but it is very painful for an ETF holder if the price of natural gas drops, as the loss is correspondingly magnified.

Another issue with beta (also called leveraged) ETFs is that they need to be rebalanced at the end of each trading day. I will not go into the details on how the rebalancing process works, however, for those who are interested, please feel free to research this topic for yourself. There's quite a bit of information readily available online. It is important for the leveraged ETF investor to know that their leveraged holding can lose value over time, and especially in a volatile non-trending market. That means leveraged ETFs are better to hold in a trending market (either up or down) and should not be held for an extended period of time like a non-leveraged ETF or mutual fund.

The following are some of the reasons why an ETF can make for a good swing trade instrument.

- Expense ratios: ETFs have a relatively low expense ratio compared to other investment vehicles such as mutual funds. You always have to "pay to play" though, so try to keep these costs as low as possible.

- Ride a sector: let us imagine you really like the biotechnology space in general. There have been some mergers and acquisitions recently in this area and all of the stocks in the sector are reacting positively. Rather than going out and trying to buy up a basket of stocks in the sector, you can purchase an ETF like XBI, which invests in S&P stocks in the biotechnology sector. This is a much more cost-effective way to invest in a number of stocks in a sector without actually purchasing small numbers of numerous stocks.

- Risk management: using the same example of the biotechnology sector being hot, let's assume you decided to go out and buy a few individual stocks in this space instead of an ETF such as XBI. One of them could have been PUMA Biotechnology Inc. (PBYI). While XBI has been climbing higher through mid-January 2018, on January 23rd. PBYI finds out they will not be getting a key drug approval from Europe and the stock falls from $94.00 at the close to $65.00 after hours. In comparison, XBI experiences a small drop of about $2.00 per share on that same day. The bad news hurts XBI a bit but this small loss is nothing in comparison to what happened to those owning PBYI stock. Which would you rather own in this situation? This is a very fundamental principle of security ownership and highlights how bad it can be if you're not diversified in your portfolio. *Diversification* means not having all of your eggs in one basket, therefore owning an ETF spreads your risk across the sector and not in one stock. Holding individual biotechnology stocks can be particularly risky when negative events occur such as seen in Figure 4.1 below with PBYI.

- Mobility of capital: using an ETF allows the investor to move in and out of sectors with a single trade. Sectors often rotate in and out of favor with investors. If you are long in one sector's ETF, and it looks like that sector is about to head lower in price, one trade can get you out of your long position. You are now back in cash looking for the next opportunity.

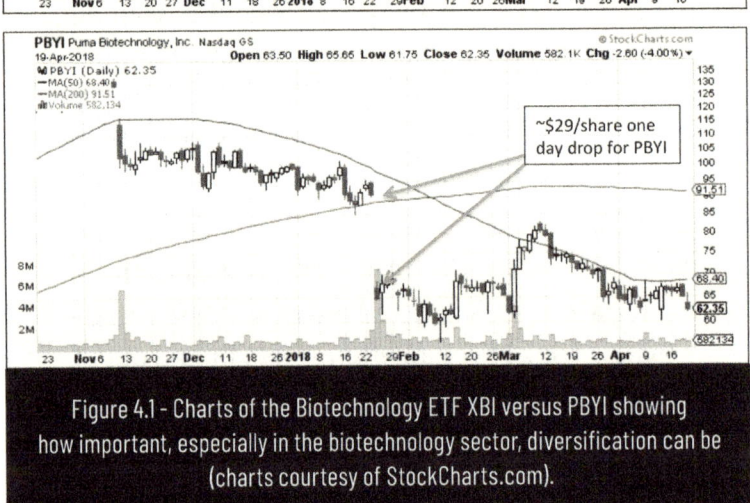

Figure 4.1 - Charts of the Biotechnology ETF XBI versus PBYI showing how important, especially in the biotechnology sector, diversification can be (charts courtesy of StockCharts.com).

Let's look at some of the more commonly traded ETFs and ones that I have traded in and out of in the past. I am not recommending that you trade any one of these funds specifically. You will need to do your own due diligence. What was traded in the past may not be a good trade today.

The Select Sector SPDR ETF is commonly referenced by professional traders and offers a good way to play a specific sector on the long side. This fund manager has an ETF that closely matches the entire Standard & Poor's 500 Index. They have also divided that index into 10 sectors and created funds that try to match the performance and yield of that underlying sector. They are listed in Table 4.1 below and offer a swing trader a good way to play the whole market or a sector trend on the long side.

Some Select Sector ETFs

ETF Name and Symbol	Focus of ETF
SPY	S&P 500 Index
XLU Select Sector SPDR	Utilities
XLE Select Sector SPDR	Energy
XLRE Select Sector SPDR	Real Estate
XLP Select Sector SPDR	Consumer Staples
XLY Select Sector SPDR	Consumer Discretionary
XLV Select Sector SPDR	Health Care
XLI Select Sector SPDR	Industrial
XLB Select Sector SPDR	Materials (commodities)
XLK Select Sector SPDR	Technology
XLF Select Sector SPDR	Financial

Table 4.1 - A list of Select Sector ETFs available to trade.

The Select Sector SPDR ETFs are fairly stable and may not move a significant amount from day-to-day but they do offer a good way to play a trend in a sector. They do not offer as much reward for the swing trader, but neither do they present as much risk of loss.

Let's look in Table 4.2 at some more volatile funds that a swing trader can use to play both long and short opportunities. Direxion is a fund management company that develops and offers "magnified" (leveraged) exposure to the underlying assets that the fund is focused on. Again, I am not endorsing these products. I am listing them here because they are popular and therefore heavily traded in the market. They offer large gains or losses should you choose to trade them due to the leverage mechanism used by the fund.

Some Popular Direxion Funds

ETF Name and Symbol	Focus of ETF
TNA	Russell 2000 Small Cap Bull 3x
TZA	Russell 2000 Small Cap Bear 3x
NUGT	Gold Miners Index Bull 3x
DUST	Gold Miners Index Bear 3x
LABU	S&P Biotech Bull 3x
LABD	S&P Biotech Bear 3x
SOXL	Semiconductor Bull 3x
SOXS	Semiconductor Bear 3x

Table 4.2 - A list of Direxion leveraged ETFs available to trade.

These are just a very small sample of Direxion funds that are offered by this one company. The 3x indicates that the fund will move approximately 3 times that of the underlying asset, so do remember that while this can offer significant gains, it can also result in much larger losses if you're on the wrong side of the trade.

You can also see that these funds offer a way to short without actually being short the asset. For example, the TZA

ETF will rise in price as the Russell 2000 market sells off. This means that even if you have not opened an account that allows you to short, you can still short the market or a sector through these types of bear ETFs.

ETFs are a good way to play sector uptrends and downtrends in both the market and a specific sector. There are even ETF products that allow you to play currencies and other countries' stock market performances. Don't be overwhelmed by the number of ETFs that are available to trade. Just be aware that they exist and can be a good option for playing a sector trend either up or down. Finally, be aware that leverage funds can erode in value day to day if the sector you are invested in is chopping along and not trending either up or down.

Individual Stocks

One of the obvious choices for swing trading is with individual company stocks. As I have discussed already, there are pros and cons to holding individual stocks. Holding an individual stock can expose you to single event risk. Suppose you are long a stock and some negative news comes out such as the loss of a big contract, an SEC investigation or a lawsuit. This is something you would like to avoid, but if you swing trade individual stocks, you are always subject to single event risk.

The advantage of holding an individual stock is that you can take advantage of a single stock setup or hot sector story that is playing out in some individual stocks. The marijuana sector got hot in 2017 but there were no good ETFs in that space at the time. There were, however, several clear leaders in the business and their stock price performance was stellar and made a lot of investors very wealthy.

Select single stocks will also occasionally perform better than their hot sector. Let's look at a comparison of Micron Technology, Inc. (MU) versus the XLK Technology Select Sector SPDR Fund. You can see in Figure 4.2 that the technology sector was a great performer through February 2018 but MU had a much higher percentage gain over the same period.

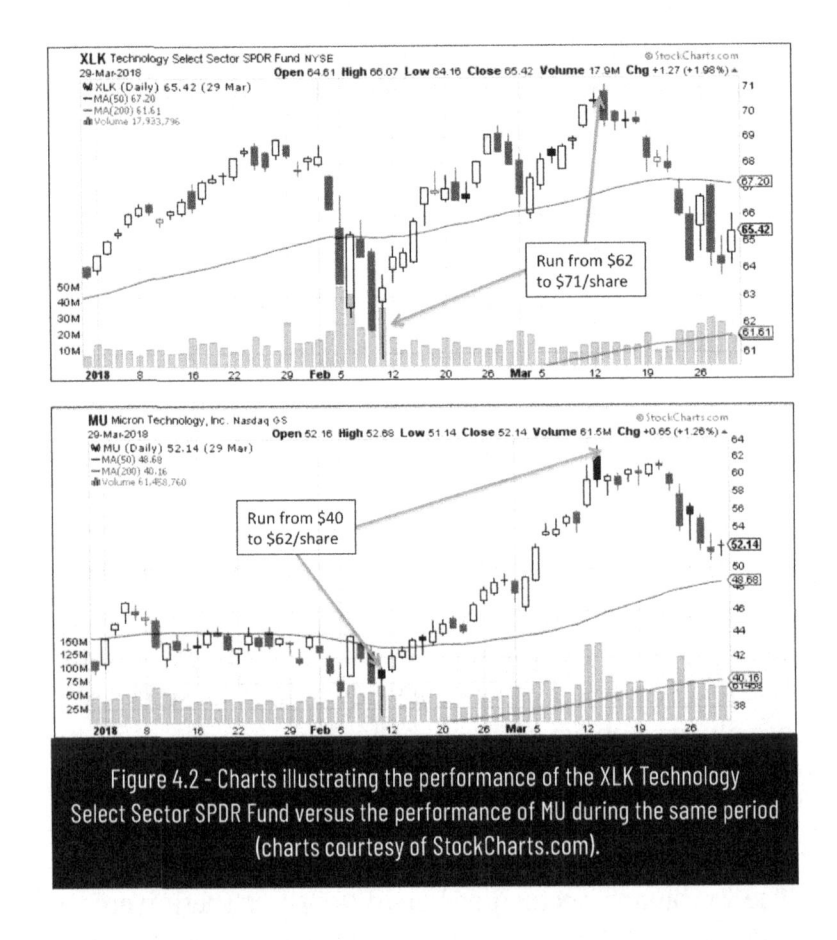

Figure 4.2 - Charts illustrating the performance of the XLK Technology Select Sector SPDR Fund versus the performance of MU during the same period (charts courtesy of StockCharts.com).

This is an example of a hot stock in a hot sector that would have made for a much better swing trade.

The ETF XLK increased by about $9.00 for a gain of about 15%, but in comparison, MU gained about $22.00 or 55% during that same period. This illustrates that you can get much better returns by investing in individual stocks but you also take on more risk by putting your money into a single stock with the potential of single event risk.

Currencies

I have also tried trading currencies in the past, but like most investments, I found that this is not a get-rich-quick proposition. With swing trading and day trading in the stock market, the Retail investor has some advantages compared to the larger players like investment funds and money managers. In the foreign exchange markets (forex), the smaller and often under-capitalized investor may be trading at a disadvantage compared to the well-financed forex traders.

The forex trader has a significant amount of leverage, which can be an advantage, however the forex trader also needs to apply the same risk management principles to their trading account and not over-invest in one position. They should keep investments to 1 to 2 % of their portfolio. On an under-funded account, this leads to small potential gains so traders will often break these risk management principles and use tight stops. Unfortunately, tight stops on forex trades will often get triggered and the investor will accumulate an ongoing series of small losses.

Forex trading as a swing trade vehicle can offer some opportunities but I do not recommend trading currencies for the beginner. If you are an experienced trader and you are interested in this trading vehicle, I recommend considerable research before you begin trading forex.

Cryptocurrencies

Trading these new currencies has been a whole new frontier and has attracted both sophisticated and very unsophisticated traders and investors. Some of the more popular coins include:

- Bitcoin
- Ethereum
- Bitcoin lite
- Ripple

There are many more cryptocurrencies and so called Initial Coin Offerings (ICOs).

Swing trading these currencies is not for the faint of heart. These trading instruments are constantly subject to single event risks with announcements about hacks, losses of coins, possible government regulations, SEC probes into ICOs, etc.

They made for great swing trades when Bitcoin and others were on a parabolic run higher. But like all parabolic runs, reality set in and prices came down as fast as they went up, leaving some overly optimistic investors in a lot of financial pain. As of the writing of this book, Bitcoin and other cryptocurrencies are very volatile.

I have heard of some traders using indicator tools such as moving averages to predict future coin price movements. These tools are also used to evaluate and predict stock price movements. Traders are using similar levels of 50, 100 and 200-day moving averages to find areas of support and resistance but I feel there is still too much uncertainty in these markets to be able to make smart trades and manage risk. I will be discussing the use of tools such as moving averages later in this book.

At this point, I believe that for the foreseeable future, there will be no big gains to be made in cryptocurrencies, and trading or holding cryptocurrencies is too risky for me personally. There are many varied predictions and opinions on the future value of these trading vehicles that range from zero to "the sky is the limit". Until a new trend emerges, I will not consider swing trading these currencies.

Options

To understand the opportunities in swing trading options, you first need to understand how options work. The following 4 items are required to define a stock option:

- the stock that the option is being applied to (AAPL, IBM, etc.)
- is it a "call" or a "put"
- the strike price
- the expiry date of the option

A "call" option gives the buyer the option to buy the underlying stock at a defined price (the strike price) before expiry. Obviously you would not exercise that option unless it was profitable for the trader.

As an example, FB is trading at around $170.00 in the middle of March 2018. If you think FB will go higher over the next few weeks, you can buy 100 FB shares for $17,000.00 or you can buy a $180.00 call option for $1.90/share that expires April 20th (at the time of writing, $1.90/share was the quoted market price to purchase this $180.00 call). Your 100-share investment in FB costs you $190.00 plus commission ($1.90 x 100 shares). Now you need FB to go up to over $181.90 per share to break-even on the trade ($180.00 strike price plus the $1.90 you paid for the options on 100 shares). Options move up or down in price with the underlying stock, so if your FB shares go up to $175.00 the following day, your option is going to be worth a lot more than the $190.00 you paid. You would likely have doubled your money or more with your $180.00 call rising significantly in value.

There is a downside though because if FB just trades sideways or drops in price, the value of your options will also drop until you get to April 20th at which time they will expire worthless if the price is not above the $180.00 strike price.

Playing a stock to the downside is also equally easy. Instead of buying a call, you would buy a put, which gives you an option to sell the stock before expiry. A put buyer benefits when the underlying stock price drops below the strike price but the same caveats apply to buying puts. They can expire worthless and your entire investment will be lost if the price of the stock does not drop as hoped for.

I do not trade options except on rare occasions and I do not recommend any trader participate in the options market without much more research than this book is providing. Regardless, it is part of the overall market and all swing traders should be aware of the following pros and cons for trading options:

Pros

- Allows for an investor to trade high-priced stocks with very little capital.
- Leverage is much higher in options so small investments can result in big rewards, but be careful, they can also result in big losses.

Cons

- There is a time limit on options and they can expire worthless, and that results in a 100% loss.
- Options have a time value so, as the expiry date gets closer, the value of the option will drop assuming there is no movement in the stock price.
- Option trading volumes are often much lower compared to stocks. This means that the spread between the bid and ask can be relatively wide making them more difficult to exit profitably.

There are also a number of different strategies traders and investors employ using options in combination with holding stocks. These are more sophisticated strategies and beyond the scope of this book. Regardless, it is good for an educated swing trader to be aware that these strategies exist in case they want to do more research and possibly employ these techniques in the future.

Chapter Summary

In this chapter, I discussed the various types of securities that you can swing trade. This book focuses on stocks, however you can use the same principles on a number of different trading instruments such as currencies, cryptocurrencies and options. Within the realm of stock trading, a swing trader can trade individual company stocks and ETFs. A summary of the chapter follows.

- There are numerous ETFs that a swing trader can use to trade. These ETFs can be used to trade almost any aspect of the market including specific sectors such as financials or biotechnology.

- ETFs can also be used to trade commodities, currencies, market indexes and market volatility to name a few.
- Trading an ETF can be less risky compared to trading stocks due to the single event risk that can happen with individual stocks.
- ETFs also can be structured by the fund owner to magnify moves of the underlying security. For example, an ETF that moves with the price of gold can be set up using derivatives to move twice as much as the price of gold moves. These ETFs are referred to as being leveraged or high beta.
- Individual stocks are another option for the swing trader. A good stock can move more than a sector of stocks does, therefore offering a swing trader a better return.
- Currencies and cryptocurrencies are another trading instrument that a swing trader can use, however, it can be more difficult to trade these due to higher volatility, the specialized markets, and the need for more capital so the trader can survive the waves of buying and selling without stopping out.
- Options were also discussed and are used by some swing traders in certain trading strategies. An in-depth analysis of these options strategies are beyond the scope of this book, but a general introduction was presented in order to help you determine if options trading might be of interest to you and therefore be something you should investigate further.

CHAPTER 5

Risk and Account Management

As a trader, the money you are investing in the market, your capital, is one of your most important and vital tools. Without capital, there is no way for you to make money, no matter how many other tools and skills you might possess. Protecting this capital should, therefore, be the highest priority for any swing trader. To protect your capital, there are 4 very important processes a successful trader must use:

- properly assessing the risk and the reward
- setting stops and targets
- managing the dollar size of the trade
- maintaining a journal of trading activity to measure and improve performance

Let's look at these 4 important risk and account management processes in more detail in the following sections. At the end of the chapter I will discuss trading psychology and how your emotions can impact your feelings about risk and, ultimately, your trading success.

Assessing the Risk and the Reward

Your most important objective in any type of trading is to manage your risk. The objective is not to buy and sell stocks – it is to make a profit. Your broker is the only winner when you are buying and selling stocks in the market. Your job is to manage your risk and your account. Whenever you click "buy" or "sell" (going short) on your trading platform, you expose your money to a risk of loss.

An unsuccessful trader will likely look at an entry and only think about how much they are going to make on a trade. A successful trader will always consider what is the upside and what is the downside on any particular trade. In other words, how much am I risking if I have to take a loss? This is not about being right on a trade or being wrong; it is about comparing the risk you are taking to the reward you hope to get from the trade. If you are risking a loss of $0.50 per share on a trade and only expect to get $0.25 per share as the upside reward, then this is NOT a good risk to reward ratio.

To have a good trade setup, you should expect to get at least 2 times the reward in comparison to the risk that you are taking. Obviously, having more than 2 times the reward is even better. If you use this risk to reward strategy in your trading, you will still be marginally profitable even if you are wrong 60% of the time.

Let's look at a setup for a good swing trade and how we can assess the risk compared to the reward. On February 11th

Risk and Account Management

a trader is looking at the chart of the ETF XBI and notices a nice setup for buying some shares (going long). The basic principles of why this trade setup looks good for a long will be discussed in the following chapters. Referring to Figure 5.1 below, an experienced swing trader would look at this chart and determine that if they went long on XBI at $87.50 per share, they would risk $1.00 per share ($87.50-$86.50=$1.00). At around the $86.50 level (the low close of a recent price move), a swing trader would consider the trade a failure and they would sell the position for a loss.

For the reward, they are hoping XBI gets to $91.00 per share (a prior *area of resistance* which I will discuss later in the book) for a possible gain of $3.50 per share ($91.00-$87.50=$3.50). In this setup, the trader is risking $1.00 per share to make $3.50 per share. That is a very good risk to reward ratio, and in this particular example you can see it worked exactly as expected, with XBI easily hitting the target price of $91.00.

Figure 5.1 - A chart of XBI illustrating a very good risk to reward ratio for a long trade setup (chart courtesy of StockCharts.com).

In Chapters 7, 8 and 9 I will discuss in depth how to recognize these setups and determine good entry and exit prices so you can determine the risk to reward of each trade you consider entering. A good trade setup will always offer a swing trader 2 times or more reward for the risk that they are taking.

Setting Stops and Targets

Now that I have discussed the concept of risk to reward, the next step is to understand how to put this into action. The stop-loss is a must for a successful trader and is one of the most important tools a trader will use to preserve their capital. A winning trader must have a belief that a stop-loss is one of their best friends. Any trading system or strategy will have losses – that is a given. A successful trader will accept it and move on from a losing trade.

Once you have done a complete assessment of a trade, and determined that your potential reward is at least or better than 2 times your risk, you will push the "buy" or "sell" button. Your capital is now at risk and you need to set your stop-loss price. This stop point is at a price level where you have determined that the trade is not going in the direction you expected. I will discuss how to determine a stop-loss price on a trade later in the book. You need to trade your plan and, if necessary, get out of the position before a small loss becomes a big loss.

As noted, the trade I outlined in the previously referenced Figure 5.1 worked perfectly as planned, but oftentimes they will not behave as you expect. XBI could have continued to trend lower, and in that case a disciplined swing trader would have stopped out, or in other words, sold their position for a loss. Remember: you must protect your capital so you can survive to trade another day.

It sounds simple to make a trading plan and follow that plan, but novice traders often get caught up in the emotion of the trade. They hate taking a loss because it seems like an admission of failure and they do not want to lose money. Rather than taking a small loss and moving on, they reassess and rationalize why they believe the trade will turn in their favor. Emotions take over.

As a swing trader, you must accept that the market is always right – no matter how wrong you think the market is! Keep your ego and emotion out of the trading equation. You, the trader, cannot control the market – you can only go with the flow. If you are rationalizing a trade or looking for justification as to why the stock or the market is not moving in the direction you expect, you are in trouble. You need to learn that losing on a trade does not make you an unsuccessful trader. There is no trader on Earth that makes profitable trades 100% of the time and you need to accept the fact that you will not be an exception.

Remember these words of wisdom from the famous economist John Maynard Keynes:

> "The market can remain irrational longer than you can remain solvent."

If you have already determined the level for your stop and it broke through that price, the chances are the security will move further against you and your losses will increase. You can likely imagine the 5 stages of grief that a novice trader will go through as they watch a trade go against them (and they have not followed their plan):

1. **Denial:** they cannot believe that the trade that looked so good when they entered did not work out as hoped.

2. **Anger:** *"The market makers hate me!"* or *"Those damn short sellers are killing my position!"*

3. **Bargaining:** *"OK, just get me back to break-even and I will get out."*

4. **Depression:** they feel depressed as they finally realize that they have lost money.

5. **Acceptance:** the pain of losing money becomes so severe, they close the trade at a much bigger loss than originally planned.

As I discussed, the advantage for a swing trader is that everything slows down. Day traders can more easily get caught up in the emotion of the moment because everything in day trading is happening so quickly. As a swing trader, you have time to sit and consider what is happening with the trade you have entered, so it should be easier to take stock of your emotion and follow your trade plan objectively. You just need to be aware of the trap that many novice traders fall into by not making and following a trading plan.

The discipline in following your trading plan also applies to taking profits at your expected target price. When a trade becomes a winner, people are inclined to immediately take a profit to reinforce their inherent need to be right. Some traders want to believe that they can achieve a high win/loss ratio, and as long as they close out a trade profitably, then they will be a profitable trader. A novice trader may see a profit in a trade, but instead of sticking with their planned exit strategy, they take profits before the target is hit, fearing that their gain will reverse and turn into a loss.

Unfortunately, taking profits too early negates the process you initially went through to determine your risk to reward ratio. By exiting a trade early, you may be barely getting a 1 to 1 risk to reward ratio. That means you now need to be right 50% of the time just to break-even. Those odds are not nearly as good as getting at least 2 times the reward in comparison to the risk you are taking. You surely do not want to spend all of that time and effort just to break-even.

There are, however, occasions when a trader might want to change their original trading plan. Again, as a swing trader, you have the luxury of time and therefore the ability to monitor your trades as they unfold. This includes constantly monitoring existing positions to ensure that nothing has changed from the time you entered the trade.

For example, assume you entered a trade in the Health Care ETF XLV in May 2015. You liked the way it was trading technically and the fundamentals were good, with the overall market consensus that the sector will continue higher. Your trade is looking good, and then a chorus of tweets hits the wire from US politicians about the greedy, evil health care companies ratcheting up prices. This immediate turn of events is not good news for health care stocks.

The successful swing trader will refer to their trade journal and review each trade on an ongoing basis to see if their assumptions about the trade have changed and gone from positive to negative. This will not happen often, but the health care news described above is a good example of a situation where you should change your plan. Having politicians use the stock sector you're invested in as a political punching bag is not going to end well. It's time to get out immediately and not wait for your stop to be hit.

Refer to the XLV chart in Figure 5.2. Imagine a trader had entered a long trade on the stock in early April 2015 and had already seen some good gains and was targeting higher, but then the bad political news hit the sector. By constantly monitoring positions, the trader would have avoided seeing a winner turn into a loser by recognizing something had significantly changed regarding the assumptions in their trade plan. An alert trader would have exited the trade quickly.

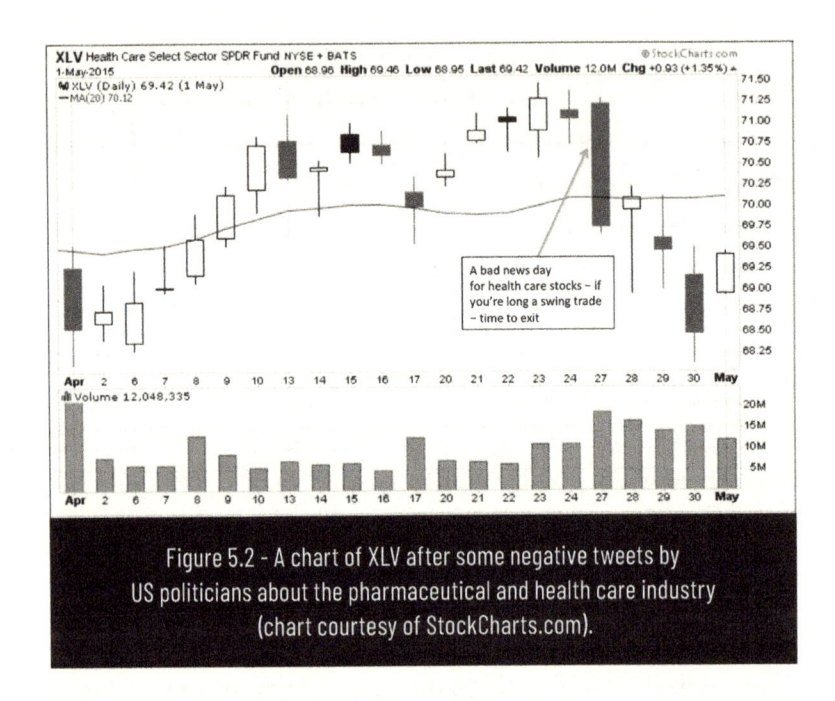

Figure 5.2 - A chart of XLV after some negative tweets by US politicians about the pharmaceutical and health care industry (chart courtesy of StockCharts.com).

As a swing trader, you need to constantly review your existing positions and trades. This does not mean you should be making changes to your trading plan daily because of every little gyration in a particular position. However, you should continue to make sure that nothing fundamentally has changed that would make you want to reconsider your stops and your target exit prices.

Managing the Trade Size

Managing and controlling how much of your capital you invest in one trade is also very important. Even with the best planning and strategies, you will never know which of your trades will become winners and which ones will turn into losers, therefore, you should not overcommit your capital to any one trade.

Most experienced traders use the "rule of thumb" that says you should not put more than 2% of your capital at risk on any one trade. This means that if you have $20,000.00 of capital in your account, you should not put more than $400.00 at risk on a trade (2% of $20,000.00). Let's take a look at how this would apply to an imaginary trade as described below.

Assume you are looking at a stock that is trading at $10.00/share. The price movements are looking like it will go higher and you want to take an entry because it looks like it could head to $10.75 where it will find some price resistance. You like this trade because it looks like there is price support around $9.75 where it made a low on some bottoming price action. So if you get an entry price of about $10.00/share, then you are risking $0.25 ($10.00 - $9.75 stop) to make $0.75 ($10.75 exit - $10.00). This is a good trade because the reward is 3 times the risk (reward $0.75 versus $0.25 risk). Remember, I said you should expect to get 2 times or more reward for the risk you take.

So, the next question is, "How much should I buy?" In other words, "What is the most money that I should put into this trade?" Using the previous example of an account with $20,000.00 total capital, you should be risking no more than $400.00. With a stop-loss of $0.25 per share below your entry at $10.00, you would purchase no more 1,600 shares ($400.00 divided by $0.25/share). Therefore, if you do get stopped out, you will lose about $400.00 based on holding 1,600 shares.

A loss of any kind is not what you are hoping for of course, however, by limiting your investment you also limit the loss to 2% of your capital. This is how managing your stop-losses and the amount you put at risk will ensure that you survive to trade another day.

Some traders might think that they can adjust the amount they risk on a trade based on how confident they feel about their trade. However, most experienced traders feel that this is still a random approach and a departure from good trading practice. All experienced traders have had trades they felt extremely confident about but ended up getting stopped out. Alternatively, these traders have had trades that gave big surprises to the upside even though they thought initially that the trades were marginally promising. In some cases, they turned out to be their best trades of the year.

For this reason, especially if you are a novice trader, you should avoid adjusting the amount you intend to risk on a trade based on your level of confidence in the setup and entry. As you develop your own trading style and strategies, you might start to feel comfortable taking larger risks on certain setups. For example, maybe double bottom patterns (which I will discuss later in the book) almost always turn into a winning trade for you and therefore you are willing to risk more of your portfolio on those types of patterns versus other patterns. Possibly you have better success with short selling versus going long on trades. You will need to make sure your confident feeling is producing the result you think by recording and reviewing all of your trades.

Decisions to change your trading strategies will come with both practice and the documenting of all of your trades so you can track what works for you and what is not working well. This leads us to the next section – maintaining a journal of your trading activity and reviewing the outcome of trades.

Maintaining a Trading Journal

In industry and other sectors we often hear the phrase, "what gets measured gets improved". This is only partially true. For example, if you are growing a vegetable garden and you want to ensure a good crop, you will want to make sure the garden is getting enough water. However, putting a rain gauge out and measuring the rainfall during your growing season is not going to be enough to ensure a good crop of vegetables. While it is important to know how much rain you are getting in your garden, it is equally important to have a plan in place and to act on the information that you collect. In the case of our proverbial garden, we measure the rainfall and if the plants are not getting enough water, then we take action to water them.

It is the same for almost any system or process – you need to measure performance (very important) and then take that information and use it to determine what actions you can take to improve on that performance. This is one of the main reasons keeping a trading journal is so important to being a successful trader.

There are many ways that you can keep a trading journal and the process that you should follow will be up to you and your personal preferences. Everyone is different, so you need to figure out what works best for your personality. Because your trades will unfold over days to weeks, it may be best to keep some sort of log – either an electronic-based or paper-based recording system.

There are also a number of web-based journaling platforms such as Tradevue, TradeBench and Edgewonk. Each platform has a free subscription level, which offers a limited number of tracking options. Fees apply to unlock additional features in each platform. If you want to consider using a web-based platform for journaling activities, I suggest you research a number of these sites to decide if one of these will meet your needs.

Regardless of what you chose to use, the following are items I suggest you keep track of before placing a trade, after the trade is placed and when the trade is closed:

- date
- market internals: i.e., conditions overall, S&P, Nasdaq, industry sector
- source of trade idea
- reasoning to enter trade
- sector alignment: is the trade you're considering aligned with the market and sector direction
- technical indicators including RSI and MACD values (discussed later in this book)
- check for upcoming events to avoid holding through
- entry price
- stop price
- target price
- a risk to reward ratio ≥ 2
- actual entry price
- actual exit price
- profit/loss
- comments: whatever seems relevant to you at the time, this may include notes on the trade as well

as your execution and your level of confidence versus the actual trade result

Remember, that if you are trading a plan that is right 60% of the time, 4 out of 10 trades are going to be wrong and you will get stopped out. You will have no idea in what order these gains and losses will occur – there may be 5 winning trades in a row, followed by 3 losers, which are then followed by 2 winners. You will not be able to predict trade by trade what will happen, however, by keeping a journal you will be able to track your success rate and come up with an average over time, and that is much more important.

As you adjust your trading style and the strategies that you decide to use, you can take my suggested list and either add items you want to track or delete items that don't seem relevant to you. Remember, market conditions change, so you have to be ready to adapt and move from one strategy to another as these changes occur.

Trading Psychology

Many new traders will start out with a simulator or fictitious account and practice making trades with "pretend money". After having some success and starting to build some confidence with a practice account, they will move to trading with their real money. Some traders who have been successful with a simulator subsequently have problems when their money is at risk and therefore do not have the same trading success they enjoyed when it was all "pretend" money. The question is, "What has changed?"

A trader who is working with imaginary funds is not as emotionally invested in the trades they are making. A key reason why many traders fail is that they take negative events and real losses in trading personally. Their confidence and peace of mind are connected to their trading results. When traders do well, they feel good. When they encounter losses, they become discouraged, doubtful, and frustrated, questioning themselves and their strategy. Instead of dealing directly and constructively with their losses, they react to the emotions triggered by personalizing the events.

Successful swing traders are focused on finding good trading setups, planning their trades, and executing a correct profit target or stop-loss level. Consistently profitable traders take every negative or positive trade they make as an opportunity to improve (which is why they keep a journal). A journal can help keep you grounded by allowing you to come back to each trade at a later time and, with as little emotion as possible, review the reason you entered the trade. You can then look at each decision in a rational way and learn from it.

Keeping a record of both your physical and mental condition may also be instructive. I believe that one of the key contributors to traders' self-discipline is their physical and mental health. People who eat well-balanced nutritional meals, exercise regularly, maintain proper body weight and fitness levels, and get adequate rest are likely to have the levels of energy and alertness that are required to make them effective traders. You may be surprised to read this, but your state of alertness, your energy level, and your overall health can have an impact on your trading results. Those who neglect these aspects of their well-being or, even worse, abuse alcohol or drugs, will find it difficult to concentrate and make good decisions.

Aspects of personal lives outside of trading can also impact your effectiveness as a trader. Changes in personal relationships such as a breakup or divorce, family issues like illness, or financial problems, can reduce a person's ability to focus and make appropriate decisions. For example, it is common for young traders to experience more stress after they have married, had children, or purchased a new home, because these added financial responsibilities create additional worry and stress (but also hopefully much pleasure!).

The swing trading strategies you might consider using, such as what are outlined in Chapter 12, Swing Trading Strategies, should improve with time. You will begin to realize that the key to being a successful trader is practicing self-discipline, maintaining your physical and mental health as well as controlling your emotions. You have to know in advance what you will do in any given trading situation and stay with your plan. It's challenging to predict what the market will do, but you have already lost if you first don't know what you yourself will do.

New trading strategies, tips from chatrooms or from this book, or even the most sophisticated software imaginable, will not help traders who cannot handle themselves and control their emotions. The swing trading advantage is that you have time to think through your trades in advance. There is no need to make snap decisions. Before entering any trade, you can take your journal and ask yourself some basic questions:

- How am I feeling mentally: am I able to make rational and non-emotional decisions right now?
- Does this fit into my trading personality and my risk tolerance?
- What strategy will this fit into?
- If this trade goes the wrong way, where is my stop?
- How much money am I risking in this trade, and what is the reward potential?

Be in touch with the results of your decisions and constantly be reviewing your performance.

- Are you trading profitably?
- Have you had 5 wins in a row or have you had 5 losses in a row?
- If you are on a losing streak, will you be in touch with your own emotions and maintain your composure, or will you let your judgment be impaired?

I cannot emphasize enough just how important the following steps are: you must take the time to prepare, you must work hard, you must plan your trades, and you must take the time afterward to review your trades.

Some of these skills are comparable to learning to ride a bicycle. Once you've learned to ride, that is a skill that can't be taken away. However, after you learn to ride and hit the road, you cannot forget or ignore the rules of the road. If you do, you are at risk of getting flattened. In a similar way, once you've learned the skill of identifying a good stock, that skill will always be with you. But remember, discipline in trading is something you will need to constantly work at and remember in order to be successful.

Chapter Summary

In Chapter 5, I discussed how the swing trader must protect one of the most important trading tools: their capital. There are a number of rules that you can follow to ensure that you do not have an issue with a significant loss of capital. Some of these rules and major points about risk management that I covered in this chapter are listed below.

- Protect your capital: without it you cannot be an active swing trader.

- Leave your ego at the door and submit to the market and price action, because that is all that is important – remember, "the market can remain irrational longer than you can remain solvent".

- Honor your stop-loss, do not let small losses turn into big losses.

- Respect your target price and do not take profits too early and thus change your original trade plan and the risk to reward ratio you had established earlier.

- Learn and respect that having some losses is part of the swing trading game. Do not take it personally.

- Constantly review your existing trades to ensure that nothing has changed fundamentally in the stock, sector or market. This is the only reason you should consider changing your trade plan.

- Actively manage the size of each trade so that you do not risk more than about 2% of your capital.

- Maintain your trading journal and review it regularly to determine what works and what needs to be changed.

- Keep your mind and body fit. Recognize points in your life where you might be stressed or sad and consider whether your mood or sentiment could affect your trading decisions negatively.

CHAPTER 6

Fundamental Analysis

What is fundamental analysis? In simple terms, it is an analysis of hard data on a company, a commodity, a financial instrument, a sector, etc. That data can include one or more of the following:

- total revenue
- earnings per share (EPS)
- price to earnings ratio (P/E)
- leverage: the amount of debt to equity
- product pipeline: future potential growth driver
- competitive advantages a company may have over competitors
- conditions that might favor or disadvantage a particular sector/commodity
- company management

- peer-to-peer comparisons
- regulatory environment and pending changes
- short interest
- hot sector manias

The fundamental measures listed above are not a complete list but they are some of the more common ones that are used when performing fundamental analysis. The challenge for many of us is that we do not have the time or the expertise to, for example, deep dive into financial statements. We should leave that work and effort to the accountants and the analysts.

Fundamental analysis has significant relevance for a value investor like a Warren Buffett. Value investors typically take larger positions and look for moves over longer periods of time because it often takes a year or more for other investors to realize the future value of a stock.

Some fundamental analysis can also be helpful for a swing trader and there is one factor that is very relevant. This involves watching for hot sector manias. In my opinion, it is one of the most powerful opportunities to make great returns on your money using fundamental analysis. I will discuss this fundamental factor later in this chapter and in Chapter 12, Swing Trading Strategies.

Regardless, a basic understanding of some of these fundamental factors can be helpful to a swing trader. In particular, you'll be better able to recognize potentially good investment opportunities in stocks. Let's look at a few of these important factors in more depth and then examine the one I feel is the big winner. I will cover the following stock fundamentals in this chapter:

- total revenue
- earnings per share (EPS)

- price to earnings ratio (P/E)
- debt to equity ratio
- return on equity (ROE)
- short interest
- hot sector manias

After reading this chapter, you should have a basic understanding of these fundamentals and how to apply them when looking for potential swing trade opportunities.

Total Revenue

A company's total revenue is important and can be easily understood even by investors with limited financial knowledge. This revenue number is a measure of a company's total sales of their products and/or services. It is often a good indicator that a company is doing well if its revenue is growing at a steady pace year over year. If the revenue numbers are flat or dropping year over year, it shows that a company is probably having trouble growing its business and that profits will likely be flat or dropping as well. Falling profits usually translate to a falling stock price.

Analysts will do projections on future revenues and these estimates are usually public information on websites like Yahoo Finance, CNBC and Estimize. The Estimize site is a good source of information because they crowdsource earnings and economic estimates from over 72,000 hedge fund, brokerage, independent and amateur analysts. Collecting and presenting estimates from a wide community of experts and amateurs often provides a more accurate set of financial numbers compared to an investor referencing only a couple of sources.

As a swing trader, you can check to see if the stock you are considering for a position has growing or declining revenues and determine if that is aligned with your trade. For example, are you going long on a stock with growing total revenue numbers?

Earnings per Share

Earnings are calculated by taking the total revenue and subtracting the direct costs of production. Positive earnings are important in the long term for any business to continue operating. However, the name "earnings" should not be confused with profit or profitability. Profits are calculated by subtracting the additional costs of doing business such as interest paid on debt. At some point in a company's history, it will need to start turning a profit or investors will lose patience, funds will run out and bankruptcy will follow.

Simply put, the long-term value of a company is based on the future cash that the company will generate in its business. The more cash it is expected to generate in the future, generally speaking, the more investors will value the company today. Think of it as making an investment in a cash generation machine. The more cash the machine generates in a year, the more it is worth.

Like the total revenue numbers discussed above, past and projected earnings numbers are readily available online. Investors are usually prepared to pay a premium share price for a company that is projected to be growing earnings. The higher the projected earnings growth, the higher the premium they are willing to pay.

However, earnings are only part of the equation. To get a real understanding of the value of a company and how it compares to the value of another company, you need to look at the earnings per share (EPS). To arrive at this number, you take the earnings and divide it by the number of shares outstanding. For example, if a company that reports $100 million in earnings for a given year has 20 million shares of stock outstanding, then that company has an EPS of $5.00 per share. Knowing the EPS of one company makes it easier to compare that company to others in a similar business. Using our example, a similar company with an EPS of $6.00 per share is earning $1.00 per share more for shareholders.

Like total revenue discussed above, stock prices of companies will usually rise if there is an expected growth in EPS numbers. Information is readily available to help you determine if your trade is aligned with the numbers.

Price to Earnings Ratio

Price to earnings ratio (P/E) is considered by many investors to be the one fundamental measure that tops all of the others in determining a company's stock price movement. The P/E gives you a view of how the market is pricing a company's shares in relation to its earnings. It is calculated by taking a company's price per share (P) and dividing by its earnings per share (E). For example, if a stock is priced at $100.00 per share and it has an EPS of $10.00 per share, then the P/E ratio is 10 ($100.00 divided by $10.00). A higher P/E ratio means investors are willing to pay more for each dollar of annual earnings. You can use this number to compare how investors are valuing other companies in the same business sector. A higher P/E in relation to other companies in the same sector indicates that investors are feeling particularly bullish on the company. If a company has no earnings to date, then it will not have a P/E ratio.

Similar to the EPS ratio, you can use this measure to determine if a company's stock price is overvalued or undervalued by the marketplace by comparing the P/E to its industry peers. EPS numbers and company comparisons are all available online for your reference. I will suggest a number of good websites to source this information later in the book.

Debt to Equity

Most companies need funds to start up and operate their business. They need money to pay employees, to purchase inventory, to buy equipment and computers, etc. That money can come from 2 sources: 1) debt and 2) equity.

Debt is essentially borrowed money that the company usually pays interest on for its use. The debt will also need to be repaid at some point in time. Equity is money that is invested in the company and, in return, the investor is given shares. Those shares represent some percentage of ownership in the company. At some point the investor is hoping to sell their shares for a profit and/or collect dividends, which are payments that come from the company's profits.

Debt and equity represent different levels of risks for a company and its shareholders. Debt comes with obligations to pay interest and repay the outstanding loan at some point. Therefore, it is a higher risk to the company compared to equity, which has no such obligations. Equity has more risk for the shareholders because if the company goes bankrupt, the debt holders usually get first pick at whatever is left of value. The equity investors get what is left over and that is usually nothing.

When considering the financial structure of a company, it is good to have a balance of debt and equity. Generally speaking, a company should not have more debt than equity. This is a significant generalization, but in most cases, financial people want to see a ratio of debt to equity of less than 1. More debt is considered to be more risky for the company and its ongoing operation.

If you do a search for stocks that are appropriate to take a long position in, you could include this factor in your scan. Look for the companies that have a debt to equity ratio of less than 1. Scanning for trading opportunities will be discussed in Chapter 12, Swing Trading Strategies.

Return on Equity

Return on equity (ROE) is a measure, expressed as a percentage, of how much profit a company generates with the money shareholders have invested. For example, if an investor puts $100.00 into a savings account that earns 1% per year, they expect their $100.00 to be worth $101.00 in a year. In a similar way, investors in a company expect to see the company make a good return on their investment. The measure of ROE indicates how well the company is doing in terms of the invested capital.

Companies with higher and growing ROE numbers tend to be more highly valued by investors. Doing a search that includes companies with higher ROE numbers is another fundamental search option that you can experiment with as a swing trader when doing your scans for trading opportunities.

Short Interest

I have already discussed how investors who feel negative about a stock can sell short. They are borrowing shares and selling them into the market and hoping that they will be able to purchase them back at a lower price at some point in the future. They are still buying low and selling high, except they are doing it in reverse.

When numerous investors and traders in the market feel that a stock is particularly overvalued, the number of shares that get borrowed and sold short increases. In theory, the maximum number of shares that can be shorted is limited to the number of shares that are available for trading – this number of tradable shares is referred to as the *float*. You will never have a situation where the entire float is shorted, but there have been some extreme cases where over 50% of the tradable shares in a company have been sold short.

Brokerages that loan shares for shorting are required to report the number of shares they have loaned out to short sellers. Most exchanges take this short information and report it to the public monthly. The Nasdaq requires this short information from brokers twice per month. Therefore, the total number of shares of a company that are sold short is available to investors and traders, albeit the data may be a little out of date. By dividing the shares shorted by the total float, the short interest can be calculated as a percentage. For example, if a company has a float of 40 million shares and 10 million of them are reported short, then the short interest is 25% (10 million divided by 40 million).

The level of short interest is an indicator of market sentiment for a stock. If the short interest is under 5%, there is some level of negative sentiment but it is not extreme. There will always be some traders and investors who feel a company is overvalued. If the short interest is over 20%, then it is an indication that a significant number of traders have a negative opinion on the stock and hold a strong conviction that the stock price will go down.

The level of short interest can have some implications for the future price action of a stock. While a high level of short interest indicates a negative sentiment, it can also be a catalyst for a strong price increase. Let us say that a stock with a high level of short interest releases some unexpected good news. Buyers immediately enter the market and purchase shares based on the news, which drives the price up. Short sellers start to worry that they are going to have to buy the shares back at much higher prices so they start to cover their short positions by purchasing shares as well. This additional purchasing adds to the buying frenzy. This event is referred to as a short squeeze and it can result in very strong upward price moves depending on how many shares are shorted and the size of the float.

I will discuss how you can use short interest information to find potential swing trade opportunities in Chapter 12, Swing Trading Strategies.

Hot Sector Manias

Now that I have covered some of the basic fundamental financial analysis that can help in assessing a stock's future value, let us look at the one that I feel has by far the greatest potential to create a good swing trade setup. This is by no means a big secret. It is a well-known fact that catching a popular sector early is like grabbing a tiger by the tail. Once you grab one, hold on for the ride. I refer to this phenomenon as "hot sector manias" because all investing common sense seems to be abandoned by investors and traders. Many traders pour money into companies with no earnings or profit on pure speculation that maybe someday they will be profitable. Other traders are just following the money and hoping not to be the last one out with a loss.

Let's examine one of the potentially profitable trading opportunities that a hot sector offered a swing trader through 2017. I will also expand on this topic in Chapter 12, where I discuss a number of different strategies to use for swing trading.

Bitcoin and Blockchain Mania

Prior to 2017, very few people knew about bitcoin, let alone the blockchain, but this budding new business opportunity was a boon for many who saw the opportunity and got in early. Like most of these hot sector trades, there was lots of time to invest and make money, even if you were not in on the ground floor. These opportunities tend to play out over time but you need to be vigilant because the earlier you are in, the better. If you are hearing about a "great investment opportunity" from a cab driver or the person who is making a latte for you in the morning – you are too late. In fact, that is a pretty good sign that the crest of the wave is coming – it's either time to get out or, at the very least, time to take profits and be very, very cautious moving forward.

As most know by now, bitcoin is a cryptocurrency created in late 2008. It is essentially a digital asset, which is designed to work as a medium of exchange. This exchange uses cryptography to control the creation of bitcoins and its management. Early in its inception, individuals participating on the bitcoin forum established the initial value of the first bitcoin transactions. It was reported that one of the first and notable transactions was the purchase of 2 pizzas for the indirect cost of 10,000 bitcoins. Imagine how many pizzas that would buy today.

Blockchain technology went hand in hand with the advent of cryptocurrency and was important in guaranteeing the digital asset was secure and not spent multiple times. The security of the blockchain is made possible because it is a decentralized, distributed, public digital ledger. This ledger is used to record transactions across many computers in a network. The distribution of records in many computers prevents the record from being altered randomly without the alteration of all subsequent blocks attached to that ledger. Any alteration requires the collusion of many computers in the entire block network.

When bitcoin and other cryptocurrencies really started to take off in 2017, blockchain also gained significant popularity for another reason. Blockchain technology was starting to be viewed as having a large potential to transform business operation models. It was felt that the blockchain distributed ledger technology had the potential to create new foundations for global economic and social systems. This would make it more of a disruptive technology with many different applications other than just cryptocurrency uses. Some potential uses include bringing significant security and efficiencies to global supply chains, financial transactions, and decentralized social networking.

All of this information about bitcoin and blockchain is interesting in itself, but it also provided some of the best opportunities to make some great swing trading returns in 2017. As bitcoin prices started to go parabolic, many companies also took interest in the underlying blockchain technology as a possible means to ramp up their business.

Riot Blockchain, Inc. (RIOT) is a great example of how a hot sector play can make you a lot of money. It is also a good example of the silliness that will occur in a hot sector. This company was a struggling diagnostic medical device maker in the biotechnology sector. They saw the blockchain space as an opportunity to shift their business and take advantage of this hot sector. On October 2nd, 2017 they unveiled a new direction for their company and Figure 6.1 below shows how that unfolded.

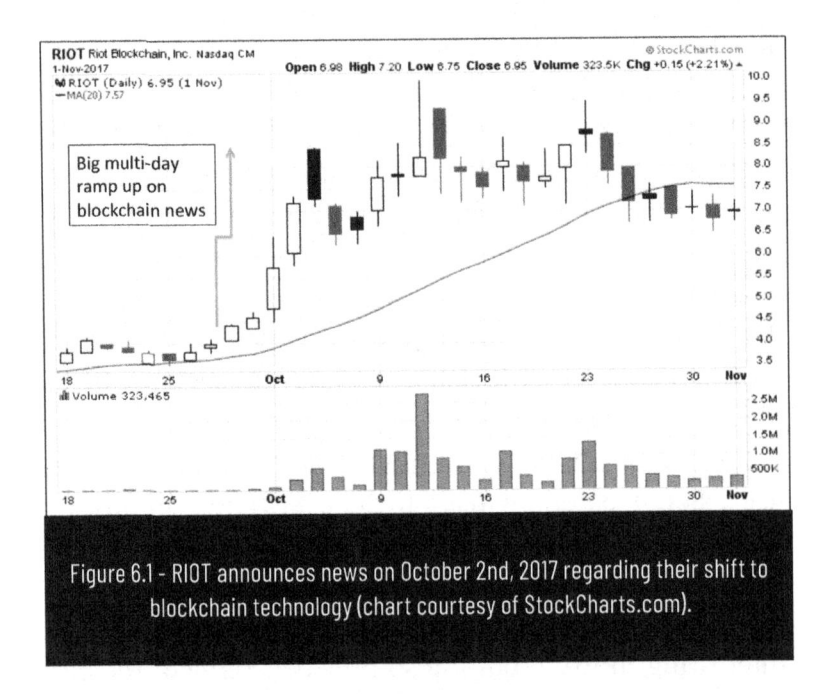

Figure 6.1 - RIOT announces news on October 2nd, 2017 regarding their shift to blockchain technology (chart courtesy of StockCharts.com).

I played this as a day trade and as a swing trade. When you get this kind of action in a hot sector, you can make some very profitable trades by getting in as early as possible and then letting the herd of traders follow.

As with all hot sector plays, there is never just one. Others in the capital market take notice and follow suit (i.e., follow the money). For example, those of us with a few gray hairs (or more) will remember the company Eastman Kodak. They were a Dow Jones listed powerhouse in the camera, film and photography business until they began to struggle in the late 90s and eventually filed for bankruptcy in 2012. Since then they have been trying to reinvent themselves and, in the process, grabbed on to the idea of adding blockchain to their business model.

In early January 2018, Kodak announced it would be getting into the blockchain business and issuing its own

Fundamental Analysis

cryptocurrency appropriately called: the KODAKCoin. The resulting price move in the stock was similar to all of the other companies that added blockchain to their name or business model. See Figure 6.2 for a chart of the KODK price action after their announcement.

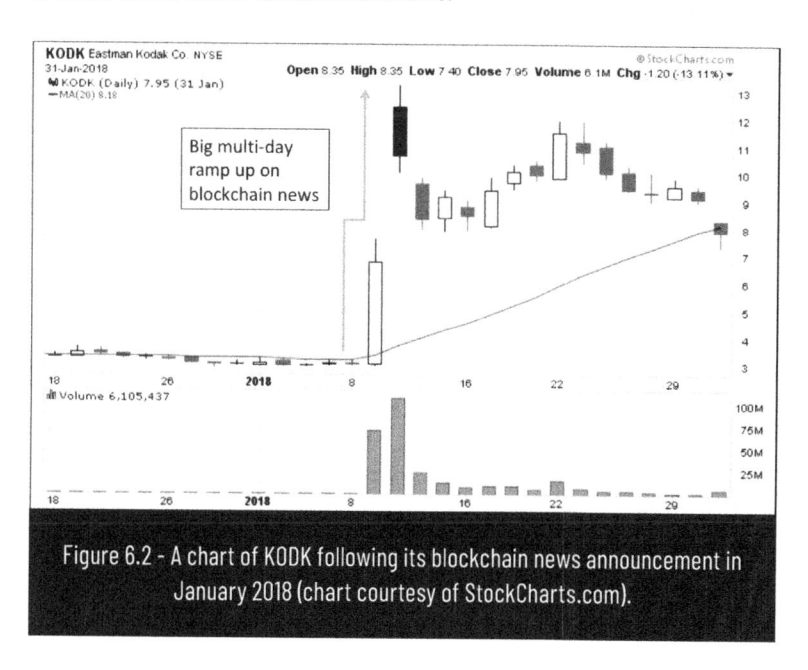

Figure 6.2 - A chart of KODK following its blockchain news announcement in January 2018 (chart courtesy of StockCharts.com).

Another blockchain convert was the Long Island Ice Tea Corp. This little-known small publicly listed company announced on December 21st, 2017 that it was now the "Long Blockchain Corp." Subsequently, the stock price leaped more than 200% at the open of the trading day. It then closed up 183% and continued to go higher in the days to come. This company, that had been a beverage maker, stated in a news release that it was "shifting its primary corporate focus toward the exploration of and investment in opportunities that leverage the benefits of blockchain technology". A company spokesperson said they would do this while maintaining their iced tea beverage business.

There are many more examples of similar great opportunities, and they all have one factor in common: it is important to take advantage of these hot sector manias when they occur. Let us stress that final phrase one more time: when they occur. Not after they occur. You only need one of these in a year to make a great return on your money. These events are one of my favorite swing trading strategies, which I will discuss in more detail in Chapter 12.

In summary, sector mania plays are the one fundamental factor I like the most. The downside is that these do not occur very often and you will need to be patient but vigilant as you wait for the next hot sector trading opportunity to come along.

Chapter Summary

In this chapter, I discussed a number of fundamental factors that can be used by swing traders to assess the potential for a profitable entry and exit. Points discussed in this chapter are as follows.

- Performing detailed fundamental analysis can take a significant amount of time and effort.
- Real in-depth analysis of a company's financial statements requires some expertise in accounting, which most swing traders do not have.
- There are a few fundamental analysis tools that a swing trader with very little accounting experience can use when searching for trading opportunities:
  - total revenue
  - earnings per share (EPS)
  - price to earnings ratio (P/E)
  - debt to equity
  - return on equity (ROE)

- These financial ratios listed above can be used to assist you when you're looking for swing trading opportunities.
- The level of short interest provides some insight on the sentiment of traders toward a stock. A high level of short interest indicates that traders are expecting the price of the stock to drop significantly. However, if some good news comes out on a stock that has a high level of short interest, it can act as a strong catalyst to drive the stock price higher with a short squeeze.
- A short squeeze occurs when traders who are short a stock buy in mass when they see the price of that stock start to rise dramatically.
- The best fundamental analysis factor for a swing trader is finding and investing in hot sector mania plays.
- Hot sector mania plays defy most fundamental analysis principles – common-sense investing is completely discarded.
- One of the best opportunities for good returns is to find these sector mania plays when they start to occur, get in early, and then get out before the inevitable pullback or collapse.

CHAPTER 7

Technical Analysis – Charting Basics

Technical analysis of securities is based on the principle that past price movements in a financial instrument are a predictor of the future moves in the price. Trading volume (the number of securities being traded) is often combined with price movement to help improve these price prediction models.

In this first chapter on technical analysis, I will cover the basics of charting. I will look at how you can construct a graph that represents the price action of a stock using candlesticks and bar charts. I will also look at how these candlesticks and bar charts can be used to get a read on the market sentiment and possible changes in the sentiment toward a stock.

Some readers of this book may be well-versed on this topic already while others may be new to trading and charting. This section is critical for new traders because many swing trade strategies are based on graphing price action and reading charts that are readily available online.

In this chapter I will cover the following topics:

1. candlesticks

2. bar charts

3. price action and psychology

4. candlestick patterns

In the following Chapters 8 and 9, I will discuss how to use these charting techniques in conjunction with a number of tools and patterns in order to gain insight into the future price movements of a stock.

Candlesticks

In the following section I will start by discussing "the candlestick". To do technical analysis you must be conversant with this type of charting tool. The Japanese began using technical analysis and some early versions of candlesticks to trade rice in the 17th century. Much of the credit for candlestick development and charting goes to a legendary rice trader named Homma from the town of Sakata, Japan.

While these early versions of technical analysis and candlestick charts were different from today's version, many of the principles are similar. The type of candlestick charting that traders are familiar with today first appeared sometime after 1850. It is likely that Homma's original ideas were modified and refined over many years of trading, eventually resulting in the existing system of candlestick charting that everyone uses today.

To help you understand the technical analysis and trading strategies discussed in the pages to come, I will start by explaining the fundamentals of candlestick charts and what they tell us about *"price action"*. Candlesticks do not just represent the price action of a stock during a period of time. When these candlesticks are put together in a timeline, they can also be thought of as a window that gives the trader some insight into the overall market sentiment or feeling about a stock's perceived value. Candlesticks convey the majority of the traders' psyche regarding that stock's valuation over the period of time being examined.

In order to create a candlestick chart, you must have several numbers, including the following:

- beginning price for the chosen time frame (also called the opening price)
- highest price in the time frame
- lowest price in that time frame
- last price for the time frame (also called the closing price)

The time frame can be 1 minute, 5 minutes, hourly, daily, weekly, or any other period you choose. Typically with swing trading, traders will commonly look at daily charts or those that cover longer periods of time because your hold time will typically be measured in days or weeks or possibly even longer intervals. From the set of numbers listed above, you can create a candlestick.

A candlestick is made up of a "body" and up to 2 "tails". The wide portion of the candlestick is called the body. The long thin lines above and below the body that represent the high/low price range are called tails (also referred to as *"wicks"* or *"shadows"*). The top of the upper tail identifies the highest price in the period and the bottom of the lower tail identifies the lowest price in that period.

Two examples follow in Figure 7.1 as follows:

- An upward move in price for the period: if the stock closes higher than its opening price during the time period being measured, the body of the candlestick is drawn with the bottom representing the opening price and the top of the body representing the closing price. On a stock moving higher, the body is usually green (the user can adjust the color in most charts based on their preference). This is referred to as a bullish candlestick because it represents an increase in price over the measured period.

- A downward move in price for the period: if the stock closes lower than its opening price, a filled (usually red) candlestick is drawn with the top of the body representing the opening price and the bottom of the body representing the closing price. The tails on the candlestick represent the absolute high and low during the period. This is referred to as a bearish candlestick because the price is dropping over the period in question.

Let us look at some other scenarios for price action in a single period. If a stock closed the period at the high of that time frame, then there would be no top tail because the high of the period was also the closing price. If a stock started at the lowest price during the period and traded last at the highest price, then there would be no tails on the top or the bottom of the body.

Some single and double candlesticks can provide an indication of future price moves. They can also be looked at over multiple periods of time to provide insight into future price movements in a stock. Before I start discussing these specific chart patterns, let's look at another charting technique that some traders prefer called the bar chart.

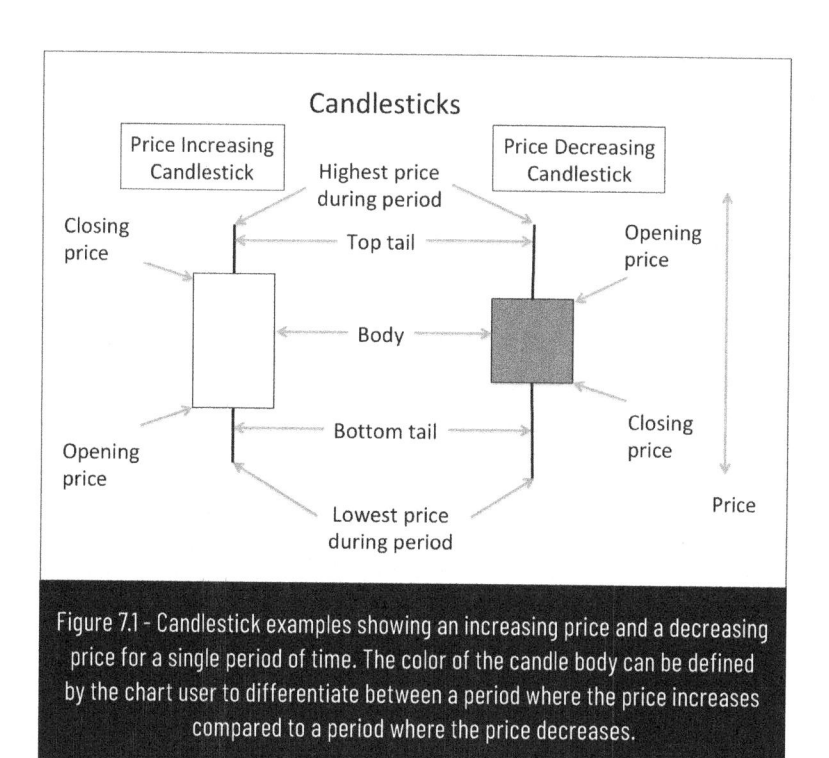

Figure 7.1 - Candlestick examples showing an increasing price and a decreasing price for a single period of time. The color of the candle body can be defined by the chart user to differentiate between a period where the price increases compared to a period where the price decreases.

Bar Charts

There is another way that some traders look at the price movement of financial instruments in a chart. It is referred to as a bar chart. Instead of creating a "body" for each time frame, there is a simple vertical line that represents the range of price movement over the time period being examined. On each side of that vertical line, there is a small horizontal line. On the left side, the small horizontal line shows the price at the beginning of that time period, and the horizontal line on the right side shows the last price traded at the end of the period. Figure 7.2 shows a typical bar chart for a price move up and a price move down. Colors can also be added to these bar charts to give you a better visual on which way the price is moving.

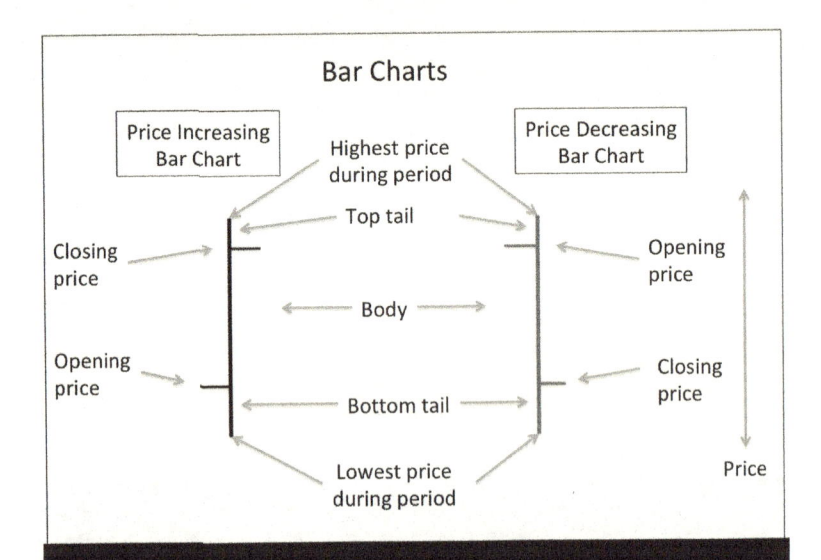

Figure 7.2 - Bar chart examples showing an increasing price and a decreasing price for a single period of time. To help differentiate the bar's direction during a time period, most charts have options that allow the user to define a color for periods where the price increases and a different color for periods when the price decreases. For example, I use green for a price increase and red for a price decrease.

Both charts show the same information and it is a matter of personal preference as to which option you choose to use. Most charting tools will provide you with multiple options regarding chart type, color, time frame, etc. I prefer to use candlesticks and you will see that my examples and illustrations will be displayed as such.

Regardless of which charting style you choose, candlestick and bar chart patterns tell you a great deal about the general trend of a stock and the level of interest between buyers or sellers of that stock. In the following sections, I will discuss how the charts showing price action can reflect the overall sentiment of traders. Specifically, I will examine which chart patterns traders look for in an attempt to predict future price moves.

Price Action and Psychology

Basically there are 3 categories of traders: the buyers, the sellers, and the undecided. As with any market, the buyers want to pay as little as possible, while the sellers want to charge as much as possible. This different perspective between buyers and sellers results in the bid-ask spread that I discussed in Chapter 2, How Swing Trading Works. The *"ask"* is the price a seller wants to sell their stock for. The *"bid"* is the price that a buyer offers to purchase the stock. The actual transaction prices are the result of the decisions and actions of all of the traders at a particular point in time: the buyers, the sellers, and the undecided.

The presence and actions of undecided traders can put pressure on either the buyers or the sellers depending on which way this group is leaning. These undecided traders could suddenly decide to take a position and make the deals that the others are considering. If the buyers wait too long to decide on a transaction, someone else could beat them to it and drive up the price. The sellers who wait too long for a higher price might be disappointed by other traders who sell at the bid, which drives the price down. Their ongoing awareness of the presence of undecided traders makes the buyers and sellers more willing to trade with each other.

The buyers are buying because they expect that prices will go up. If there are more buyers than sellers, then the result is that buyers are willing to pay higher and higher prices and subsequently will bid on top of each other. When this occurs it is said that the "buyers are in control". They are apprehensive that they will end up paying higher prices if they don't buy now. When undecided traders see the price increase, they may also decide to become buyers, which creates a feeling of urgency among all of the buyers. The price of the stock then starts to accelerate further upward.

The sellers are selling because they expect that prices will go down. When a stock price is dropping it means that the "sellers are in control". The result is that sellers are willing to accept lower and lower prices to get out of their positions. They are concerned that they will end up selling at even lower prices if they miss selling immediately. Undecided traders who are holding the stock see the selling pressure and they decide to sell as well. This added selling creates a sense of urgency among the sellers, causing the stock price to drop faster.

Your goal, as a successful swing trader, is to discover the balance of power between the buyers and the sellers and then bet on the winning group. Fortunately, candlestick charts reflect this fight in price action between the buyers and sellers. The price action shown in the charts reflects the sentiment of the majority of traders and investors over a period of time. A successful trader will use their charting tools to interpret the sentiment of the traders in a particular stock. Who is in control – is it the buyers, the sellers or the undecided?

In the next section, I will provide you with a quick overview of several of the most important individual candlestick patterns for swing trading. In the following 2 chapters, I will explain how you can trade using these patterns in one or more of your swing trading strategies.

Candlestick Patterns

Now that I have discussed candlesticks and bar charts, let us look at some specific patterns that these charting methods create and how a swing trader can use these patterns to assess potential long and short trades.

I will look at the following patterns in this section:

- basic bullish and bearish candlesticks
- reversal patterns
- gap patterns

A detailed discussion on each of these patterns follows.

Basic Bullish and Bearish Candlesticks

Figure 7.3 shows 2 different bullish candlesticks where the closing price of the stock was higher than the opening price during the period. The larger the body of the candlestick and the shorter the upper tail, the more bullish the candlestick and possibly the overall trend. In the figure below, the candle on the right is much more bullish compared to the one on the left. It means that the buyers are in control of the price action, and it is likely that they'll keep pushing the price higher.

A seasoned swing trader will also confirm the bullish move by checking the volume (the number of shares being traded during that time period). Increasing volume relative to previous periods will confirm that the trend is strong. The volume of shares traded is represented by a bar located under the candlestick. The height of the bar is proportional to the number of shares traded.

Figure 7.3 - An illustration showing 2 bullish candlesticks. The candlestick on the right is more bullish in comparison to the one on the left. The figure also shows the volume bars underneath the candlesticks with the tall bar representing a larger number of shares traded in comparison to the smaller bar.

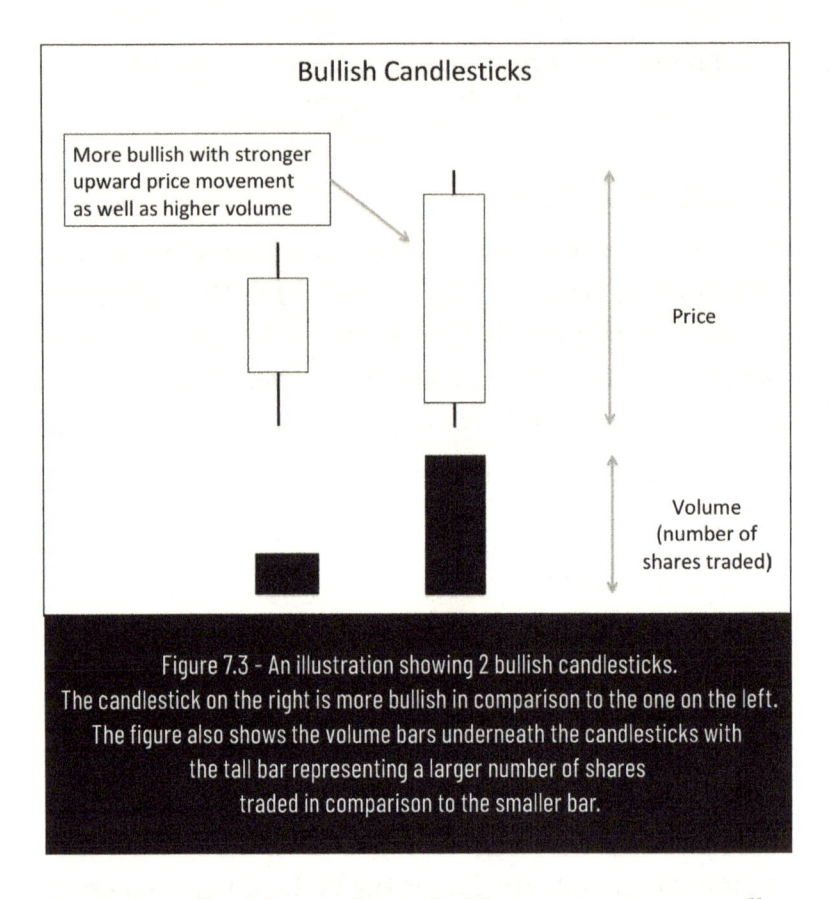

Bearish candlesticks, as shown in Figure 7.4, are any candles that show a bearish body. These candlesticks tell you that the sellers are in control of the price action in the market because the closing price was lower compared to the opening price during the period. The candlestick on the right is much more bearish. A small bottom tail on a bearish candlestick means the price closed the period at or near the low of that period.

As with bullish candlesticks, a seasoned trader will again check the number of shares traded in the period to see if during the selling the volume was increasing relative to previous periods. This is another confirmation that the sellers are firmly in control of the price movement.

Technical Analysis - Charting Basics

Bearish Candlesticks

More bearish with stronger downward price movement as well as higher volume

Price

Volume (number of shares traded)

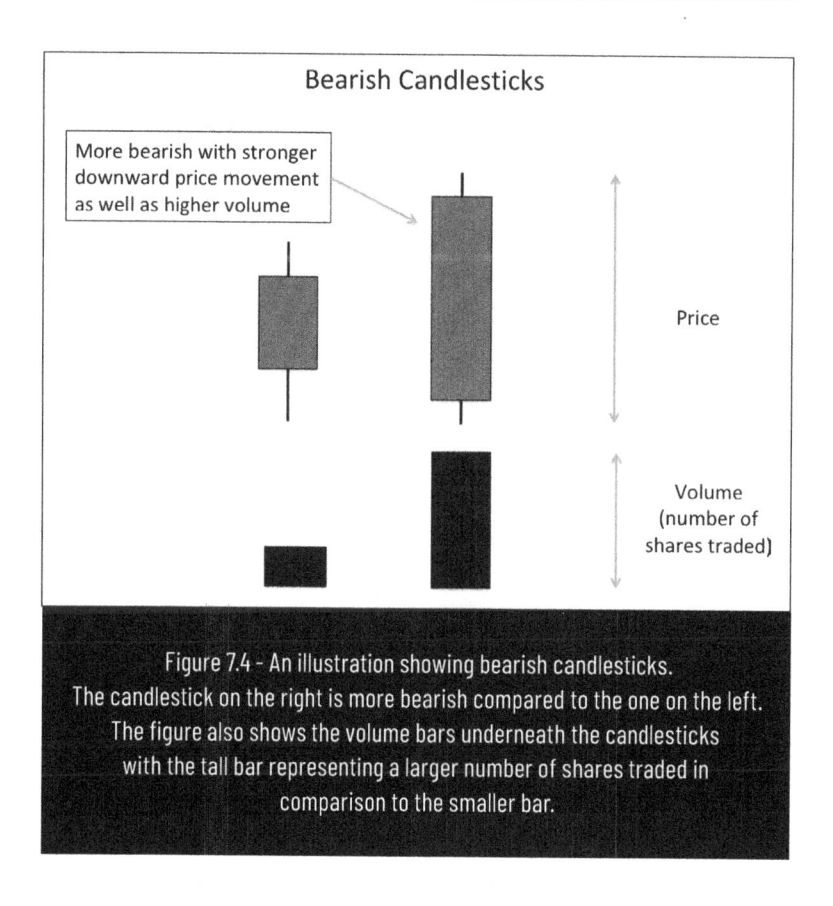

Figure 7.4 - An illustration showing bearish candlesticks. The candlestick on the right is more bearish compared to the one on the left. The figure also shows the volume bars underneath the candlesticks with the tall bar representing a larger number of shares traded in comparison to the smaller bar.

By learning to read these candlesticks and the patterns that they generate over a period of time, you will begin to understand which group of traders is in control of the price action. Is there overall buying pressure pushing the stock price higher or are the sellers in control and pushing the price lower? The price action or price movement seen in the charts represents the mood of these buyers and sellers over a period of time.

Your primary goal is to discover the balance of power between the buyers and the sellers and to bet on the winning group. If the buyers are in control, you should buy and hold. If the sellers are in control, you should sell your position or even sell short. If the price action indicates a lack of conviction between the buyers and sellers, then you will wait or look for another opportunity. You should let the bulls and the bears fight with each other and then enter a trade only when you are reasonably certain which side is likely to win.

You never want to be on the wrong side of the trade. This is why you need to learn how to read candlesticks or bar charts and then be constantly interpreting and reassessing the price action while you are in a trade. In the following section, I will outline a few favorite swing trade chart patterns that can indicate who is in control or who is about to take control.

Reversal Candles

Reversals are one of the most basic types of strategies that you can use as justification to enter a swing trade. In fact, there are dozens of different candlestick patterns but several are fairly consistent in predicting future price direction, especially when used in conjunction with other indicators. These patterns include the following:

- engulfing pattern
- doji: harami cross
- doji: gravestone and dragonfly

Let's examine the characteristics of each of these patterns in more detail.

Engulfing Pattern

One of these popular trading pattern setups is referred to as an engulfing candle. This engulfing candle pattern illustrates a potential change in control between the buyers and sellers. The engulfing pattern can either be bullish or bearish, which means either the buyers are taking control (bullish) or the sellers are taking control (bearish).

As with many indicators, both price and volume are taken into consideration to assess a possible trade opportunity. A short candle followed by a longer candle characterizes these reversals with this longer candle moving in the opposite direction of the previous price trend. It is referred to as engulfing because (in the case of a bottom reversal) the price will start lower than the previous period's close and end above the high of the previous period. The current candle engulfs the previous period's candle indicating a decisive change in control between the buyers and sellers. Figure 7.5 shows a simple illustration of both a bullish engulfing candle and a bearish engulfing candle.

The trading volume is used to confirm a change in control with this indicator usually being displayed at the bottom of a chart as a bar. The short candle has lower volume indicating that the buying or selling action is getting exhausted. The longer reversing candle will have a higher volume of trades, which indicates that control has changed hands and there is likely a decisive shift in the direction of the stock price.

An example of an engulfing trade is shown below in Figure 7.6 when TZA made a strong reversal from a downtrend in price (bearish) to a trend higher (bullish) with an engulfing candle.

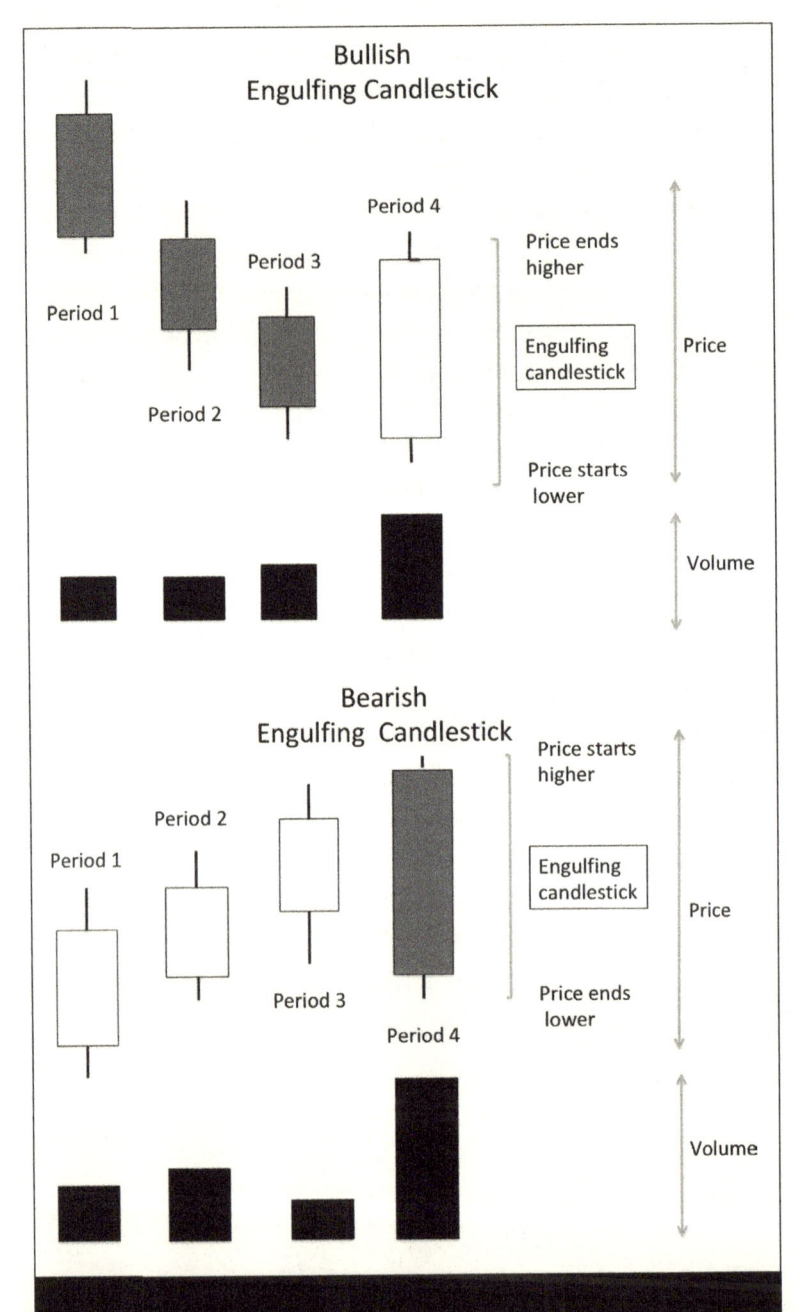

Figure 7.5 – Two illustrations showing a bullish engulfing candlestick and a bearish engulfing candlestick.

Technical Analysis - Charting Basics   113

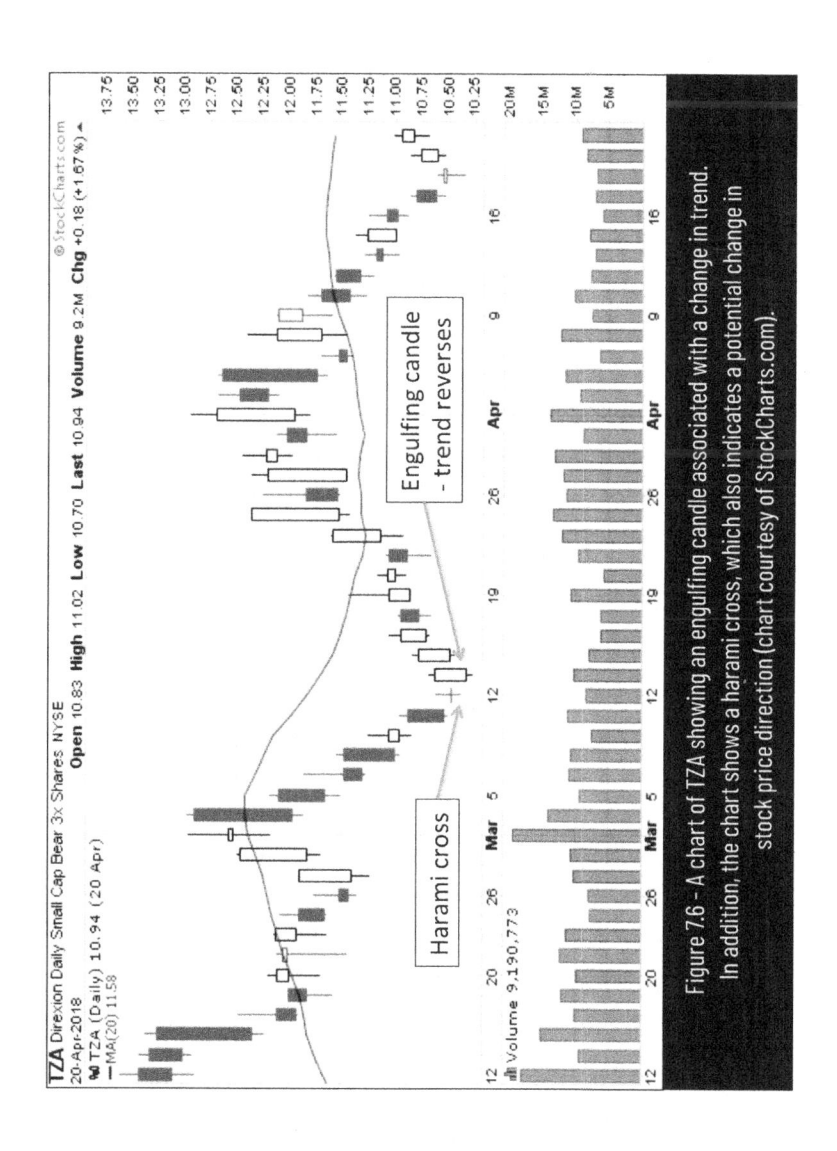

Figure 7.6 - A chart of TZA showing an engulfing candle associated with a change in trend. In addition, the chart shows a harami cross, which also indicates a potential change in stock price direction (chart courtesy of StockCharts.com).

How to Trade Engulfing Candles or Bars

These engulfing candlesticks can be bearish or bullish. A bullish engulfing candlestick suggests that the bulls have taken control of the price action. Leading up to the engulfing candlestick it was the bears who would have had control of the stock, keeping the price action in a downtrend. The bullish engulfing candlestick accompanied by a spike in volume indicates either a large new interest in owning the stock or possibly the covering of short positions held by traders.

A swing trader should start by checking other indicators to get some confirmation that a potential reversal in price action is happening. Other confirming indicators can include the Moving Average Convergence Divergence (MACD) and the Relative Strength Index (RSI), both of which are known as momentum tools. I will discuss these tools in the following Chapter 8, Technical Analysis – Indicator Tools.

It is important to get into a reversal trade early to ensure that you have the best possible risk to reward ratio. You should look at your chart to identify areas of resistance or support in the stock or market. With the engulfing pattern, if you are going to take a long trade, then your stop out price should be no lower than the low of the engulfing candle. Some traders might set the stop out price even higher, at the low of the previous candlestick that was engulfed.

Once you know your stop out price level and potential entry price, you can then determine your potential reward by looking at where you would expect to sell. You now have enough information to calculate your risk to reward ratio. If there is at least 2 times more reward compared to risk, it could be a good setup to examine more closely for an entry.

You can also try to assess if there have been some fundamental factors behind a possible reversal. Look for news or other events that might be causing a reversal in order to confirm the trade you are considering.

Doji - Harami Cross

The "doji" candlesticks can provide trading information on their own or they can be read as part of a series of candlesticks. A doji pattern is formed when a stock's opening price and closing price are equal or almost the same. The length of the upper and lower tails can vary depending on the price action during the period and the resulting candlestick can end up looking like a cross, inverted cross or plus sign. Any reading into bullish or bearish price action is usually based on the preceding price action and volume. Figure 7.7 shows doji candlesticks with long and short tails.

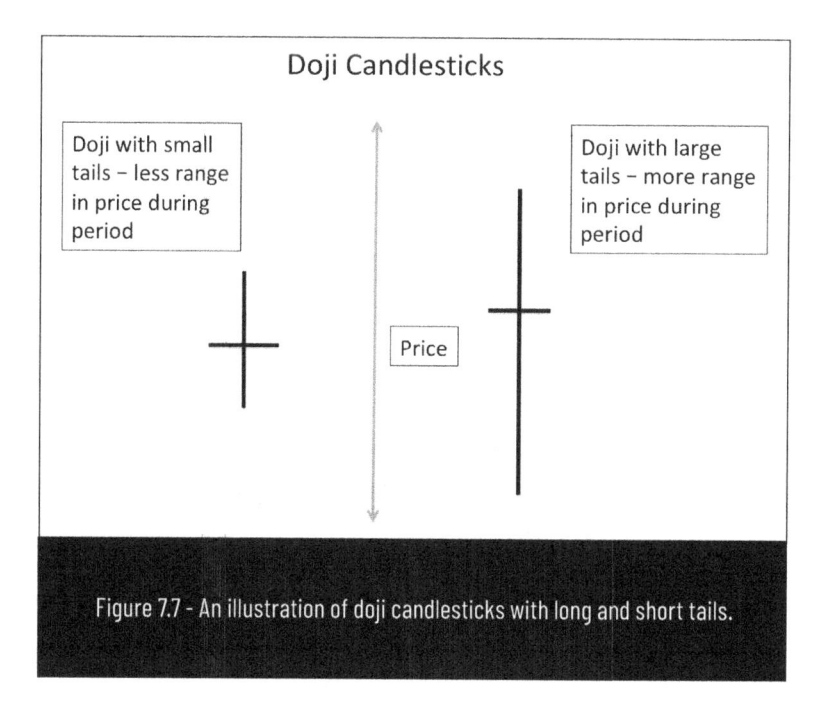

Figure 7.7 - An illustration of doji candlesticks with long and short tails.

One particular type of doji that shows a potential reversal in price action is called the harami cross. The key to reading this pattern is to look for the trading volume confirmation. You should see strong volume on the preceding days followed by a drop in volume with shorter tails on the final harami cross candlestick. This change in volume and price action usually indicates a shift in traders' confidence on the continued direction of the stock price. An illustration of a bullish and bearish harami cross is shown in Figure 7.8.

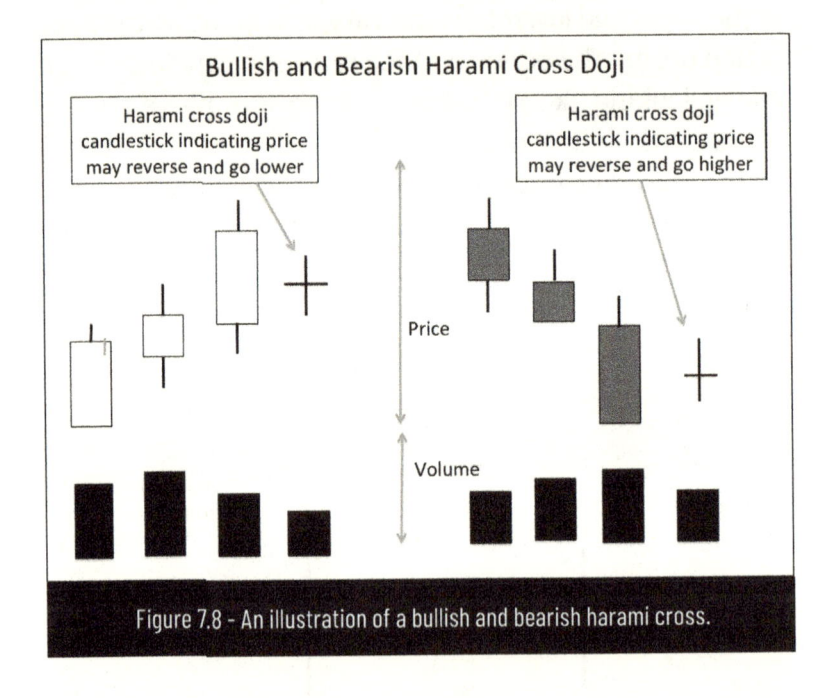

Figure 7.8 - An illustration of a bullish and bearish harami cross.

Referring back to Figure 7.6, you can see how a harami cross appeared just before an engulfing candle in the chart of TZA, indicating the price was ready to reverse and move higher. The engulfing candle confirmed this signal and shows how this indicator can be used in combination with other indicators.

Doji - Gravestone and Dragonfly

A gravestone and dragonfly are doji patterns that are also associated with reversals in sentiment between buyers and sellers. They are both characterized by opening and closing prices that have long tails and are near each other. While the opening and closing prices don't have to be precisely the same for either pattern to be valid, they should be relatively close. Figure 7.9 below shows both types of doji.

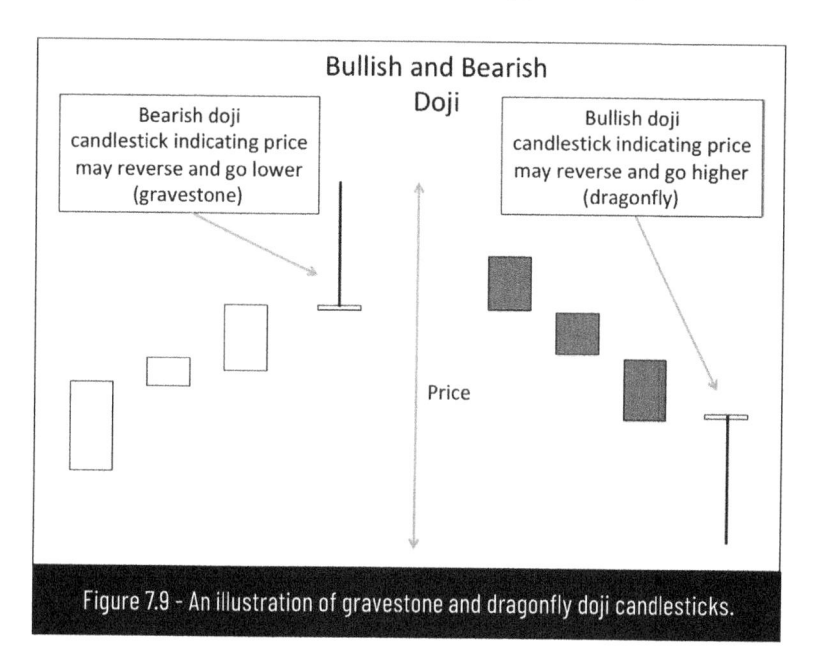

Figure 7.9 - An illustration of gravestone and dragonfly doji candlesticks.

The gravestone doji can be found at the end of an uptrend as shown on the left side of the figure. The long upper tail suggests that the bulls took control early but later in the period it was the bears who were in control, pushing the price back down to the open.

The dragonfly doji is the opposite of the gravestone in that it is the bears who start out in control of the price by pushing it lower at the open. As the period continues, the bulls take control of the price movement, returning the price back to the open.

Traders will sometimes scan for these patterns and then take long positions or initiate short positions based on this setup although it is important to use other technical analysis tools as a confirmation of this reversal signal. Some research on this pattern has shown them to be less reliable compared to other patterns.

Traders should also look at the volume of shares traded with the doji and compare that volume to the previous period – ideally the volume will be equal to or larger during the period that the doji occurred. The following chart in Figure 7.10 shows a gravestone doji in Pfizer, Inc. (PFE) stock following a significantly high volume uptrend. This doji was the start of a significantly bearish reversal in the price of PFE until a dragonfly doji appeared and the stock reversed again with the price starting a trend higher.

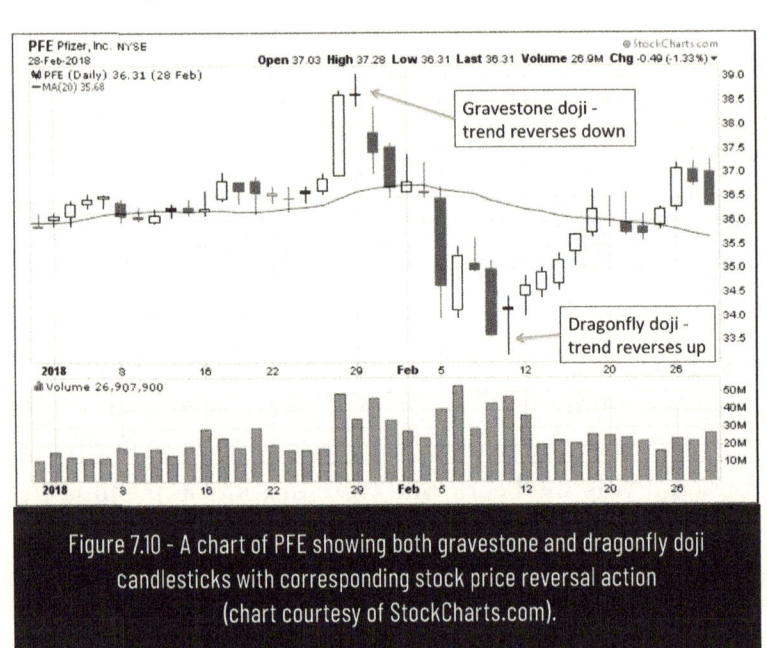

Figure 7.10 - A chart of PFE showing both gravestone and dragonfly doji candlesticks with corresponding stock price reversal action (chart courtesy of StockCharts.com).

How to Trade a Doji

Doji patterns can be traded in a similar way as to how you would trade an engulfing candle. The first objective is to get in as early as possible when you recognize the pattern appearing. For example, on a dragonfly doji, a swing trader could go long with their stop at the bottom of the tail. A tighter stop for a more conservative trader would be about 50% of the tail. Let's say the stock started and finished the day at $25.00 with a tail tracing down to a $24.00 low of the day. That would put the 50% stop at $24.50. Recall that your reward needs to be at least 2 times the risk that you are taking, so for this price stop level, you would need to expect at least $1.00 in reward per share.

Again, you should check other indicators to get some confirmation that a potential reversal in price action is happening. Also, you should assess if there have been some fundamental factors behind a possible reversal.

Gaps

There are 2 types of gaps made by candlesticks when a stock price moves suddenly. One is referred to as a *"gap up"* and the other is called a *"gap down"*. A gap up occurs when the opening price of a stock is higher than the previous close. If the opening price of a stock is lower than the previous close, then it is a gap down. Figure 7.11 below shows examples of these 2 types of gaps.

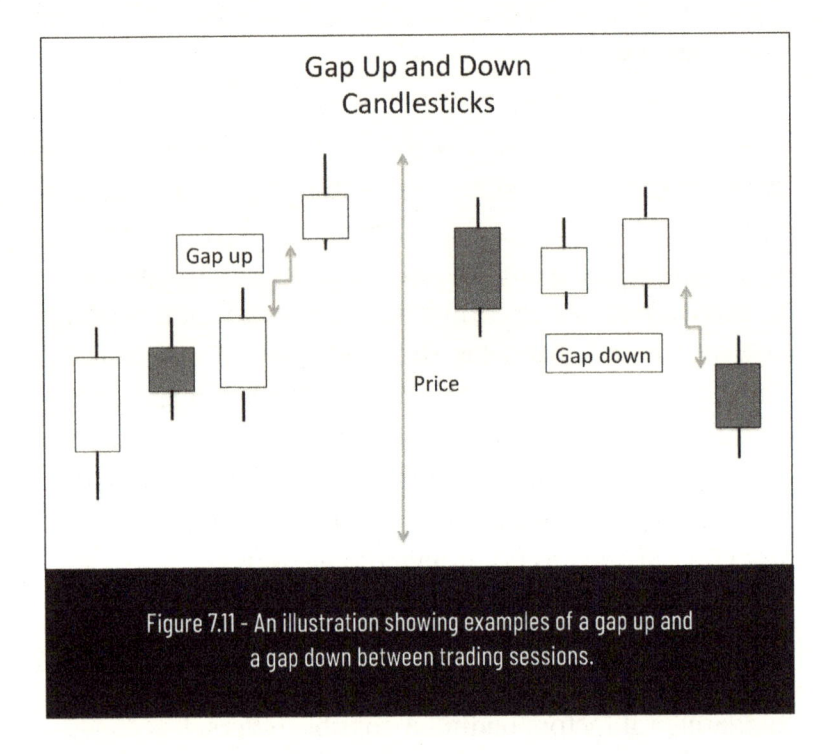

Figure 7.11 - An illustration showing examples of a gap up and a gap down between trading sessions.

Gapping price action normally occurs between trading sessions. The size of the gap is often very small but at other times it can be very large. Larger gaps are usually caused by some new information that has come to light, which affects the sentiment of the traders and investors toward the stock. It could be negative news such as a drug test failure or it could be good news such as the announcement of a new product launch. After a gap has occurred, 1 of 3 things will happen:

5. gap and go

6. gap and consolidate

7. gap and pullback (called "filling the gap")

I will look at these 3 possible scenarios in the following sections.

Gap and Go

The gap and go happens when it takes several days for the market to settle on a new valuation for the stock. This usually happens after a major announcement or event. Overly exuberant buying or selling will drive valuations to such extremes that an eventual pullback will occur.

These types of scenarios will likely play out on extremely good news or in markets that are very bullish or bearish in sentiment. For stocks gapping higher, if there is a high number of traders holding short positions (over 20% of shares are shorted for example), then panic covering of these short positions creates additional buying that drives the price even higher. This is referred to as a *"short squeeze"*, which I discussed in Chapter 6, Fundamental Analysis.

Gap and Consolidate

Some gaps are 1-day events and all of the news gets priced into the stock in the session immediately following the event. After that, the stock's price will move sideways with a bit of up and down action as investors take profits or losses and new investors come in to take new positions. After a period of sideways consolidating price action, the price will start to move higher or lower. The direction the stock goes after consolidation depends considerably on the event and the overall market direction.

If the news was good but the overall market is trending lower, then eventually the market direction may override the event and take the stock's price lower. If the news has long-term implications for the stock (either positive or negative), the stock will likely continue to move in the direction of the gap after consolidation.

Gap and Fill

Some gaps are not sustainable. Traders and investors will take profits in the gap and it is possible that short sellers will see an opportunity to sell high and buy low. Long traders will sell into a pop up in price and the short uptrend will reverse with the stock *"filling the gap"*.

Figure 7.12 - A chart of NETE showing the gap up and follow through for several days, followed by a gap and fill (chart courtesy of StockCharts.com).

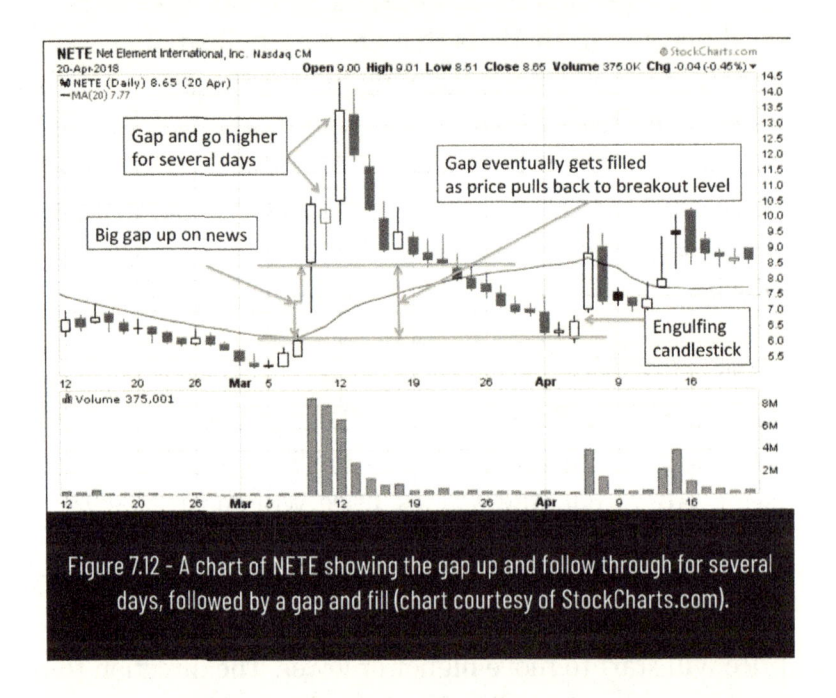

Figure 7.12 shows a gap and go as well as a longer-term gap fill on Net Element International, Inc. (NETE). You can see there was a large gap up on the news from the open on the first day, but it would have been difficult to determine a good stop price unless you got an entry right at the open on that first day.

This chart also shows another example of an engulfing candlestick that I discussed earlier. As often happens, the stock price found support after dropping back to the point it broke out from (areas of support and resistance will be discussed in Chapter 8).

How to Trade Gaps

For a swing trader, gaps can be difficult to trade after they have already happened. Gaps can result in overreactions to some news and those overreactions can last a day or they can last for several days. In an uptrending market, a swing trader can take a position during the first day of the gap up. They could take a position near the end of the day if the stock continues to trend higher and closes out the day close to or at the high. There is a good chance under this scenario (a strong market and a strong stock price action) that the price will gap up again on the following day. I will discuss this particular strategy of playing gaps in more detail in Chapter 12. In the NETE case, even though the trade looked good for a follow-through day, the next day the stock opened lower in price, however it did eventually break to a new high.

Another way to play gaps is to use the gap and fill principle. Often the points where a stock gapped higher or lower become, respectively, levels of resistance or support. Looking at the NETE chart shown in Figure 7.12, you can see that as the price started to drop back, the price movement seemed to pause briefly around the $8.50 level. This is where it opened on the first gap up day. These levels are often respected and traded by market participants, but once it broke that support level, the price continued to drop back to where NETE started its journey higher. Knowing where there will likely be levels of resistance and support, a swing trader can make trades based on this principle regarding these levels. I will discuss using support and resistance techniques in Chapter 8.

Overreactions in the market happen all of the time and eventually these overreactions will correct themselves. A swing trader can watch for top or bottom patterns in a stock that would indicate the buyers or sellers are exhausted and that a reversal in price is about to happen (which will represent a trading opportunity). I've discussed reversal engulfing and doji patterns as specific patterns to watch for. I will cover additional tradable top and bottom patterns in the following 2 chapters.

Chapter Summary

In this chapter, I covered the basics of constructing a candlestick and a bar chart. Charts containing these figures are readily available online. I also looked at some basic candlestick patterns that many technical traders watch for and base their trades on. In the next chapter, I will look at some more advanced charting patterns and some additional tools that a swing trader can use to find good trade setups. The following topics were covered in this chapter.

- Candlestick basics: how a candlestick or bar chart is constructed and what it tells you about the opening and closing price during a period as well as the highs and lows of that period.
- How to construct or identify a bullish candlestick (price moving higher) and a bearish candlestick (price moving lower).
- Several reversal candlesticks were discussed including the following:
  - Engulfing candle: one large candle that fully engulfs and moves in the opposite direction of the previous candle.

- Harami cross candle: has the appearance of a cross with a very little body and often approximately equal top and bottom tails.
- Gravestone doji: shows that the price of the stock opened low, it rose in price, but then dropped back and closed fairly near to the open price, its long upper tail indicates possible bearish action.
- Dragonfly doji: shows that the price of the stock opened high, it dropped in price, but then increased and closed fairly near to the open price, its long lower tail indicates possible bullish action.

- Engulfing candlesticks and doji can indicate a trend reversal. You can trade these as a trend reversal and especially with other confirming indicators like the MACD and RSI. You can also look to see if there has been some fundamental shift that has caused the stock or sector to reverse. There are additional reversal patterns that I will cover in the next chapter.
- Gap ups and gap downs were described in the chapter. I discussed why they happen and what can happen after the event that caused the gap.
- Gaps can be traded as a continuation trade (the uptrend or downtrend continues for an extended period of time) or watched for an overreaction. You can watch for a topping or bottoming pattern due to an overreaction in price action (which indicates that the buyers or sellers are exhausted and that a reversal in price is about to happen) and then take a reversal trade.

CHAPTER 8

Technical Analysis - Indicator Tools

As I discussed in the previous chapter, the technical analysis of stocks is based on the principle that past price movements are a predictor of the future moves in price. Trading volume (the number of stocks traded) is often combined with prior price movement to help improve these price prediction models.

With the advent and then increased use of computers over the past decades, a wide range of different technical analyses has become much more accessible to every individual Retail trader. Imagine how labor intensive it would have been 25 years ago to sit down with a pencil, paper and calculator to plot out an average comprised of 200 numbers. How about 50 years ago, doing it with a slide rule?

Today, many Institutional trading firms are using computers to make purchase and sale decisions on different markets. These computers run *"algorithms"* (essentially a computer program) that monitor price and volume, perform ongoing technical analysis, and then make actual trades based on the results of that analysis. The programmers design the algorithms to perform functions at a certain point or technical event. One can imagine the impact that these algorithms might have if a number of different firms were all running programs with similar action parameters. Moves would certainly be somewhat predictable.

There are now hundreds of different technical studies that are readily available to all traders and machines. These studies analyze and attempt to predict stock price movements. Below is a short list of some commonly used technical studies:

- moving averages (simple and exponential)
- support and resistance lines
- momentum indicators
- trading patterns

Because machines and their algorithms make technical analysis ever more important today, these studies are very useful to swing traders, and essentially create self-fulfilling events. In other words, an expectation about a stock price movement event can affect the buying group's behavior toward that movement, which will then cause the expectation to be realized.

As an example, traders and machines that do technical analysis commonly watch a 20-day simple moving average of a stock's price. When a stock's price is on the rise, the 20-day moving average price will follow along on the uptrend, while remaining under the current price. Let's assume there is some profit-taking and the stock starts to drop. Unless there is some fundamental reason for the change in attitude toward the stock, people and machines wait at the 20-day moving average price to buy. When the stock hits that price or close to it, the buyers come in and the price rebounds, continuing to reinforce that the 20-day moving average event is almost always an area of support.

The large number of studies now available for use by traders can be overwhelming and leave you to wonder which one or ones you should use. I suggest that you find a couple of tools that you feel comfortable using and then focus on them rather than getting bogged down with trying to manage and find alignment with too many indicators.

In this second technical analysis chapter, I will look at some specific tools that you can use to identify potentially profitable trading opportunities. The tools I will look at are ones that I use on a regular basis and include the following:

- support and resistance levels
- moving averages (simple and exponential)
- Relative Strength Index (RSI)
- MACD: convergence and divergence
- Average True Range (ATR)

After reading and studying this section, you will have some excellent tools to use to identify trading opportunities. There are also many other swing trading tools available, so I encourage you to continue looking at other measures as you further develop your trading skills and strategies.

Support and Resistance Levels

Now that you understand the candlestick and how it shows price action in the market for a stock, I will examine how support and resistance levels can be used to predict future price movements in a stock. This is one of the easiest forms of charting and does not require any formulas or complicated calculations. All you need is your eyes and a small amount of creativity.

When stocks move up, they tend to find price levels that are hard to break through. For stocks heading higher, these levels are called areas of resistance. Conversely, stocks that are dropping will eventually find price levels where buyers come in and prevent the price from moving lower. These are called areas of support. If you look at a chart that contains a series of candlesticks over a long period of time, you should be able to identify where these areas of support and resistance occur. You can do this for a 1-hour chart, a daily chart or even a weekly chart. Sometimes these support and resistance levels are common to all time frames.

Support and resistance line charting is the first and most basic charting tool you should be able to master as a new swing trader. Once you start doing scans, which I will discuss in Chapter 12, Swing Trading Strategies, you will start identifying potential trade ideas for numerous stocks. The next step will be to scan the price charts of these stocks. Your eye will quickly become trained to identify previous areas of support and resistance, and that will help you assess key price levels for entries and exits on a trade.

Horizontal support or resistance trading is simple but very effective. My years of trading experience have shown and taught us that the market remembers price levels, which is why these support or resistance lines make sense. You might ask – why does the marketplace remember these levels? Again, it is a self-fulfilling prophecy. Most of the knowledgeable traders and machines are looking at the same charts and drawing the same lines and they all arrive at roughly the same values for support and resistance. So naturally, when one of those price levels is reached, there is additional buying or selling pressure depending on whether it is an area of support or resistance. Minor support or resistance areas will often cause price trends to pause. Major areas of support or resistance will often cause the prices to at least temporarily reverse.

Support is a price level where buying is strong enough to interrupt or reverse a downtrend. When a downtrend hits a support level, it bounces. Support is represented in a chart by a horizontal line connecting 2 or more bottoms. *Resistance* is a price level where selling is strong enough to interrupt or reverse an uptrend. Resistance is represented in a chart by a horizontal line connecting 2 or more tops.

Figure 8.1 and Figure 8.2 shown below illustrate how levels of support and resistance can clearly be seen on the daily charts of the SPDR S&P 500 ETF (SPY) and Sun Life Financial Inc. (SLF). Identifying these past levels can give you a clear indication of where future price levels will either bounce or be rejected.

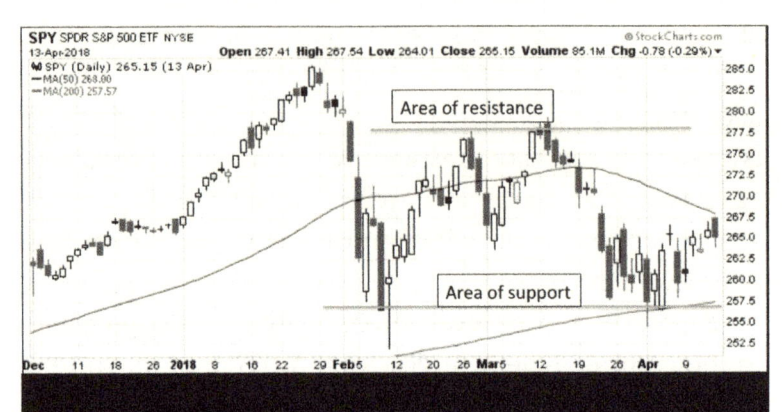

Figure 8.1 - A chart of SPY that shows both support and resistance levels from February through to April 2018 (chart courtesy of StockCharts.com).

Figure 8.2 - A chart of SLF that shows how levels of support and resistance were respected a number of times in the past (chart courtesy of StockCharts.com).

Listed below are a number of items that you should be aware of when drawing support or resistance lines in hourly, daily or weekly charts:

1. The more recent levels of support or resistance are more relevant in comparison to levels that are from further in the past.

2. Levels of support or resistance that are tested often are stronger than levels only tested once and therefore they are harder to break through.

3. Look for individual indecision candles in the area of support or resistance because that is where the buyers and sellers are fighting to take control. An engulfing candle or doji at support or resistance will help confirm a possible price action reversal.

4. Often half-dollar ($0.50) and whole dollar numbers act as a support or resistance level, especially in lower than $10.00 stocks.

5. Support or resistance lines do not give you an exact price. They are more of an "area" where you will find this level. For example, if you drew a line in a stock chart and found an area of support at $21.20, you should not expect the price to go to and bounce exactly off of that $21.20 level. However, if you picked your line correctly, there is a good chance that somewhere around that level there will be some buying support. The stock might actually bounce at the $21.45 level or it could drop to $21.00 before bouncing back. Some factors that might affect the exact bounce level include overall market conditions on that day, the price of the

stock (does it trade at $10.00 or $100.00 per share) and its Average True Range (how much the stock price varies day to day on average) to name a few.

6. The level of support or resistance should provide a very clear indication that it is in fact a level of support or resistance. If after reaching that price the stock flounders around that price level, and does not clearly reverse direction, then it may not be respecting that level. A common phrase is "the trend is your friend" – floundering around a price level will, more often than not, result in the price action continuing in the direction it was going initially.

7. If the price of a stock breaks through a level of resistance and continues higher, then that level of resistance now becomes a level of support if a downturn in price occurs. The same applies for downtrending stocks that break a level of support. That level of support now becomes a resistance level should the stock turn and try to move higher.

8. For swing trading, you can use other tools to confirm support or resistance. You can look at moving averages like the 20, 50 and 200-day moving averages because an apparent level of support or resistance may also be happening at one of those levels. Other tools I will discuss later in this chapter, such as the Relative Strength Index (RSI) and the Moving Average Convergence Divergence (MACD), may also be used to confirm your assumption about a level of support or resistance.

Diagonal Lines

Some traders who work with charts also look for and rely on diagonal trendlines. You will typically find these in stocks and other financial instruments that are in long-term trends, either up or down. These can be useful because stocks never go straight up or down: they move in waves. These waves of price action can slowly move a stock up or down depending on whether the buyers or sellers are in control.

The challenge with diagonal waves is that they tend to be more subjective and open to interpretation by the creator. Other indicators like moving averages and momentum indicators can provide similar information but are not as open to interpretation by the chartist. This is why I prefer not to rely too heavily on any diagonal trendlines, however I am aware that numerous technical chart analysts do use them in assessing stocks that are trending higher or lower.

Diagonal lines can also be drawn in a stock that is either trending up or down to create a channel of trading in that trend. These diagonal channels of stocks in a long-term uptrend or downtrend can be used to keep you in a position for an extended period of time to maximize profits. You need to recognize that if you are using diagonal channels in this manner, your hold time may be much longer than a typical swing trade. Your trade could become a long-term hold and that may not be a bad thing if you are continuing to build wealth.

Shown below in Figure 8.3 is an example of a diagonal line chart pattern that could have been used to keep a trader in a stock for a very long time. This figure shows Amazon.com, Inc. (AMZN) slowly grinding higher in waves of buying and selling. A break in the horizontal trendline provides a longer-term swing trader with an indication that the uptrend may be ending and it would be time to take profits on a long trade or go short to take advantage of a drop in price.

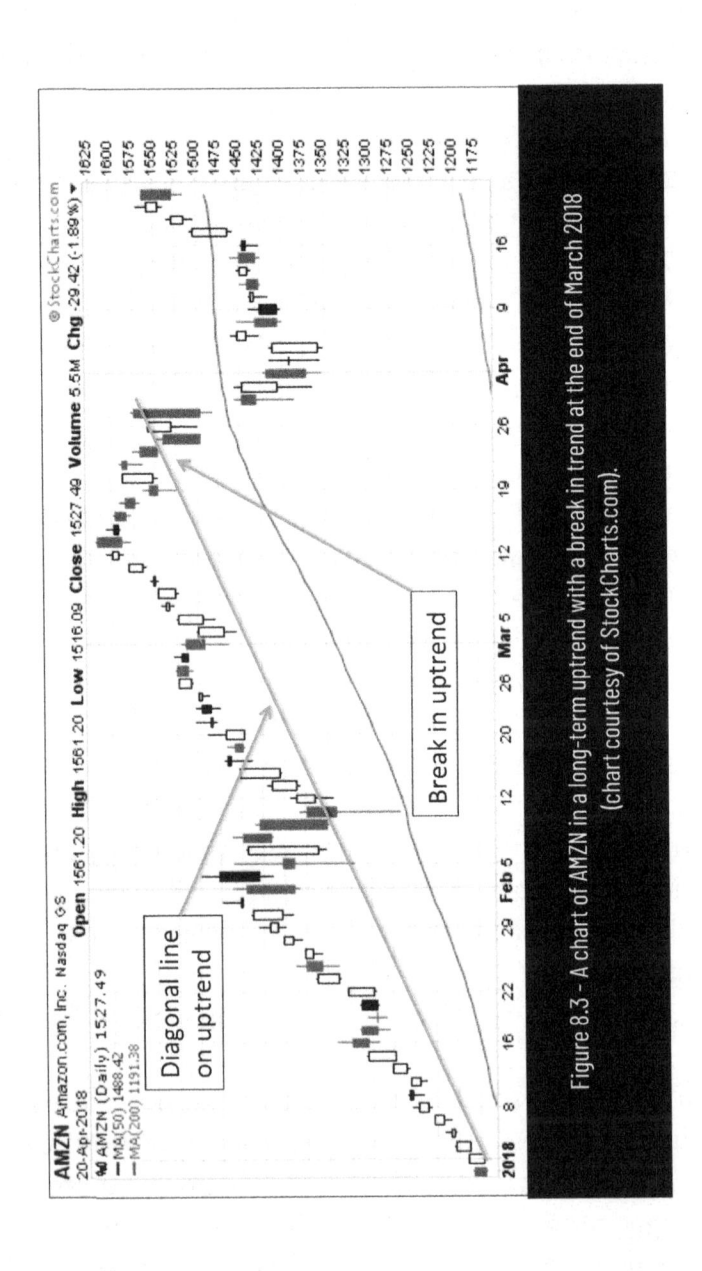

Figure 8.3 - A chart of AMZN in a long-term uptrend with a break in trend at the end of March 2018 (chart courtesy of StockCharts.com).

How to Use Support and Resistance Levels

You will often start with a scan of the market to identify possible trade opportunities. I will discuss how to do these scans in Chapter 12, Swing Trading Strategies. Once some potential trades are identified, you should look at the charts to see if you can identify levels of support and resistance.

Let's imagine you have a particular stock that during a scan has been identified as a potential long trade. You look at the chart and notice that the current price is close to a level of prior resistance. This is a price where it has not been able to break higher in the past. You would probably want to pass on going long on this stock because this is an area of prior price resistance.

Alternatively, if you find a stock that is trading just above a level of prior support, this may provide a good long entry from a risk to reward perspective. Your risk would be the price difference from the support level to the entry price. Next, you would look to find where you might expect the stock price to meet some resistance and then calculate your risk to reward ratio. Recall that your potential reward should be at least 2 times the risk you are taking on the trade.

Let's take a look at Figure 8.4 as an example of how you could have traded using levels of support and resistance. This daily chart of FireEye, Inc. (FEYE) clearly shows areas of support and resistance. The stock price fluctuates between these 2 levels giving opportunities to go long and to go short as shown in the figure. At the break of support in August, you would have quickly been stopped out or not have taken that trade at all due to the gap down and erratic price action.

The chart in Figure 8.4 also shows how support becomes resistance once the support is broken. There is a pause at the previous level of support before news related to the stock results in a gap and go price movement. The news was particularly good because the upper prior level of resistance did not stop the stock from moving higher after a very short pause.

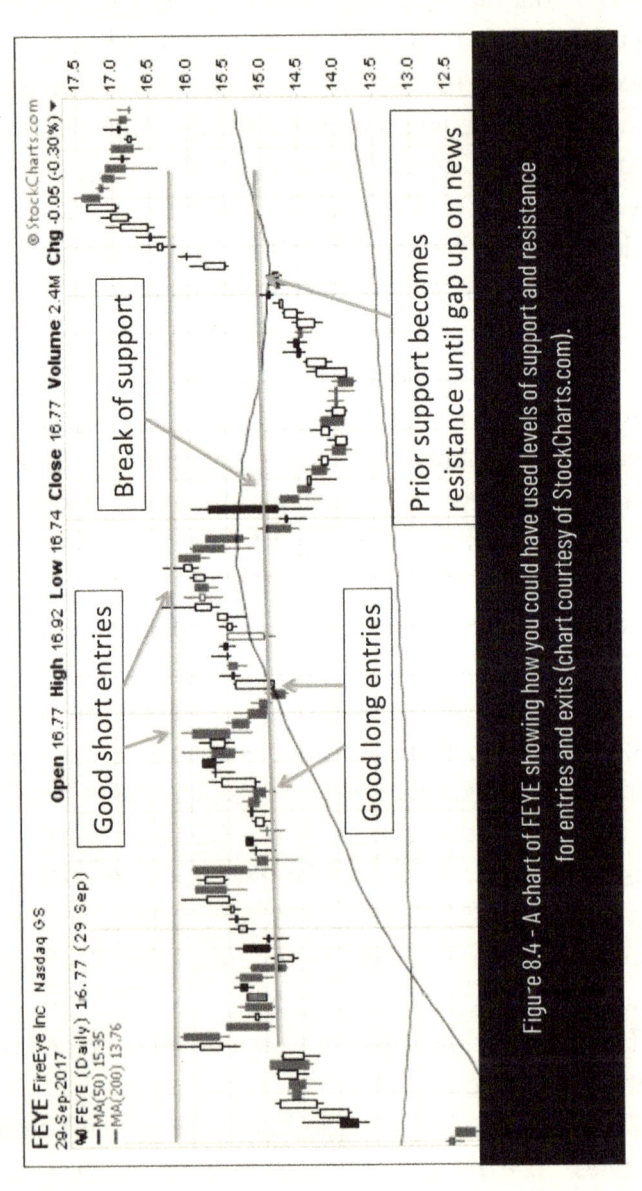

Figure 8.4 - A chart of FEYE showing how you could have used levels of support and resistance for entries and exits (chart courtesy of StockCharts.com).

Levels of support and resistance will often provide you with good reference prices for risk and reward calculations assuming you get the entry price in your trade plan. Having a good risk to reward ratio is crucial to your success as a trader.

Moving Averages

Moving averages are another very popular and relatively simple trading tool that can be used by a swing trader. They can assist you in getting a good entry on a stock and further help you to stay in a position to take advantage of a long-term trend. They can also provide a good signal for when you should make an exit.

Moving averages come in 2 primary types: simple and exponential. Both of these moving averages can be calculated using different periods of time. The longer the time period used, the more likely the average will lag behind a stock price in an uptrend or downtrend. Let's start by looking at the difference between the simple and exponential moving averages, and then look at different time periods, and then, finally, consider how best to use them with your swing trading strategies.

Simple vs. Exponential Moving Averages

The difference between the simple moving average (SMA) and the exponential moving average (EMA) can be significant and your choice of which one you choose to use can make an impact on your trading. An SMA is calculated by starting with a period of time. Let's use 20 days as an example. You take the closing price for each of the previous 20 days, add these price numbers together, and then divide by 20. This gives you the average price for those 20 days.

The next day you repeat the same process with the new set of numbers: the oldest day from your previous calculation gets dropped out because it is no longer in your 20-day range and the most recent closing price replaces it. As each day passes, you calculate a new 20-day SMA number that you can plot on a graph against the time. For the 50-day and the 200-day SMAs, you go through the same process with the corresponding number of days.

If the stock price you are plotting is constantly moving down, then the moving average prices get dragged lower as well. This gives you a trendline that you can monitor for trend changes. In our example, if the price reverses and starts to move higher, then the stock price will eventually cross the moving average, which has been lagging behind the current price movement. This cross provides a possible indicator of a change in sentiment.

Figure 8.5 shows a plot of Micron Technology, Inc. (MU) trending lower with the moving averages following the price down until it starts to reverse. On August 14th, MU's price crosses over the 20-day SMA. This is a sign of a possible change in investor sentiment with a new uptrend beginning. In our MU example, the price consolidates (churns sideways) for almost 2 weeks until the price starts to break above the 50-day SMA. After this event, the price trend change is clearly established and MU's stock price moves higher.

The chart of MU also shows how for a number of times the 20-day SMA acts as a support as the stock moves higher with waves of buying and selling. This illustrates how moving averages can be used to get a good entry in a trade and also to keep you in the trade in order to maximize profits.

Technical Analysis - Indicator Tools

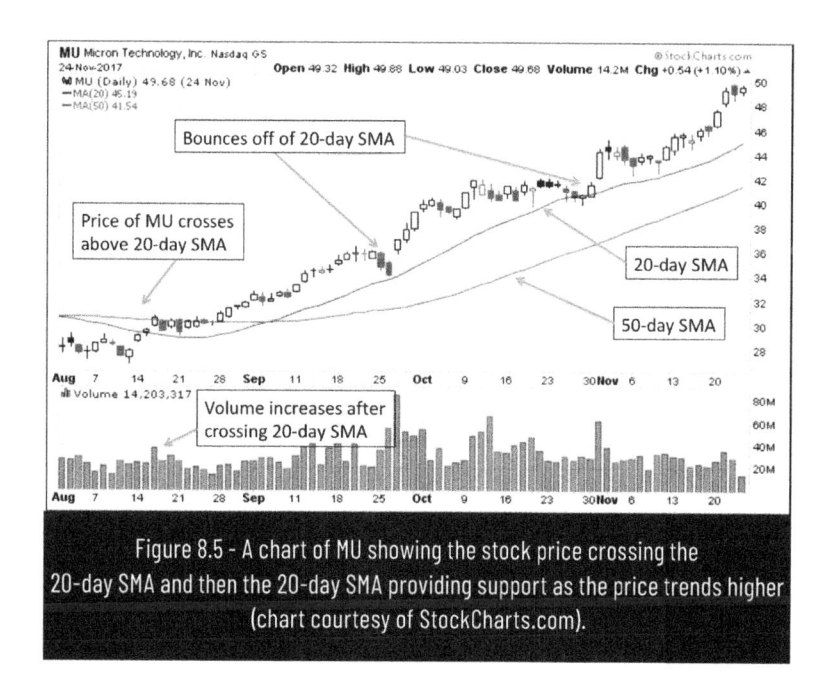

Figure 8.5 - A chart of MU showing the stock price crossing the 20-day SMA and then the 20-day SMA providing support as the price trends higher (chart courtesy of StockCharts.com).

The exponential moving average calculation is a little more complicated so I will not provide an explanation of it in this book. The formulas used are readily available on the Internet. The important thing to know when comparing the 2 different moving averages is that the EMA is more sensitive to recent changes in the price of the stock. This means that the EMA will react more quickly and, depending upon the situation, may or may not be good.

Because the EMA reacts faster when the price changes direction, it can provide an earlier signal of a possible change in trend. But, especially during times of higher volatility, this quicker reaction can also give the wrong signal. Stocks move in waves regardless of what direction they are moving: up, down or sideways. If a stock in a downtrend starts to bounce higher after a wave of selling, the EMA could start pointing up and potentially send a signal that there is an overall change in direction of the stock's price. This may not be the case if it is just a temporary bounce higher before continuing on a downtrend. Therefore this early indicator can result in a false trend change signal.

Because the SMA moves more slowly, it can keep you in a winning trade longer by smoothing out the inevitable bounces or pullbacks that normally occur during a long-term trend. Conversely, this slower moving trendline may also keep you in a trade when the trend has actually changed, so you may have to use other tools or fundamental analysis to decide if this trend is changing to the other direction. You will more often use the SMA when you are in your trades for longer durations and you are thus wanting to stay with a trend for as long as possible.

Due to the different levels of sensitivity between the 2 types of moving averages, you should consider adjusting which one to use based on the particular market environment. In volatile markets, where prices are bouncing up and down, an SMA may be a better tool. In less volatile market conditions, you would consider using the EMA to get earlier entry signals on trend changes.

Referring to Figure 8.6, you can see the difference between using the 20-day SMA versus the 20-day EMA. You'll notice that the EMA gives a slightly earlier signal as the MU price first crosses the faster reacting moving average. In this case, you may have got a slightly lower entry price on the trade, however, given the great run on MU it would not have made a big difference in your total return on the trade.

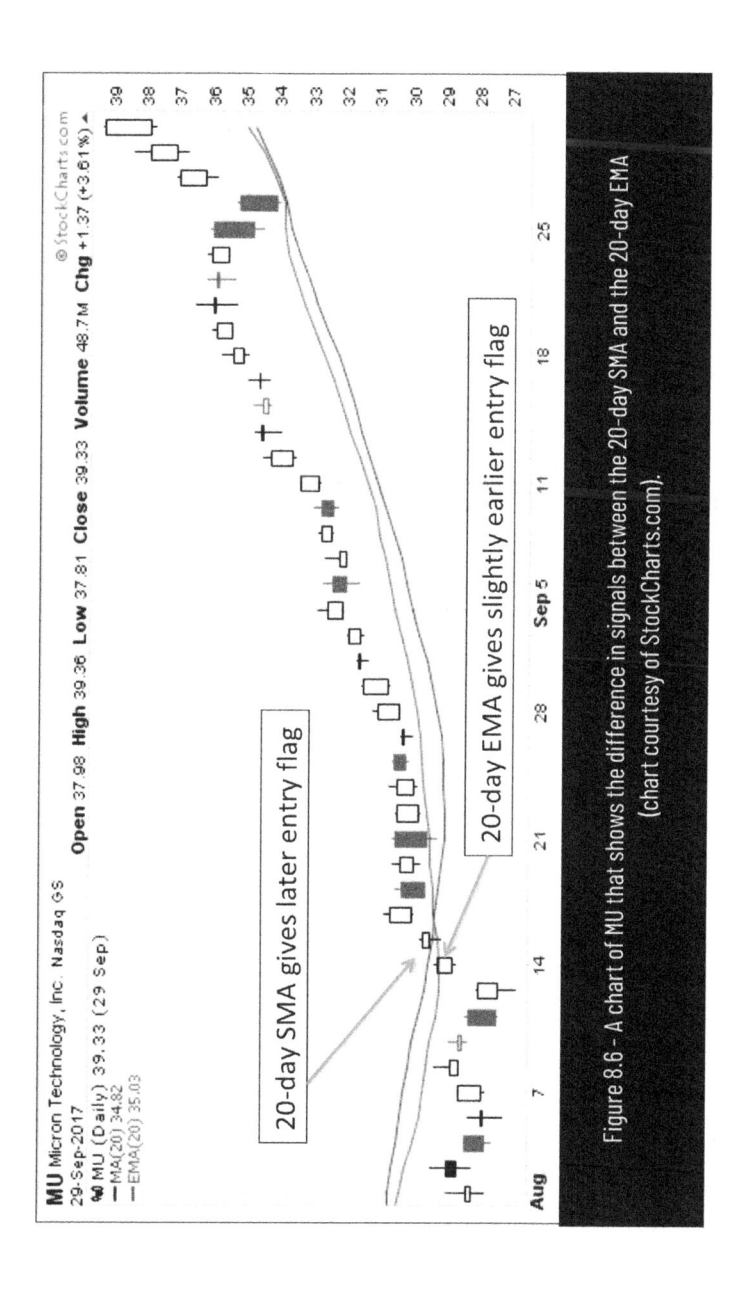

Technical Analysis – Indicator Tools 143

Figure 8.6 – A chart of MU that shows the difference in signals between the 20-day SMA and the 20-day EMA (chart courtesy of StockCharts.com).

Moving Average Time Periods

As a swing trader using moving averages tools, you will need to consider what periods of time you want to use that give the best signals for your trading style. The first thing you should do is to stay with some of the periods that are commonly used by traders and computers. As I have discussed already, these moving averages work as technical indicators because they are, in effect, self-fulfilling prophecies. Many other traders and machines are looking at the same indicators and they work in part because of that fact.

The shorter the number of days used to calculate the moving average, the sooner you will see a change in direction because the short time periods more strongly reflect current price action. Like the EMA, these shorter time frames can be good in identifying a shift in sentiment between the buyers and sellers, but they can also give false signals by reflecting the waves of buying and selling that occur within the typical wave action movements of a stock's price.

The most common periods used by swing traders are 20-day, 50-day and 200-day SMAs. Because traders are watching price movements in relation to these averages, they usually offer areas of support and resistance. The 200-day SMA is highly revered and normally provides the strongest level of support when a stock is selling off and the strongest level of resistance when a stock is starting to move higher from a low.

Traders also use the percentage of stocks in the market that are trading above their 200-day average as a gauge to determine the overall health of the stock market. The higher the percentage of stocks above their 200-day SMA, the more the overall market is biased to trending higher, therefore, the better trades for a swing trader may be long trades versus going short.

Below are some further thoughts to consider in developing your strategies related to using moving averages when swing trading:

- The 20-day SMA is a good tool to use for a short-term swing trade. In a trending stock, the price action will often respect this level and it will also quickly identify a shift in sentiment and thus a reversal in trend.

- The 20-day EMA is a faster reacting tool that can be used for short-term swing trades. It can get you into a trade earlier but in more volatile markets, it can also give you a false trend reversal signal.

- The 50-day SMA is also a popular gauge for a longer-term swing trade and it will allow you to ride a potentially profitable trade longer in order to make additional gains. It is a good intermediate balance between the shorter 20-day and the longer 200-day SMAs.

- The 200-day SMA represents almost 1 year of past price action (there are about 250 trading days in a year). In a downtrending stock, this SMA may provide significant support and therefore be a good entry for a long position due to it being a very popular level for traders (remember the discussion on self-fulfilling prophecies). The risk on this sort of trade is when the price finds a support level just below the 200-day SMA and the trader is then stopped out.

The Golden Cross and the Death Cross

One other way to use moving averages to determine a directional price change is to watch for what traders refer to as a "golden cross" or a "death cross". This indicator uses the 50-day and 200-day SMAs. For example, let's consider a stock that has been in a long-term downtrend. Due to this trend, the 50-day moving average is creating a line that is below the 200-day SMA line. A golden cross signal on this stock will occur when the 50-day SMA crosses the 200-day moving average from below to above. When this happens, it is an indication that the negative sentiment is possibly changing with the downtrend in price shifting to an uptrend. This cross happens because the 50-day SMA is reflecting more current price action while the 200-day SMA is lagging further behind, reflecting prices that are further in the past.

The death cross is the opposite of the golden cross. It occurs when a stock is in a general uptrend and the price action starts to trend lower. Once again, the faster-reacting 50-day SMA starts to turn down faster than the slower reacting 200-day SMA and they eventually cross. The 50-day SMA crosses from above the 200-day SMA to below it, showing a change in sentiment and stock price direction.

Figure 8.7 is a chart of the Consumer Staples Select Sector SPDR Fund (XLP). You can see where the 50-day SMA crosses the 200-day SMA. However, you can also see from this chart that the signal is a relatively late indicator because both of these moving averages are longer-term indicators and therefore they take longer to reflect changes in sentiment. The event of a 50-day SMA crossing a 200-day SMA is something you can scan for when looking for potential trades but it is important to recognize that they reflect longer-term trends. In Chapter 12, I will discuss finding these events by performing market scans.

Technical Analysis – Indicator Tools

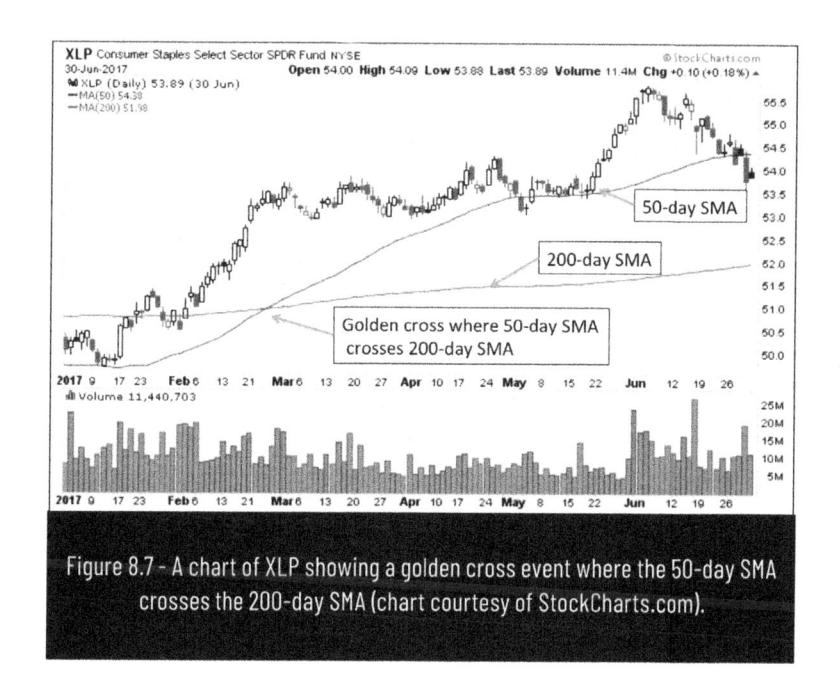

Figure 8.7 – A chart of XLP showing a golden cross event where the 50-day SMA crosses the 200-day SMA (chart courtesy of StockCharts.com).

Moving Averages in Range-Bound Stocks and Markets

As a swing trader, you need to be aware that SMA and EMA tools do not work well in markets or in stocks that are trading in a limited range (where the price makes relatively small moves between support and resistance). This type of market or stock is referred to as being *"range-bound"*, and the price action is commonly referred to as *"churning"*. In these range-bound trading cases, all of the different time period SMA and EMA lines ripple sideways between levels of support and resistance. The price action does not respect these lines, therefore, these tools are most effective when trends are occurring: either higher or lower.

How to Use Moving Averages

The first way you can use moving averages is to scan for opportunities in the market based on the SMA tool. I will discuss scanning techniques in Chapter 12, Swing Trading Strategies. You can search for events such as the 20-day SMA dropping below the stock price while the 50-day and 200-day SMAs are still above the price. This event could be an indication of a stock price reversal, with the faster reacting 20-day SMA indicating the sentiment shift while, in comparison, the longer-term moving averages have yet to reflect the change in sentiment.

You can also monitor these averages once you have entered a trade in order to help you to decide whether to exit a trade completely at a target price or to take some of the position off at one target and continue to hold the rest as the stock price continues to move in your favor. This is referred to as *"scaling out"* and will be discussed later in the book.

The SMA can be used to find a potential area of support or resistance. For example, if you are holding a short position, you might consider covering all or some of that short position as the price of the stock approaches the 200-day SMA, which is watched by many traders and trading machines as an area of significant support.

Moving averages can be used as an indicator to enter a trade, to exit a trade and to stay in an existing trade. Therefore, it is a good tool in your arsenal when markets and/or stocks are trending up or down.

Relative Strength Index

The Relative Strength Index (RSI) is another indicator that you can use to help you pick a good entry or exit on a stock. The index was developed by J. Welles Wilder and is an indicator that measures the speed and change of price movements. Some traders refer to it as a "momentum oscillator".

Many professional technicians believe that stocks are constantly moving between a position of being overvalued or undervalued and that their true value lies in the middle of these wave actions. Occasionally, stocks will become extremely overvalued or undervalued. The RSI is one way to measure how much over or undervalued a stock might be.

The RSI calculation generates a number that ranges between zero and 100. I will not discuss or show the formula that is used to calculate this number but, for those interested, it is readily available on the Internet. Almost every trading platform will do this calculation for you. As a swing trader, you only really need to understand what the RSI number is telling you about a stock's price action.

The RSI will never actually reach zero or 100 but traders who use the RSI get interested in stocks that are either below 30 or above 70 on the index. A number above 70 will indicate that a stock's price has been rising strongly to the point it may be getting overbought or extended to the upside in price. Conversely, a RSI number that is below 30 indicates that a stock's price has been in a strong downward move and might be getting oversold or extended to the downside. Index readings above or below these numbers provide an indication that the stock price may be due for a reversal in price trend. In the case of a stock selling off with an RSI of 23 for example, it might mean the stock could reverse and the price will start to move higher, even if only temporarily.

While some traders use 30 and 70 as levels to watch, I prefer 20 and 80 for swing trading because these are more extreme levels of overbought and oversold and therefore give a more definitive signal on potential topping and bottoming price action. The downside of using these more extreme levels of 20 and 80 is that some changes in sentiment could be missed and a reversal will happen before the RSI reaches these levels.

In an uptrending market, the RSI value will run between 45 and 85, with the 45 area on the index acting as support. A downtrending market will result in RSI values of 15 to 55, with resistance being around 55.

The RSI indicator, when plotted on a graph under the price action of a stock, can also form patterns such as the double top or double bottom. I will discuss these patterns in the next chapter, Chapter 9, Technical Analysis – Patterns. Another chart event to watch for occurs when the stock's price action and RSI number are not in sync. An example of this is if the price action is making a new high or low and the RSI does not also make a new high or low but instead moves in the opposite direction. This is a good indication that some topping or bottom action is occurring in the stock and a trend change could follow.

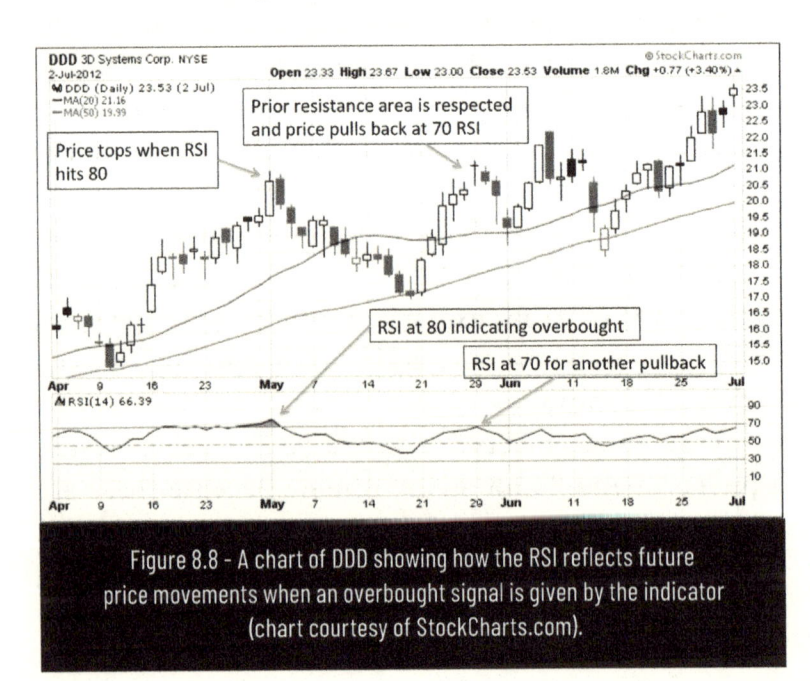

Figure 8.8 - A chart of DDD showing how the RSI reflects future price movements when an overbought signal is given by the indicator (chart courtesy of StockCharts.com).

Figure 8.8 is a chart of 3D Systems Corporation (DDD) and shows how the extreme level of the RSI (over 80) predicted a subsequent drop in the price of DDD. On the next wave of buying in DDD, the RSI only reached the 70 level before another drop in price occurred.

How to Use the RSI Indicator

The RSI is a good indicator for you to employ and can be used to scan for potential trades on its own or in combination with other indicators. It can be used to indicate when stocks have been either overbought or oversold. When a stock is getting overbought and the RSI reaches 80 or higher, the price has risen to an extreme level and may be due for a price drop. When the RSI drops to 20 or below, then the price action on a stock is getting very oversold and may be due for a reversal and a subsequent bounce higher.

These trend reversals can be temporary and the stock may return to the original trend or it could indicate some bottoming or topping action in the stock price. I do not suggest that the RSI is a good stand-alone indicator as it is better used in combination with the other tools and indicators discussed in this book to confirm if a bottoming or topping in price action is happening.

MACD: Convergence and Divergence

As I discussed in the previous sections, spotting a reversal offers an opportunity to take advantage of a profitable trade in a stock. Spotting a trend change consistently and getting a good entry on that change is equivalent to finding the Holy Grail of swing trading. Another common reversal tracking tool used by traders is the Moving Average Convergence Divergence, which is commonly referred to as the MACD.

This tool measures the momentum of a stock and is intended to help you spot a change in the sentiment of the market or in a stock.

Although the momentum of a stock will trend just like the price, changes in momentum will often precede changes in price. Imagine you get in your car, put it in drive and push down on the accelerator - you begin to move forward and pick up speed. If you keep your foot on the gas pedal, you will keep going faster until the resistance outside of the car builds up to a point where you are in equilibrium between the resistance of the wind and the force applied by the engine. If you now take your foot off of the gas, you will start to gradually slow down. The car is still moving forward but it is decelerating in speed.

Now think of your car's movement in terms of the price of a stock. Your foot is off of the gas, and the car is still moving forward (the stock price is still going up), however, both the car and the stock price are slowing down. Eventually, the car stops (the price stops moving up) and if it is on a hill, it starts rolling backward (the price starts dropping). The MACD calculation allows you to see this gradual change in sentiment between the buyers and the sellers before the price reflects this change happening.

The MACD was developed by Gerald Appel to chart the momentum of a stock by measuring the increasing and decreasing space between short-term and long-term exponential moving averages. Traders use different time frames to calculate their 2 moving averages depending on their preferences but typical periods are the 12-day and the 26-day. The shorter period moving average (12-day) is always closer to the current price when a stock is consistently moving one way or another. The longer period moving average lags a trending stock's current price. Therefore, as the price starts to level off, these 2 moving averages start to converge or come together. The price of the stock may continue to rise or fall but the rate may be slowing which causes the convergence or coming together of the 2 moving averages.

If the stock price is accelerating higher, the 2 averages will move apart or diverge with the short-term moving average moving more aggressively higher compared to the longer-term average.

A visual representation of the MACD is a graph that shows the distance between the 2 moving averages as seen in Figure 8.9, a chart of the Consumer Staples Select Sector SPDR Fund (XLP). There are 2 lines that represent the 2 different SMAs and a bar chart that represents the distance between the 2 moving averages. The bars that are increasing in size mean that the moving averages are moving further apart and thus representing a continuation in the price trend (either higher or lower). When the bars start to decrease in size, the distance between the 2 moving averages is decreasing and a possible reversal in trend may be coming.

In Figure 8.9, the chart of XLP shows how the MACD tracks the price move higher while the RSI starts to signal that the stock is overbought. If a long trader was just looking at the RSI alone, they would have missed a big price move up, as the MACD continued to show good price strength. As the price movement started to top around June 5th, the MACD bars became shorter, indicating the moving averages were converging and the uptrend price action was running out of momentum and that it was a good time to exit if you were long.

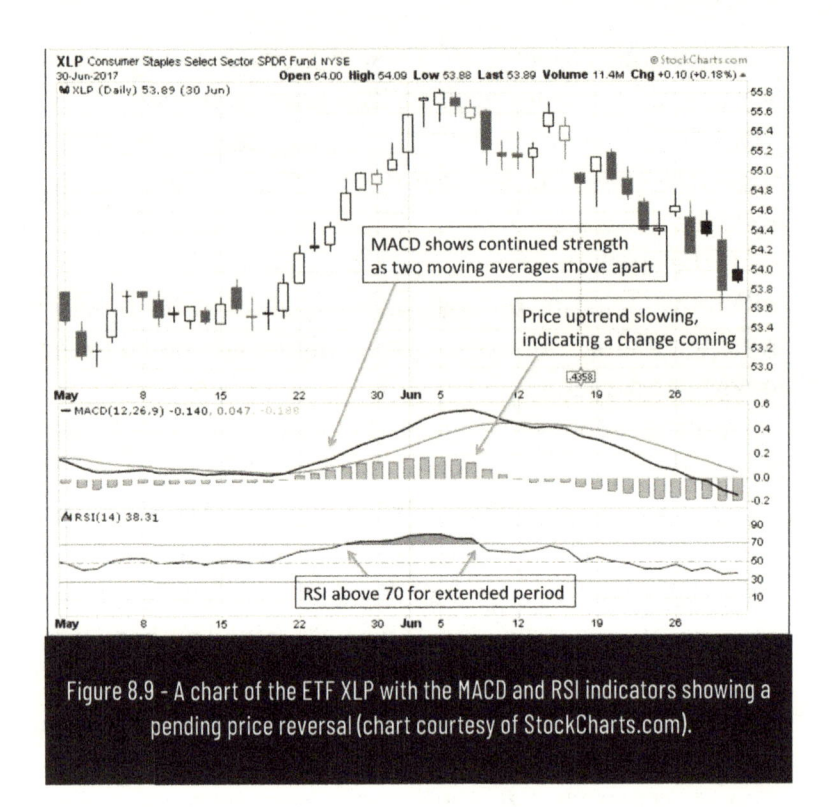

Figure 8.9 - A chart of the ETF XLP with the MACD and RSI indicators showing a pending price reversal (chart courtesy of StockCharts.com).

Since both the RSI and the MACD are momentum indicators, you might ask, what is the difference between the 2 measures? The main difference lies in what each is designed to measure. The MACD is primarily used to gauge the strength of price movement while the RSI provides an indication as to whether the market or a particular stock is in an overbought or oversold condition in relation to recent high or low prices.

You should be aware that the 2 indicators are measuring different factors and, therefore, they sometimes give opposite or contrary indications. The RSI may be over 70 for a sustained period of time, indicating an overbought condition in relation to recent prices, while the MACD may indicate that the buying momentum in the same stock or market is still increasing.

Regardless, either indicator may assist you by signaling an upcoming trend change. When both indicators are aligned, it can provide you with a good indication of a continuing trend or reversal.

How to Use the MACD

Although the RSI is more commonly used as a momentum indicator, the MACD is another indicator that you can use to check the momentum of a stock's price action. When looking at charts of potential trade setups, the MACD and RSI charts can be overlaid to see if there is an alignment between these 2 momentum indicators. If there is, this will give you more confidence in taking a position.

It should be noted that some scanning tools include the RSI but do not include the MACD. Both are good indicators to support a swing trader's conviction for entering a trade. There are a number of different specific MACD strategies that some traders use for determining entries and exits that are beyond the scope of this book. As you develop your swing trading business, you may want to do a more in-depth study on MACD trading strategies, however, the tools that I discuss in this book should provide ample opportunities to find and make profitable trades.

Average True Range

The Average True Range (ATR) indicator was also developed by J. Welles Wilder. Initially aimed for use in trading commodities, it has since become more widely accepted as an indicator for other financial instruments such as stocks.

The ATR is an indicator that measures the "volatility" of price action or, in other words, how much a stock price can swing over a certain period of time (such as a day). Wilder designed the ATR with commodities and daily prices in mind because commodity price action can be more volatile than stock prices. Commodities will often gap up and gap down between trading sessions, therefore, a volatility formula based only on the high-low range during a trading session (ignoring the gaps) would fail to capture all of that volatility. The ATR indicator takes into account those gaps as well as the swings in price throughout a normal trading session.

I will not provide the details on the formulas used to calculate this indicator but they are readily available on the Internet for those wanting more details. Wilder started with a concept called true range, which takes into account the previous day's close to capture any gaps that might have occurred between trading sessions. Absolute values are used because he was interested in measuring the distance between 2 points and not the direction. Absolute values are all positive numbers, so in the case of a drop in price which is negative, the number becomes a positive (for example, -$0.75 becomes a +$0.75).

Figure 8.10 shows the price movement of Micron Technology, Inc. (MU) with a corresponding graph below showing the ATR value for each day. The ATR indicator will change over time as shown in the chart and is dependent on the level of volatility that the stock is currently experiencing. As the daily price variation increases, so does the ATR.

Because the ATR represents a range in the price of the stock, lower-priced stocks will have lower ATR values than higher-priced stocks. For example, a $25.00 stock will likely have a much lower ATR value than a $250.00 stock. This is because a 1% move in the higher-priced $250.00 stock will be much larger than a 1% move in the lower-priced $25.00 stock, which means that the ATR values are not comparable unless they are converted to percentages of the stock's price.

Technical Analysis - Indicator Tools

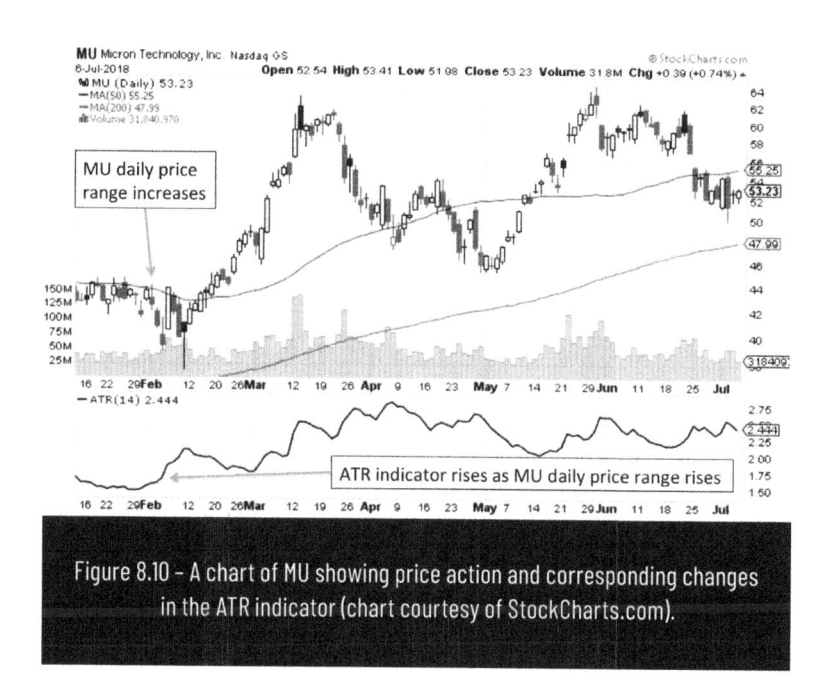

Figure 8.10 – A chart of MU showing price action and corresponding changes in the ATR indicator (chart courtesy of StockCharts.com).

How to Use the ATR Indicator

If you are willing to take on more risk as a swing trader, the ATR indicator can be used to find stocks with extremely high volatility. In addition, the ATR indicator can be used to illuminate high volatility stocks in your scan in order to assist you in finding less volatile stocks that may not move as much in any one session. The more volatile the stock, the higher the ATR, and therefore the more the price is going to vary over each period of time. Less volatile stocks are not going to move as much over a period of time and may very well behave in a more predictable fashion.

For example, you may find 500 stocks if you do a simple scan to search the stocks that are in an uptrend. In a second scan, you may decide to eliminate the higher volatility stocks from the results, which may further reduce down to 100 the stock opportunities presented by the scan.

The ATR indicator can also tell you how much variation in price you can expect to see from day to day. Understanding daily volatility and movement on any one day will help keep you from being stopped out on a position because of the normal price variation that you would expect to experience given the ATR value for a particular stock. For example, let's imagine a stock with an ATR of $1.50. If you use a stop-loss of $0.50 from the current price, then it is more likely you will get stopped out due to the normal volatility of the stock.

There are other more advanced strategies for using the ATR as a trade decision tool. Some traders will use it as an exit indicator for an existing position. If a stock price closes more than one ATR value away from its most recent close, it is possible that a significant change in the sentiment of the stock has occurred.

Other traders have used the ATR as a trailing stop for a stock. Using a long position example, they will take the highest high since taking the position and subtract 2 times the ATR to determine a trailing stop price for their position. The use of the 2 times multiplier is somewhat subjective. Others will use 3 times the ATR to determine their stop out price level.

As a new swing trader, you will likely want to be aware of this indicator only as a measure of volatility. Once you gain more comfort and experience with the various indicators, you can look at expanding your use of the ATR.

Chapter Summary

In this chapter, I discussed a few of the technical tools that are derived from doing calculations on the past price action of a stock. These technical tools often work because many traders and computers are watching them and they all trade off of key events such as a price hitting the commonly watched 200-day SMA. They therefore become self-fulfilling events. Below are highlights of the chapter for your review.

- Horizontal support and resistance lines are one of the most common tools and are relatively easy for novice swing traders to learn how to use.

- When a swing trader refers to a stock's chart, it should be apparent that, in the past, there were areas of support where its price traded down to a certain level, and then it either paused or reversed to go higher. This would be a level of support.

- There should also be areas that can be identified where a stock moved higher to a point and then the price movement either stalled and consolidated or dropped back. This is an area of resistance.

- By connecting the areas of support and resistance with horizontal lines, a swing trader can identify these price levels which will likely be in play with future price moves. A break above a prior level of resistance or a break below a prior level of support indicates a trend continuation and possible entry for a trader.

- Diagonal lines can also be drawn in a stock that is either trending up or down to create a channel of trading in that trend. A break of the channel may indicate a change in sentiment.

- Moving averages are another tool that is commonly used by swing traders and computers. The 2 common moving averages are the simple moving average (SMA) and the exponential moving average (EMA). The EMA responds faster to potential changes in price direction, which can get a trader into a trade sooner. The upside is a potentially more profitable trade but the downside is that it could be providing an indication of a false trend change. A false trend change indication often happens when the market is more volatile with more price swings.

- There are a number of different time periods that the moving averages are commonly calculated for. These include the 20-day, 50-day and 200-day periods. The shorter periods respond faster to price changes and shifts in sentiment.

- Moving averages can be used in market scans in a number of different ways, which I will discuss in Chapter 12, Swing Trading Strategies.

- The Relative Strength Index (RSI) is a momentum oscillator that can be used to determine if the price of a stock is at an extreme level compared to its recent price. Stocks move between levels of being overbought or oversold and on occasion these situations become extreme. Whenever the RSI is below 20 (oversold) or over 80 (overbought), a possible reversal trade opportunity is being represented.

- The Moving Average Convergence Divergence (MACD) measures the momentum of a stock's price movement and can be an indicator of a trend reversal using 2 EMAs. A shorter period EMA is compared to a longer period EMA and the distance measured between the 2 can be used to flag either a price trend reversal or continued strength in a trend.

- The Average True Range (ATR) is an indicator that measures the "volatility" of price action. It measures how much a stock price can swing over a certain period of time such as a day and incorporates the gap up and gap down action that can occur between individual trading days. The ATR is a good number to know so that stops are not set so close to the current price that they will get triggered on an average day of price swings.

CHAPTER 9

Technical Analysis – Patterns

In the previous chapter, I covered a few of the technical indicators that are derived by doing calculations based on the past price action of a stock. Now let's look at another type of technical analysis that can be used to help you make swing trade decisions. This indicator requires you to recognize certain classic chart patterns that reoccur time after time. Getting used to seeing these patterns as you look at candlestick or bar charts will help you to find good entries for profitable trades. Often as you look for and find these patterns, your technical analysis calculations that I discussed in the previous chapter will confirm your assessment of a possible trade entry.

Listed below are a few of my favorite classic chart patterns that you should be aware of and watch for when you are reviewing charts for potential swing trades. These classic patterns include:

1. double bottoms and double tops

2. bull and bear flags

3. bull and bear pennants

4. ABCD patterns

5. head and shoulders patterns

There are many more patterns but I do not want you to get bogged down in looking for too many of these setups. I feel that looking for the patterns listed above will provide you with ample trading opportunities as a swing trader. All of these patterns work in part because other traders are watching for them and trade the trend off of them. You should stay with the trend in swing trading because the trend is your friend. A trend may very well be your only friend in the market. Let's look at each of these patterns in more detail.

Double Bottoms and Double Tops

Double bottoms and double tops are classic patterns that indicate a potential reversal in price trend. I will discuss the double bottom pattern with the understanding that the double top is just the reverse of a double bottom and the same principles apply. The difference between the 2 is that the double bottom refers to a stock or market that is in a downtrend and potentially signaling a reversal to the upside. A double top is an upward trending stock that is signaling the potential to turn and start a downtrend in price.

The double bottom pattern resembles the shape of a "W" when looked at in a chart. A stock in a downtrend reaches an initial bottom, bounces higher for a short period of time,

Technical Analysis - Patterns

and then retests the low it made on the initial bottom. That initial low, if it holds on the second pullback, will now become a significant level of support and often indicates a level where the sellers are exhausted and the buyers may believe that there is value in the stock at that price.

There is some market psychology involved with this "W" pattern. Once the initial bottom is put in and the stock moves higher, the buyers of the stock at much higher prices may see the bounce as an opportunity to cut their losses and get out at this higher price (fearing the stock is going to continue lower). Others who bought in on the first bottom may be short-term holders who are happy to take their small gain on the bounce.

As the stock price drops back after the initial bounce higher, the value investors may be looking to get a second chance at buying the stock at this lower price. These buyers wait and then buy in at the initial support level created by the first bottom. The stock then starts to move higher again and forms the familiar "W" pattern. Traders who have been short the stock may add to the buying pressure once they see a strong level of support has been established. Short sellers will then buy to cover their positions and that fuels the price rise on the second leg up.

This pattern also works in reverse. The double top forms an "M" pattern instead of a "W" in the chart. The initial push higher and subsequent pullback is seen by some investors as an opportunity to take an entry or add to their existing position. Unfortunately for these new longs, the first top acts as a level of resistance and the second attempt to move higher fails. Some traders who are long the stock will see this failure to break higher and start to sell. Other traders who short stocks might also start selling because they see that an area of resistance has developed.

The added short selling will create additional downward pressure on the stock price. The stock then continues lower on a reversal in price action.

Let's look at Figure 9.1, an example of both a double bottom pattern and a double top pattern on Micron Technology, Inc. (MU). On February 9th, 2018 you can see a second bottom form as support develops around the $40.00 per share level. A doji is also formed on the second bottom, which provides additional confirmation that a trend change is about to happen and that going long here is likely going to be a profitable trade. From this second bottom, MU's price develops a strong uptrend through the rest of February and into March.

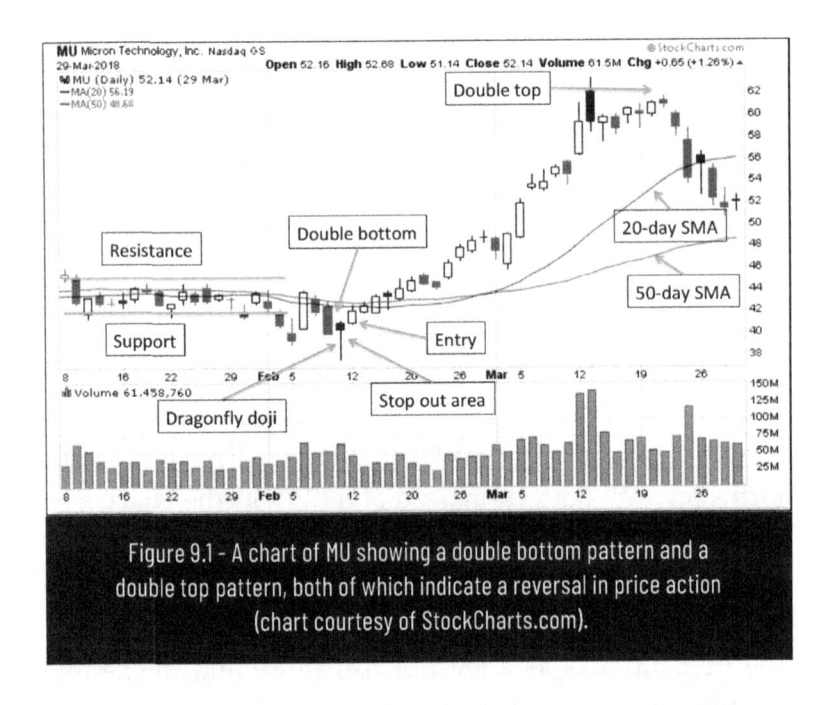

Figure 9.1 - A chart of MU showing a double bottom pattern and a double top pattern, both of which indicate a reversal in price action (chart courtesy of StockCharts.com).

After March 13th, MU's upward price movement stalls and the price pulls back. Some traders might have seen this pullback as another bull flag but, on the bounce higher, MU fails to break to a new high. This second top is put in on March 21st, which creates the double top pattern I look for as a trader. From this second top, the sellers take control of the price action and MU's stock price drops quickly.

This example in Figure 9.1 shows that either a double bottom pattern or a double top pattern is very tradable for a swing trader and that alignment with other indicators like a doji provides further confirmation of the trade setup.

How to Trade Double Bottoms and Double Tops

One thing that makes double bottoms and double tops attractive is the ability to easily define the risk to reward ratio. Establishing the stop price on your potential trade is the key to managing your account and the risk that you take in a trade. Once a double bottom pattern is traced out, the low on the "W" pattern becomes the stop-loss price. Prior levels of resistance can be established as exit points, thus making it possible to calculate a risk to reward ratio.

If you can catch an entry near the second bottom on a long trade, then the difference between your entry price and that bottom price on the "W" should be relatively low. That low price difference creates a situation where you do not require a lot of upside in the price to get that 2 times reward you need in order to make this a good trade. Getting a good entry on a stock can make a big difference in your risk to reward ratio.

The opposite applies to taking a short trade on a double top. Try to get an entry as near as possible to the second top which should give you the most desirable risk to reward ratio. Your stop will be around the high price of the topping pattern. If the price does start to continue higher, you should cover your short promptly to limit your losses.

In summary, ensure your long entry is as close to the second bottom as possible and, for a short sale, ensure your entry is as close to the second high as possible.

Bear and Bull Flags

A flag pattern can be bullish or bearish and needs to be considered in the context of the overall trend of the stock. The "flag" is a period of consolidation before the overall trend continues higher or lower. It is referred to as a flag because visually in a chart it resembles a flag on a flagpole.

A bull flag chart pattern starts with a strong price move up that looks like a flagpole. This flagpole pattern is followed by a diagonal seesaw pullback, which forms the flag. The diagonal upper trendline of the flag forms a temporary level of resistance but, once this level is broken, the buyers take control once again. A push through this line of resistance triggers the beginning of the next leg of the trend higher.

Alternatively, a bear flag pattern is the reverse and starts with a steep price drop. The flagpole portion of this pattern, representing an initial strong price movement in one direction of the other, is what separates these patterns from other typical breakout or breakdown patterns. Let's examine both the bull flag and bear flag patterns in more detail.

Bull Flag

The bull flag starts with a strong price spike higher that often catches traders who are short the stock off-guard. The many market scanners do their work and identify the long opportunity, so momentum traders then get in long to help feed the buying frenzy and push the price higher. Eventually, the initial price spike runs out of steam and the price action starts to form an orderly pullback where the highs and lows are close to parallel with each other. Drawing the diagonal support and resistance lines forms a sort of tilted rectangle. The tilt on the rectangle can have various levels of slope with some being almost flat.

The breakout happens when the upper resistance line is broken as the price surges higher again. As the stock's price breaks through the high of the formation, it triggers yet another breakout and uptrend move. The sharper the spike higher on the flagpole, the more powerful the bull flag move can be. Figure 9.2 shows an illustration of the typical bull flag with options marked for an entry buy. When the resistance and support lines are almost horizontal, the 2 entry points are close to being the same.

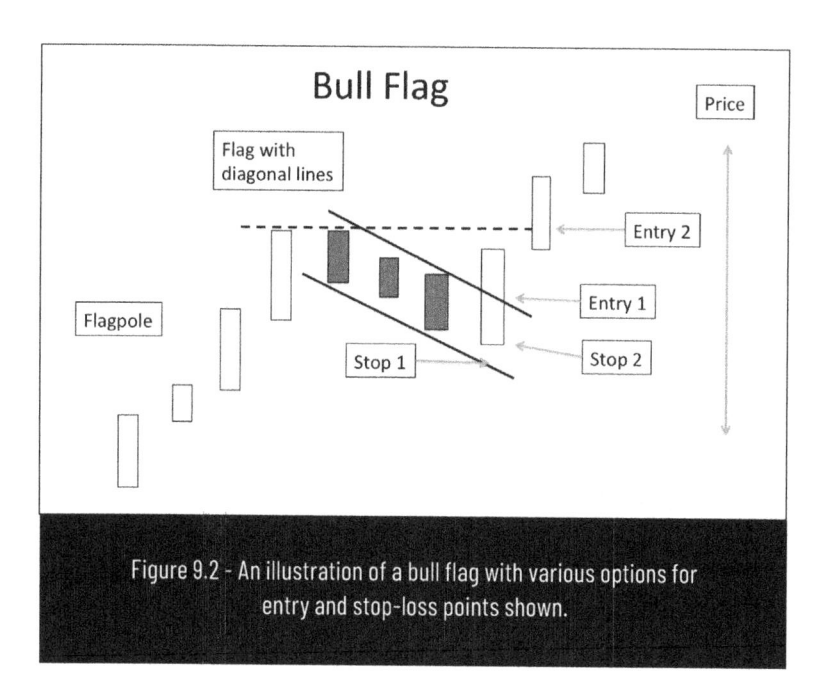

Figure 9.2 - An illustration of a bull flag with various options for entry and stop-loss points shown.

Bear Flag

The opposite of the bull flag is referred to as the bear flag. It has the same chart pattern as the bull flag except it is inverted and results in the continuation of downward price action in a stock. The upside down flagpole starts with an almost vertical price drop due to the sellers being firmly in control of the price action. Downward moves in price can be much more aggressive than upward price action. However, nothing drops forever and at some point the traders who shorted the stock look to cover their positions and the value investors see a potential opportunity. The appearance of some buying results in a selling reprieve. This results in the seesaw price action that forms a parallel upper resistance line and lower support line. These lines form the familiar flag pattern.

When the lower support line eventually breaks, the sellers emerge once again and the downtrend resumes with another leg down. Similar to the bull flag, the severity of the previous price drop on the flagpole determines how strong the bear flag will be for a continuation of the trend. Figure 9.3 shows an illustration of a bear flag with the possible entry points for a short position as well as the price point where you would be stopped out if you had decided to go short.

Similar to the bull flag, if the support and resistance lines are closer to horizontal, then the 2 entry points will be closer as well.

Technical Analysis – Patterns

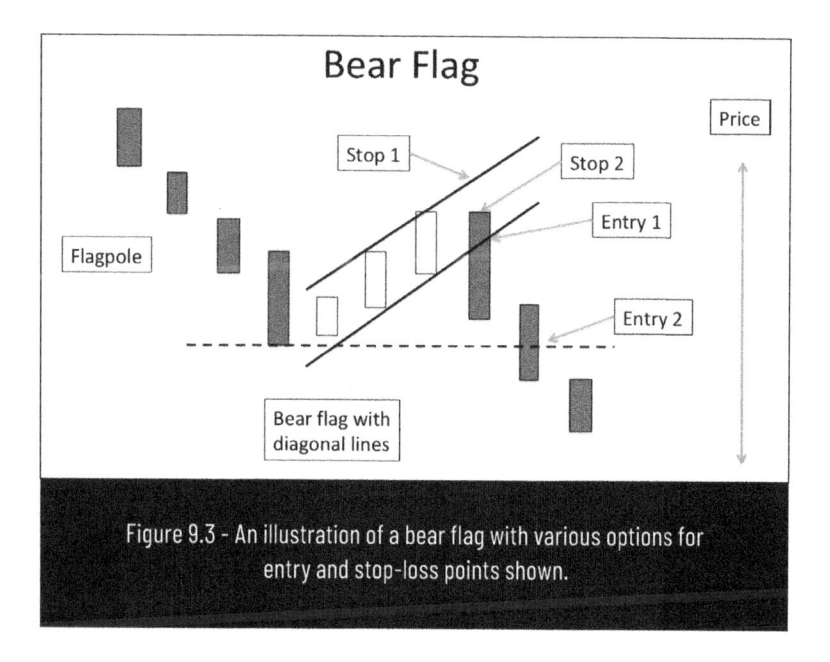

Figure 9.3 - An illustration of a bear flag with various options for entry and stop-loss points shown.

How to Trade Flag Patterns

Flag patterns require a little patience while you wait for the flag to form after the initial run up or drop. Once you have recognized the beginning of the pattern, you should start to plot the upper and lower trendlines as they form. These trendlines will be one of your potential entry points and/or stop out levels.

You will usually have 2 possible entry spots on any flag formation in order to play the continuation of the trend. The first possible entry is on the break of the trendline. The second entry option occurs when the price action breaks the high or low of the flagpole (depending on whether it is an uptrend or downtrend continuation). Both entry options are illustrated in Figures 9.2 and 9.3 above.

The first entry will get you into the position a little earlier, which will allow you to profit more on the next surge in price action (up or down). The downside of getting in earlier is that there is always the potential for the stock to have a failed breakout and not move in the direction you expect. Waiting a little longer for the break in the top of the flag results in a little higher probability of a successful trade.

These flag patterns also give you 2 stop-loss price level options to use in case the stock does not move in the direction expected. If the stock fails to follow through and continue the trend, then the trendlines can provide a price level for a stop. On a downtrend, you would use the upper resistance line in the flag and in an uptrend you would use the lower support line.

The second stop-loss option is to use the low of the lowest candle in the bull flag and the high of the highest candle in a bear flag. Both stop-loss options are also shown in Figures 9.2 and 9.3.

If you are a more conservative trader, you would use the closer stop price to keep losses to a minimum. However, this may result in getting stopped out of a trade that is becoming more volatile as the trend starts to continue. This means that, while you may take a smaller loss with this stop out price level, using this level may result in missing the move you were intending to play by getting stopped out due to some volatility in price.

This volatility component is why some traders will give the trade a little more room to avoid having their stop triggered due to some volatility as opposed to a real direction change. Therefore, they will place their stop at the lower support trendline on uptrends and at the higher resistance trendline on downtrends.

A more sophisticated or experienced trader might use multiple entries and exits to offset some of the risks of entering the trade too early. A smaller percentage of the total trade in shares can be used as a starter position and then added to at the second point above or below the flagpole.

Technical Analysis – Patterns

Figure 9.4 shows a chart of Caterpillar, Inc. (CAT) in a nice uptrend with 4 bull flags over a month-long period before the trend reverses. Notice the double top that takes place as I discussed in the previous section, giving a clear indication that the upward trend is out of energy and a reversal in price is about to happen. After the reversal, there are several bear flags formed on the overall trend down as bargain hunters think the bottom is forming and they go long. Traders who went short at the double top start taking profits, giving a temporary lift in the stock's price before the selling continues.

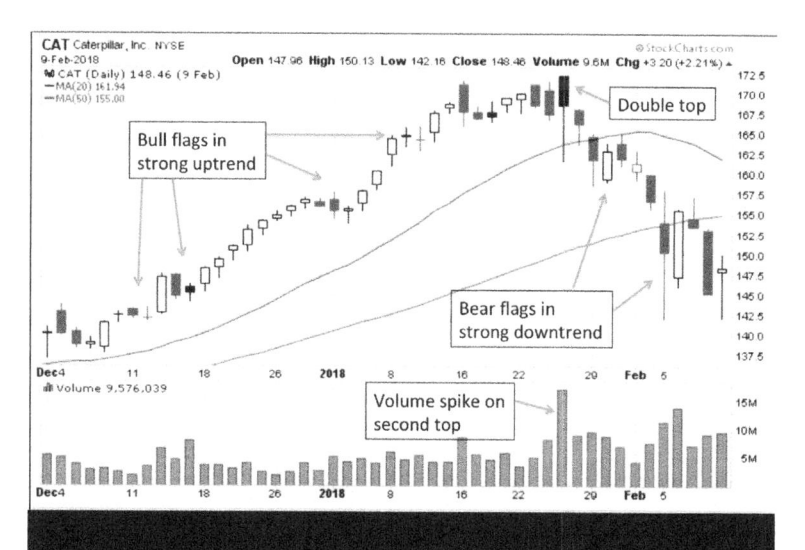

Figure 9.4 - A chart of CAT with both bull and bear flags giving you some options to enter and exit a position in this stock (chart courtesy of StockCharts.com).

Target Price Levels

Before you enter a flag pattern, as an effective swing trader you should also be planning your targeted exit price or prices. This will allow you to calculate that very important risk to reward ratio that I have discussed previously. You should be expecting at least 2 times the reward for the given risk that you're taking in the event that you get stopped out. You should look at prior longer-term levels of resistance as possible exit points if you go long and areas of support to exit if you go short.

If you chose to enter at the break of the trendline, then your initial target can be set at the high or low of the flagpole. However, if the flag was close to horizontal, then that may not give you enough reward for the risk you are taking. You will have to look for other good exit points to get that 2 times reward you need to justify your trade. Other factors you may want to consider are the strength of the trend, overall market trends and the possible strength of the fundamentals driving the move.

You may also consider scaling out of the position, which means taking some initial profits at the top of the flagpole by selling some of your position and then letting the remainder ride to your next expected level of resistance or support. In this case, you must never let a winner turn into a loser. Lock in your profits and set your stop on the remainder at or near the entry price.

Bear and Bull Pennants

The bear and bull pennants are similar to the bear and bull flags I described above. They start with a strong price move either up or down and then pause for a period of consolidation. The difference between the pennant and the

Technical Analysis – Patterns

flag is in the shape that the price action creates during this period of consolidation.

With a flag, the highs and lows of the consolidating price action create 2 parallel lines of support and resistance that I illustrated in Figures 9.2 and 9.3. With a pennant, the range of price action narrows over the passage of time. When support and resistance lines are drawn off of the highs and lows, they come together in a point as illustrated in Figure 9.5. The buyers and the sellers have been fighting it out and when the price action narrows to this point, often a winner finally emerges.

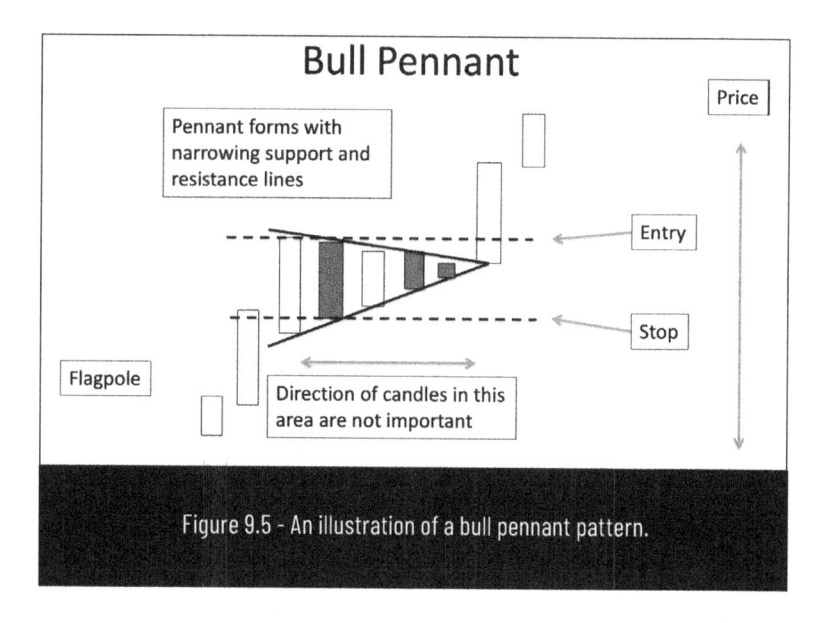

Figure 9.5 - An illustration of a bull pennant pattern.

Usually the trend will continue after this narrowing period of consolidation, however, you should wait for a signal before taking an entry. Do not assume that the trend will continue and take an early entry. While you wait for the pattern to play out, take time to look at the daily charts and identify areas of support and resistance that have occurred in the past. Find potential profit target prices so you are prepared to do your risk to reward calculation in case you eventually consider an entry.

The narrowing price action is often compared to a coiled spring getting ready to pop one way or another. You can find this narrowing price action on stocks that have been consolidating for days or weeks. These are also good stocks to watch because eventually either the buyers or sellers emerge in control and the ensuing price action can be strong.

How to Trade Pennant Patterns

My illustration in Figure 9.5 shows how you should trade a pennant pattern. You will wait for a confirmed break in the narrowing price action and take an entry on that move. This breakout move will likely be accompanied by a spike in volume and will provide you with further confirmation that a new trend is being established. Your stop out price will be where the narrowing price action started, as also shown in Figure 9.5.

Let's look at an example of how you could have traded 3D Systems Corporation (DDD) in January 2018. Figure 9.6 shows a pennant forming over about 10 trading days as DDD's price action narrows to around the $10.75 price level. At that point, the stock breaks down in price, giving a good signal for an entry to short the stock. Let's assume you got an entry at $10.50, which was about the close of the first day in the breakdown.

Technical Analysis – Patterns   177

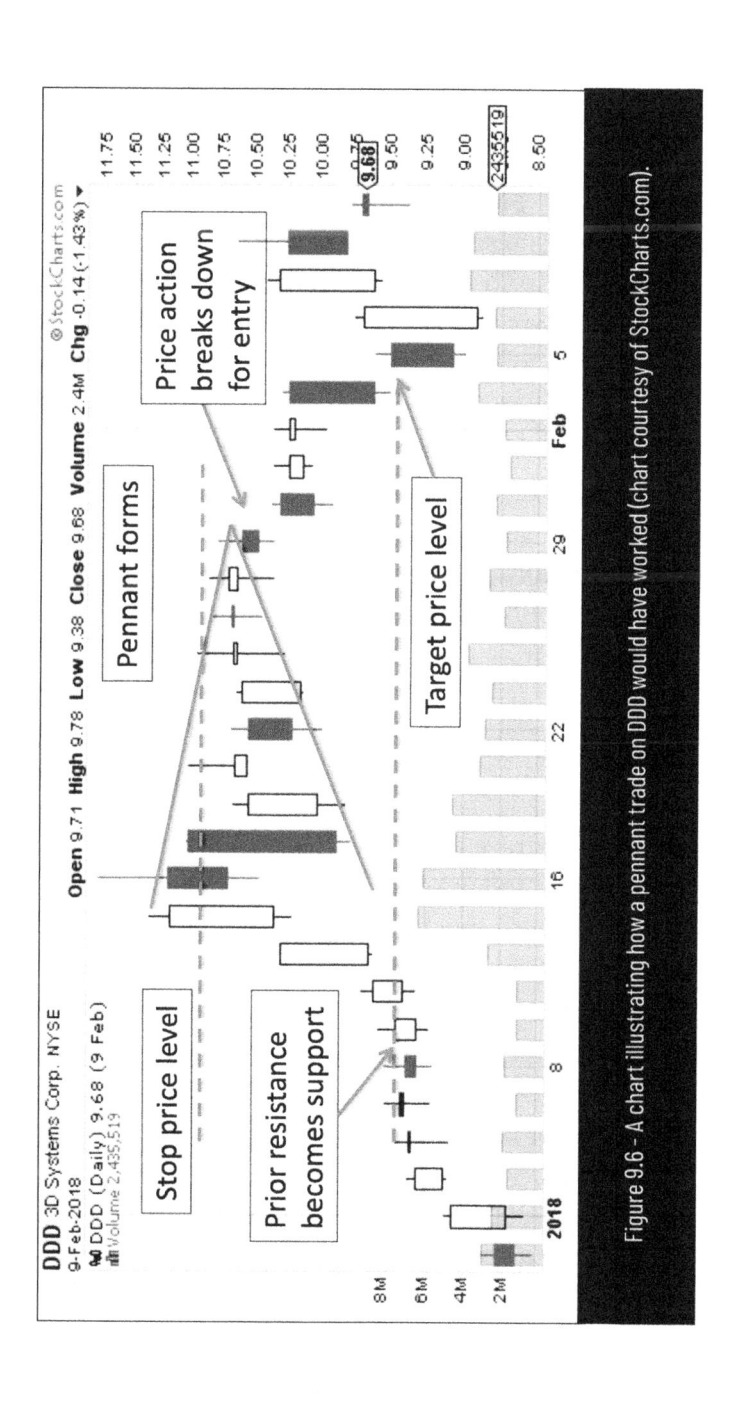

Figure 9.6 – A chart illustrating how a pennant trade on DDD would have worked (chart courtesy of StockCharts.com).

As with every trade, you need to ensure that your reward will be at least 2 times the risk you are taking. Your stop out price would be set around $11.00 based on the fact that the price was experiencing resistance to go higher at that level. Your profit target would have been down at a point of previous resistance, which has now become support at around the $9.50 level. Therefore, this is an acceptable trade because you are risking $0.50 ($11.00 stop minus $10.50 entry) to make $1.00 ($10.50 entry short minus $9.50 cover buy) and your 2 times reward ratio has been met.

Notice that in the case of DDD, the trend did not continue upward but instead reversed and went lower. This illustrates why you need to have patience to let the trade unfold before taking a position. Do not take an entry early on the assumption that the trend will continue out of a pennant pattern.

ABCD Patterns

The ABCD pattern is another one of the basic and relatively easy patterns to recognize and trade. It is essentially a price move higher or lower, followed by a flag and then a continuation of a trend. As with much technical analysis-based trading, it often works because so many traders and computers are watching for the pattern and subsequently trading this setup. It becomes another one of those self-fulfilling prophecies I discussed previously in this book.

This pattern is based on the principle that stock prices move in waves. These waves are due to the fact that price control is continually moving between the buyers and the sellers. If you examine a daily price chart of any stock, you will see waves of fluctuation up and down. Then, if you compare that daily chart to a weekly chart of the same stock, you will also see waves, but they will likely have larger price ranges

Technical Analysis - Patterns

because you're looking at a longer period of time. Within each one of those weekly bars there are 5 1-day bars, creating smaller waves inside bigger waves.

Knowing that stocks are moving in waves allows you to play on those waves much like a surfer. As a swing trader, you are waiting to catch and ride a wave, but like surfing, timing is very important. You will never see a surfer starting to paddle like crazy at the top of a wave to catch a ride. They wait to begin their ride as the wave is just starting to approach. Similarly, a trader needs to anticipate the next wave and get on board at the beginning of the next move in price action. Figure 9.7 shows a representation of the 2 types of ABCD patterns (bearish and bullish).

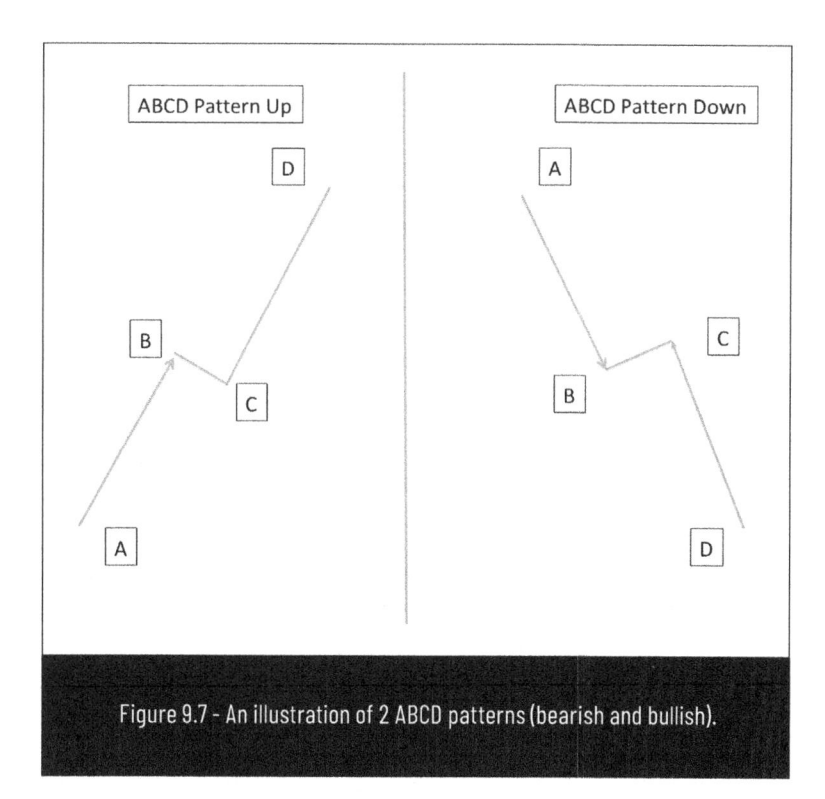

Figure 9.7 - An illustration of 2 ABCD patterns (bearish and bullish).

Bullish ABCD patterns start with a strong upward move. The buyers are aggressively buying a stock from point A and consistently making new highs of the day (point B). You should not enter the trade here because at point B the price action is very extended. More importantly, your stop-loss will be way below your entry, giving you an extremely poor risk to reward ratio. As I discussed earlier, you should be looking for at least 2 times the reward for the risk that you are taking. Using our surfer analogy, that wave snuck up on us and passed us by, so we wait for the next wave.

At point B, the traders who bought the stock earlier start selling it for profit and the price comes down. You should still not enter the trade because you do not know where the bottom of this pullback will be. However, if you see that the price does not come down from a certain level, such as point C, it means that the stock has found a potential support. You can now plan your trade in the same manner that I described previously for trading flags and pennants. You should decide on an entry price, a stop out level and an exit point(s) for a profit.

Bearish ABCD patterns are the reverse of the bullish pattern, with the stock price heading lower initially, and then there will be a bounce, which will be followed by a continuation lower.

Let's look at an example of an ABCD trade on Advanced Micro Devices, Inc. (AMD) in Figure 9.8. The price action on this stock creates a very tradable pattern for a short trade. AMD pulls back from a high at point A to level B. It then forms a nice bear flag and also creates a double top when it fails to break through the previous high. I have already discussed the double top and flag patterns. The alignment of these patterns are all telling you the same thing, making this an excellent setup for you to take a short position on AMD.

Technical Analysis - Patterns

The stop-out price level on the short would be a break higher at about the $12.50 level. A failure of the stock to move higher would have allowed you to hold the position as it moved lower, possibly scaling out instead of selling the position for a profit all at once. By scaling out, you can lock in some profits and keep moving the stop out price lower as the price moves lower to maximize the gain on the trade.

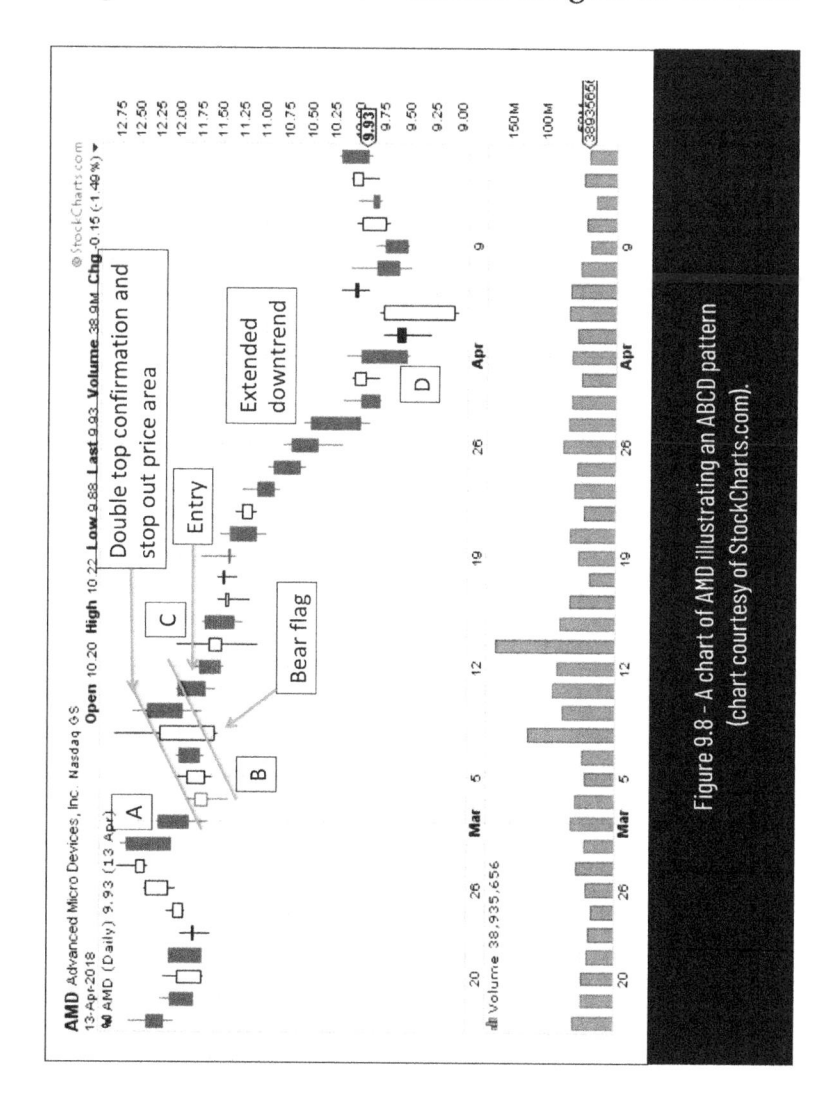

Figure 9.8 - A chart of AMD illustrating an ABCD pattern (chart courtesy of StockCharts.com).

How to Trade ABCD Patterns

The real key to trading this pattern is to watch for the pullbacks that inevitably occur when a stock makes a push higher or lower. Look for those bull or bear flags to form and plan your entries, exits and stops accordingly, as I discussed earlier in the previous section.

These patterns will often end with a double top or double bottom pattern. This is another pattern I have discussed earlier and like to use as a trade setup. A topping pattern will usually have one or more gravestone type doji and the price action will struggle to make a new high and then ultimately fail and move lower. A bottoming pattern will be the reverse – one or more doji will make a dragonfly pattern signaling that the sellers are exhausted and the buyers are starting to take control. These signals do not necessarily have to appear but they help to confirm a setup for an entry on a trade.

To summarize my trading strategy for the ABCD pattern:

- You look for stocks in a strong uptrend or downtrend. You will find these by using a scan (discussed later in this book) or through some other source such as social media.
- You then watch for the stock to transition into a consolidation period where the price action becomes choppy for a period of time.
- As the choppy price action continues, you draw your lines of support and resistance and plan your trade with an entry point, stop-loss price and exit strategy for a profit.
- You enter the trade when the price hits your entry point and then you follow your trading plan, taking profits either by a single sale or by scaling

out if you think the trend will continue. If the trade does not go as expected, you stop out, take the loss and move on to the next opportunity.

Head and Shoulders Patterns

The head and shoulders chart pattern can be a top reversal signal and the so-called "inverted" head and shoulders pattern can be a bottom reversal pattern. This pattern is generally thought to be one of the most reliable swing trading patterns and therefore should be on your radar for stocks tracing out this type of price action.

The general pattern for the topping head and shoulders starts with a general uptrend in price action, which hits a peak and then slightly falls back or chops sideways for a period of time. The stock then pushes higher through the previous peak and makes a new high before failing once again. Selling price action takes the stock back to the previous low after the first peak and the price action stays flat or bounces a little.

This price action in a chart traces the outline of a head and 2 shoulders; thus the name. A horizontal trendline can be drawn across the 2 lows on the pullbacks and is referred to as the neckline. Once the price of the stock drops below this neckline, an established downtrend is in place and shorting the stock is now a tradable option. Figure 9.9 is a chart of Advanced Micro Devices, Inc. (AMD) that illustrates a topping head and shoulders pattern with a following strong sell-off in price.

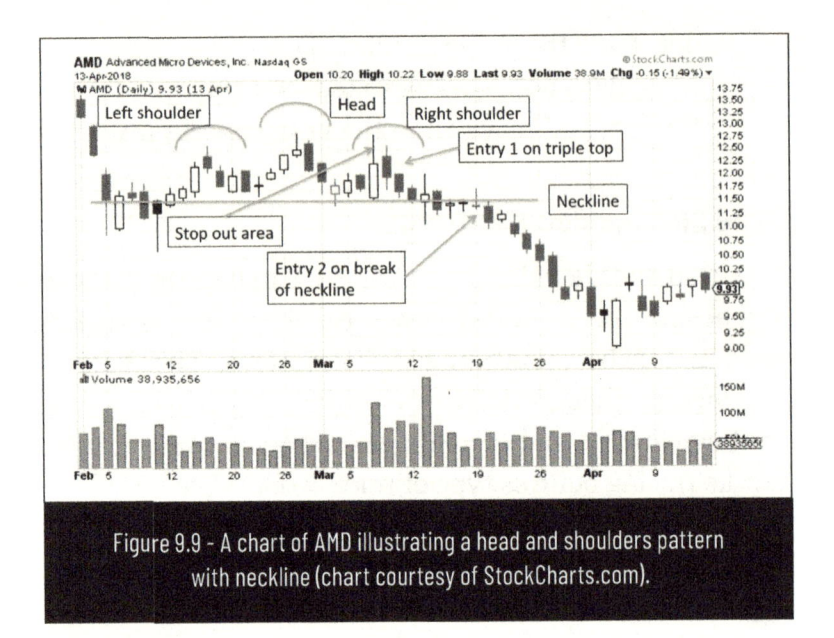

Figure 9.9 - A chart of AMD illustrating a head and shoulders pattern with neckline (chart courtesy of StockCharts.com).

The head and shoulders pattern shown in Figure 9.9 could also be considered a sort of triple top. Similar to the double top, the buyers and the sellers fight for control of the price. Some believe that this pattern gives an even stronger indication that a price trend reversal will happen.

Let's look at another chart, this time with a bullish inverted head and shoulders pattern. Figure 9.10 shows a chart of Cheesecake Factory Inc. (CAKE). Once again, this chart pattern depicts the underlying fight between the buyers and the sellers. The sellers in the stock try to take the price lower 3 times, with the third low higher than the previous low. An area of resistance forms around the $50.00 level (remember that these resistance areas like whole numbers). This resistance level creates the neckline of the inverse head and shoulders. Once the neckline is broken, the stock moves higher.

Technical Analysis - Patterns

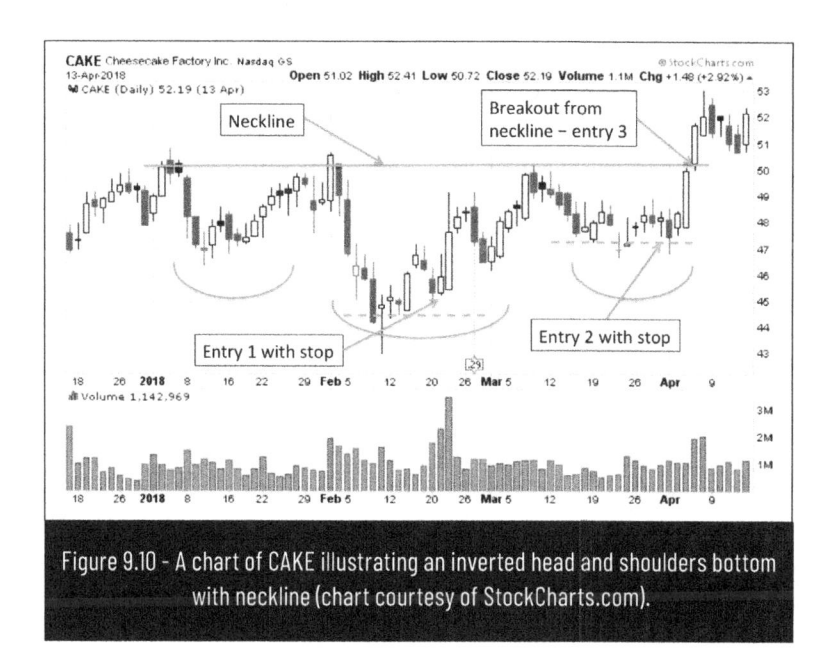

Figure 9.10 - A chart of CAKE illustrating an inverted head and shoulders bottom with neckline (chart courtesy of StockCharts.com).

How to Trade Head and Shoulders Patterns

This pattern offers a number of different entry options. It is possible that you can pick it up as a double bottom if the second move was not that exaggerated. In other words, if the head part of the pattern was not too extended from the right shoulder. This entry gives you the best risk to reward because you are getting an entry near the lowest point of the pattern and the risk is clearly defined as the extreme price of the head.

The second possibility for an entry is at the left shoulder. This entry is not as attractive because your stop out level could still be at the extreme high or low of the head portion of the pattern. If the left shoulder is trading sideways for an extended period, you can draw a line of support on the bottom or top of the pattern and use that as a stop out price level.

Many traders will use the break of the neckline to go short on a head and shoulders or to go long on the inverse of the pattern. Once the price breaks through the neckline, strong moves usually follow. This allows you to set your stop price around the neckline, which will exit you from the trade on a failed move. Figure 9.10 includes entry points for this trade as well as levels where you should stop out if the price action does not follow through as hoped.

Chapter Summary

In Chapter 9 I looked at the more common patterns that repeat in charts. Once you are familiar with these patterns, they become easy to pick out and they offer an opportunity to get entries on stocks that will hopefully turn into profitable trades. The patterns I discussed are as follows.

- Double bottoms and double tops are very good patterns to trade off of for a long or short position respectively.
- The psychology of the double bottom trade is relatively simple and is based on the assumption that on the second bottom, the sellers are exhausted and the buyers are taking control. Once a second bottom is confirmed, a trader can often get a long position with a good risk to reward ratio. The stop on the trade is a price just below the second bottom.
- The double top is the reverse of the double bottom. The second top indicates where the buyers are exhausted and the sellers are taking control. Once a double top is confirmed, swing traders can short the stock with a stop price just above the high of the second top. The risk to reward ratio is often very good because the entry is relatively early in the downward move from the second high.

- Bull and bear flags are important to recognize for a swing trader. They can provide a good entry point for a trade or they can be recognized as a pause in a longer-term trend before an additional move in the trend direction.

- A bull flag starts with a strong trend higher, followed by a period of consolidation where the price of the stock churns sideways before continuing higher. Entries can be made on the price break higher after the period of consolidation, with the stop price set at or just below the low of the period of consolidation.

- A bear flag starts with a strong trend lower, followed by a bounce higher as shorts cover and bargain hunters buy because they think it is a bottom. After the short bounce and consolidation, the price breaks down as buyers disappear and the stock goes lower. The entry and stop are at the low of the price break lower and the stop out price level is at the high of the period of consolidation.

- A pennant is also a consolidating price action similar to a flag. The distinguishing difference with a pennant is that the support and resistance lines drawn off of the highs and lows slowly converge to a point. Usually during the narrowing process, either the buyers or the sellers will emerge as the group that takes control and if that trend continues, you will have a good entry for a trade.

- ABCD is a common pattern seen in a longer-term trend and is based on the principle that stock prices move in waves where the buyers and sellers are in a constant fight for control of the price. The pauses often result in flags or pennants that can be tradable setups.

- As a swing trader, knowing that these waves of buying and selling occur will let you hopefully stay in a trade longer by recognizing that stocks rarely go straight up or down for an extended period of time without the occasional pause.

- The head and shoulders pattern is appropriately named because of the shape that the price action makes in a chart. Over a period of time, the candlesticks or bars trace out a left shoulder, followed by a head. The price then drops back to the level where the first shoulder was formed which creates the right shoulder in the chart. A neckline can be drawn in the chart and once broken provides for a good entry for a short. Stops can be back at the neckline or at the high of the shoulder if the trend does not continue lower as expected.

- The inverse head and shoulders pattern is created by the opposite price action, where the trend reversal indicates the stock is going to move higher, so a swing trader would consider taking a long position with a similar entry and stop out price level.

CHAPTER 10

Swing Trading Guiding Principles

Swing trading is a type of trading in which you hold positions in stocks or other investments over a period of time that can range from 1 day to a few weeks or more. Before I discuss various strategies that can be used to swing trade, let's look at the basic guiding principles that I build these strategies on. They are as follows:

1. Keep it simple.

2. Treat your swing trading activity like a serious business.

3. Develop a work plan and stick with it.

4. Actively manage your risk to reward ratio; focus on the entry.

5. Measure your results and adjust accordingly.

Each of these principles is discussed in more detail below.

Keep it Simple

You may have heard of the term "paralysis by analysis". This happens when you analyze something to the point where you cannot make a decision. Some swing traders overcomplicate their analysis of a security by using multiple indicators that all have to line up for them to enter a trade. In real life, everything does not often line up perfectly and you have to go with what you feel is right.

I have thus far covered many different tools and indicators you can use to help you to make a decision. You do not need to use all of them to be a successful swing trader. Once you find 1 or 2 that work well for you, you should then stick with those. If you decide to use a few different tools that all need to align, it will likely mean that you are not going to be trading very often. That is not necessarily a bad thing though. It is better to sit on your hands and wait for a good trade versus jumping in and out of marginal trade setups and slowly lose your money. The only one who wins in that case is your broker, as they collect fees for all of your trades (the successful ones and the losing ones).

Find several indicators that work well for you and focus on using them. Don't trade often, but trade smart, by knowing why you are entering a trade and, most importantly, knowing your risk to reward ratio and exit price points. As you gain more experience in swing trading, you will be able to better recognize trades that are going to work out even if everything is not perfectly aligned.

Having said this, when you do happen to find a number of indicators that are all aligned with the trade you are considering taking, it can certainly provide some level of confidence that you have a potentially profitable trade.

Treat your Swing Trading Activity Like a Serious Business

Should you decide that swing trading is a right fit for your personality, and that it is able to fit into your life along with all of your other interests and responsibilities, then you need to treat this activity as a very serious business. It will require an investment of time and effort, which hopefully will lead to some very good rewards.

Have a designated area where you do your research and keep all of your records. You are essentially becoming a professional money manager for yourself, so you should keep your work organized at all times. Everything you do with your business should be oriented toward making sure you are a success. If you feel like a professional, then you are more apt to trade like one.

Develop a Work Plan

Have a work plan and stick with it. Your work plan should include checking the market at the open and before the close. During this time you should monitor your positions, set alerts and possibly enter orders at target levels that you think might get filled during the trading day.

I also recommend that you review your portfolio and market performance every night from Sunday to Thursday to ensure your assumptions about your positions and portfolio are still valid. On the weekend, you should try to do a more thorough review.

It is important to establish a work plan and keep it consistent. By keeping your work plan relatively consistent, you can measure your performance without introducing additional variables. Measuring your performance allows you to find areas to improve and make changes as you see fit.

I will discuss the routine of a swing trader in Chapter 14, which you can adopt or use as a guide to developing your own plan that works for you and your specific situation.

Actively Manage your Risk to Reward Ratio; Focus on the Entry

As a swing trader, your first and most important tool is your capital or cash. As I have said before, without cash you cannot be a trader. I have written at length already about the necessity of assessing the risk to reward ratio on every trade and also on how much capital you should put into each trade. Following your rules on these points will prevent you from quickly losing all of your capital. You will be wrong on your trades some of the time and you need to make sure you live to trade another day.

Just planning and knowing your stop-loss and profitable exits are not enough for swing trading. Your entry becomes the next important step in your trade. You have already determined your stop-loss point and your target price(s) for a profitable exit. However, you calculated the risk to reward ratio based on an assumed entry price point.

Let's assume you found a good setup during a scan in the evening after the market has closed. The security closed the day at $10.50 and you see an upside to $12.00 with support at $10.00 where you would stop out. Therefore, you have a potential $0.50 loss compared to a $1.50 gain to the upside. That is a 1 to 3 risk to reward ratio, which is very good, and you are ready to pull the trigger and place a buy order in the morning. The market opens the next morning and the security you are ready to buy opens up at $11.00. What do you do? The novice trader is already invested mentally in the trade so they buy.

Unfortunately for them, their risk to reward is now 1 to 1 with the downside to $10.00 and upside to $12.00. This is no longer a good trade at that entry point.

The rational trader reassesses the situation. They may put a buy order in at $10.50, hoping to catch the entry they wanted on the security during the normal daily price gyrations in the market. This will give them the risk to reward ratio that they need to make a good swing trade. If they do not get a fill, then they need to reassess again, and maybe move on to finding another trade with a more appropriate risk to reward ratio.

The bottom line, do not get emotional and chase a trade. The *"fear of missing out"* can motivate you to make a bad trade and you should be aware of this when picking your entry price on a trade.

Measure your Results and Adjust Accordingly

As a trader, you must track your results to measure your performance. Nothing gets improved that does not get measured first. Every trader should use a tool to record the different aspects of each trade, from initial assessment through to the risk to reward expected, the entry point, and, finally, the exit. The tool can be a spreadsheet, it can be done on paper or it can be web-based. It does not matter how you do it as long as the process allows you to track the details of each trade as well as your performance.

Once you have your trades recorded in detail, you can go back at any time and review how the trade worked. You can compare your performance on using the different indicators, i.e., is one working particularly well versus the others that you use? Are you getting good entry points on your trades or do you need to exercise more patience? Are your exits working or are you consistently exiting a trade too early and not getting all of the money you could on a profitable trade? Are you respecting your stops?

Having all of this information to review will help you adjust your trading process and plan accordingly to maximize your performance without letting emotion enter into your decision-making. I will discuss the details of using a journal to track your trades in Chapter 14, Routines of a Swing Trader.

Chapter Summary

In this chapter, I discussed the key principles that you should build your swing trading strategies and business around. These principles included the following.

- Keep your strategies relatively simple. There are lots of tools available and much analysis that you can do, but the more you include, the less likely you will find alignment on all of them. Focus on finding and using several tools that work for you.
- Focus on finding and trading only what you consider to be high-quality setups. You do not have to trade often to make a good return on your money.
- Develop a consistent work plan and routine that you follow. Try to keep your trading process and procedures consistent so that you can measure your results without introducing other variables.
- Make sure your trades are offering a good reward to the risk that you are taking. Manage the size of the risk that you are taking so a large part of your capital is not at risk. Honor the levels you have decided to exit a trade at if it does not work out the way you had hoped.

- Measure and review your results regularly using a journaling process.
- Adjust your trading plan or strategies if something stops working. The market changes constantly as sectors come in and out of favor and overall trends change. Be prepared to change and adjust with the market.

CHAPTER 11

Swing Trading Rules

Before discussing specific strategies that can be used for swing trading, let's go over a few rules that I usually follow and why I have them. These are my general rules, which have evolved through experience and knowledge gained over the years. It is up to you to develop your own set of rules, which may include some or all of these.

The rules are based on 2 factors that I consider important in order for a trader to keep their capital and have a profitable business. These factors include the following:

- risk of holding a security
- over-the-counter stocks

Each of these factors is discussed in detail below.

Risks of Holding a Security

As a swing trader, under the right conditions you can see significant gains just by holding overnight or up to several weeks, which is what makes this type of trading attractive. Every trader has seen the "gap ups" or "gap downs" that happen when the market opens and then thought to themself, I wish I had bought and held that stock yesterday. Hindsight is always 20:20.

However, with the potential for large gains comes the added risk associated with holding a position after the market closes. Events can happen after the market has closed that may negatively impact your position, leaving you stuck holding a loser. By the time the market reopens, the position you have taken could end up resulting in a big loss if it gaps up or down against you. You will never get big rewards without taking on risk at the same time.

The following are the kinds of after-market events that can take the wind out of what you thought was a good-looking swing trade position:

1. earnings reports
2. announcements about a product or service
3. secondary offerings
4. downgrades, upgrades and short sellers reports
5. other announcements such as Securities and Exchange Commission (SEC) investigations, key management turnover, etc.
6. changes in overall market sentiment

Let's look at each in a little more detail.

Earnings Reports

I view earnings reports as a crapshoot. In other words, a security will probably move after an earnings release but it is hard to predict which way it will go. I never hold a long or short swing position through an earnings report – I have been burned too often on these events in the past. There are certainly good long position gains to be had if the company exceeds on every line item and beats market expectations, but there is always the potential for losses.

Even if a company reports good total revenue and profit numbers, there can still be some negative comments made on *"forward guidance"* for earnings that the market did not expect. One negative comment could easily send the price heading lower even if all of the other results were very good. This would be great if you were short the stock, but not good if you were long and hoping for a move higher after the report.

There are other ways to play earnings report events such as using *options* to limit risk and potential losses. Options strategies are more advanced and are not covered in this book.

Announcements about a Product or Service

Any positive or negative announcement about a product or service provided by the company has the potential to move the price significantly, either up or down. Pharmaceutical companies are a great example of this type of announcement. Events such as the results of a drug trial can cause a stock price to swing dramatically one way or the other depending on the outcome. If the results are negative – look out below – because small pharmaceutical companies have been known to lose 75% or more of their value overnight. If you happen to have a long position in the stock, you will have a substantial loss. Just like earnings reports, the problem with this situation is that the trader does not know which side to take prior to the announcement.

Other events, such as a product recall that would negatively impact your position, can also take you by surprise. Alternatively, you might be holding shares in a small company that wins a contract with a large company. Singular events like these are harder to predict and can be primarily managed by limiting how much of your portfolio is invested in any one position.

Secondary Offerings

Companies that need to raise money to sustain their operations while they develop a product or service often do secondary offerings. Announcements about an offering are usually done after normal trading hours and might come as a surprise to many holders of the stock. These offerings are often done when their stock price is moving higher, which would have led you to think you're "on a good roll" with your long position.

Secondary offerings are almost always done below market prices and are dilutive (more shares get released for trading), which means that the stock's price usually "gaps down" when the market reopens. The amount of the gap down will depend on how far below the current market price of the stock the offering was completed at. For example, if a stock ends the trading day at $30.00 per share and the company announces a secondary offering at $23.00, that is probably going to be viewed by existing shareholders as very negative. Recent investors at around $30.00 are going to be really unhappy and selling will likely follow. If the secondary offering was done at $28.00 on the other hand, then that is not so bad because the new investors are paying much closer to the market price.

The offerings are not made public until they are completed and so there is no way to know when a company might do a secondary offering. This makes them hard to guard against as a swing trader. The best you can do is understand it is a risk and companies that burn a lot of cash with little current incoming revenue are the most susceptible to this risk.

Downgrades, Upgrades and Short Sellers Reports

Brokerage firms and analysts are constantly upgrading and downgrading companies and modifying their performance expectations. Some brokers have specialists that follow only one stock such as Apple. Other firms have specialists that research and report on a sector like semiconductors. A rating downgrade or upgrade by a brokerage research firm can cause a stock price to move one way or the other depending on the sentiment expressed in the report.

There are also a number of firms that specialize in looking for companies where they can make an argument that the business model is flawed or where there is the potential for fraud being committed. These firms focus on finding companies to short and then release their arguments as to why they feel the company is overvalued. I recommend you watch "The China Hustle" (which is available on Netflix at the time of writing) if you have any doubts about how fraud can happen relatively easily in our regulated markets.

Citron is an example of a short selling research firm that can move the market price of a stock. They have the potential to make a small fortune shorting stocks and then release a report questioning a company's outlook. Their record is not perfect in the long term as, for example, they suggested Nvidia Corporation was overpriced in December of 2016 and it fell about 6% to $108.00 on that day. Nineteen months later, it was trading around $254.00 per share. Citron and other "research" firms like them can move markets and getting caught on the wrong side of one of their calls can be painful.

These analysts will normally release their reports outside of normal market trading hours, therefore, unfortunately for a swing trader, it is impossible to see these reports coming. Like many other unique events, the only way to protect yourself from a big loss is to practice your risk to reward strategies and limit how much of your total portfolio is invested in one position.

Other Announcements

Any other negative announcement such as a data breach, an SEC investigation, or a new lawsuit can hurt your position if you're long. A positive announcement such as the introduction of a new product, a partnership with another company, or the resolution of a lawsuit can negatively impact your account if you are short.

Unanticipated events are one of the challenges a swing trader faces and, as with all other unexpected occurrences, the best way to protect yourself from these is to practice your risk to reward plan. There is always the possibility that a singular event will work in your favor, such as being long a stock that announces a major partnership. You are there to capture the upside but you need to follow your trading plan and your risk to reward plan to protect your account on the downside.

Changes in Market Sentiment

Events and announcements can change market sentiment overnight. Regular reports such as the Institute of Supply Management's Manufacturing Purchasing Managers' Index (known as the PMI) are used as an indicator of the overall economic condition of the manufacturing sector. A release of an unexpected number can cause the overall market sentiment to become more positive or negative. With the PMI, a reading above 50 indicates that that particular sector of the economy is expanding, and a reading below 50 indicates it is generally contracting.

There are numerous other government and non-government reports regularly released such as housing starts, non-farm payroll numbers, inflation numbers, and Federal Reserve announcements, and each has the ability to impact overall market sentiment. A swing trader should be aware of these coming events and whether or not the market participants are putting a lot of weight on the release of an upcoming number. These events are easily accessible on a variety of websites including Estimize (under its Calendar tab). A screenshot of this calendar is included below as Figure 11.1.

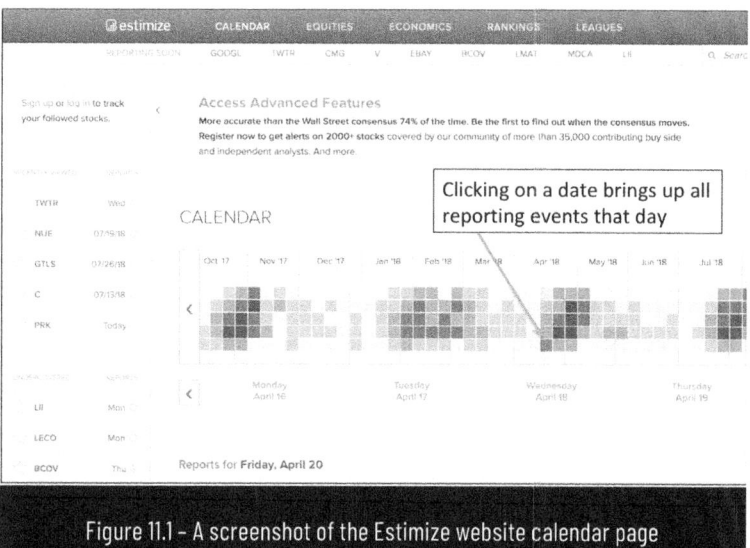

Figure 11.1 - A screenshot of the Estimize website calendar page showing upcoming news releases.

In summary, there are many events that can turn your potential winning position into a big loser and many of these announcements will happen when the markets are closed. On the positive side, you can minimize a few of these risks with a little research and some good money management, which I discussed in Chapter 5, Risk and Account Management. Below are 4 of my rules for swing trading based on the risks of holding securities overnight or for an extended period of time:

Rule #1: avoid holding positions on a stock through an earnings report.

Rule #2: avoid holding positions through known events. (For example – the date a pharmaceutical company is scheduled to release a trial result.)

Rule #3: research the company you are investing in and determine if the basic fundamentals support your forecast for the stock price.

Rule #4: follow your risk to reward plan and do not over-invest in one position.

Over-the-Counter or Penny Stocks

Over-the-counter trading happens off of the regular exchanges like the NYSE, Nasdaq and NYSE American (formerly known as AMEX). These transactions happen between dealers and can include stocks, bonds, currencies and other financial instruments. The stocks traded can include both company shares that are listed on recognized exchanges like the NYSE and stocks that do not have a recognized listing on an exchange. These unlisted stocks are primarily referred to as over-the-counter (OTC) equities.

These unlisted equities are traded through dealers because they are too small to get a regular listing on a recognized exchange and therefore they are unlikely to meet an exchange's requirements for listing. Unlike listed companies that are required to make regular filings with the SEC, OTC equities may not file as often or with as much detail, which means there could be limited information available about the company.

OTC equities may also trade in just a small number of shares per day. This limited trading activity means that there is a greater potential for share price manipulation by insiders and that it could be difficult to exit a trade once you have a position.

I avoid trading any OTC equities for the reasons listed above. I also try to avoid trading penny stocks (stocks under $1.00 per share), as they can also be more easily manipulated by insiders and are therefore less predictable. On occasion, I may consider a stock trading under $1.00 if there is a strong case for going long, but it would be a rare exception to my rule.

There is no need for a Retail trader to trade listed stocks OTC. If a stock is not listed on a regular exchange, then I do not trade those equities. This leads us to my next rule:

Rule #5: avoid trading over-the-counter (OTC) equities or stocks trading for under $1.00.

Chapter Summary

In this chapter, I provided an overview of my own swing trading rules. The following is a summary of the chapter for your review.

- There are a number of things that can impact a swing trader due to the fact that they hold securities from days to weeks to even longer periods of time. To address any negative events that might happen while holding a security, I presented a number of rules for swing trading as follows:

- **Rule #1:** avoid holding positions on a stock through an earnings report.
- **Rule #2:** avoid holding positions through known events. (For example – the date a pharmaceutical company is scheduled to release a trial result.)
- **Rule #3:** research the company you are investing in and determine if the basic fundamentals support your forecast for the stock price.
- **Rule #4:** follow your risk to reward plan and do not over-invest in one position.
- **Rule #5:** avoid trading over-the-counter (OTC) equities or stocks trading for under $1.00.

◘ A swing trader should monitor the overall market sentiment. Changes in overall market conditions can impact all stocks and a trader should make sure that the market sentiment remains aligned with their existing positions as well as the trades that they are considering.

CHAPTER 12

Swing Trading Strategies

In the previous 2 chapters, I discussed the guiding principles and some rules that you should consider following with your swing trading business. Now I will discuss some of the different strategies that you can use to identify trading opportunities. The strategies that you decide to use will depend both on market conditions and, of course, your own personal preferences.

The following 3 strategies are the ones that I primarily employ:

1. regularly scanning for trades

2. short-term gap trades

3. hot sector manias

These strategies do not work at all times and therefore you will need to be constantly tuned to the overall market to ensure that the strategy you are using is appropriate for the existing market conditions. As I have alluded to before in this book, sometimes the best trade is "no trade" at all.

In keeping with my first guiding principle outlined in Chapter 10 - keep it simple - I have limited my strategies to 3 distinct approaches. I feel that these 3 strategies will offer you many opportunities to enter trades on good setups.

Let's look at these 3 swing trading strategies in more depth below.

Regularly Scanning for Trades

Swing traders often have a daily or weekly routine of scanning for trading opportunities in the market. Scanning can generally be done on your broker's platform because most brokers now offer scanning software. If your broker does not offer this service, scanning can be done through a very good website called Finviz (finviz.com). Finviz provides you with a wealth of information as well as allowing you to scan for stocks that meet your own defined parameters. This is not the only option you have for scanning the market though. ChartMill (Chartmill.com) is another site that offers a similar free scanning service.

You do not need the subscription version of these websites unless you plan on doing more sophisticated scans and backtesting. Backtesting is the process of trying out a trading strategy on historical data. This helps you to confirm that the strategy you have developed has a good chance of success before you put your actual capital at risk. I am confident though that the free Finviz or ChartMill website service will meet most of your needs.

Let's look at the Finviz site specifically and see how it can be used to scan for and find trading opportunities. ChartMill works in a comparable fashion and, if you choose to instead use your broker's site, then you will likely go through a similar process as follows:

1. review overall market conditions
2. review performance of market sectors
3. screen for opportunities
4. review the short list of opportunities

Let's go through each step in the process as outlined above.

Review Overall Market Conditions

When you open up the Finviz home page you will see an overwhelming amount of information – let's keep it simple and look at what I feel are the most important pieces of data. You will see 3 bar charts at the top of the page that show the DOW, Nasdaq and S&P performances for the day. However, as a swing trader, you should be more interested in the data just under those charts, which includes:

- % advancing versus declining (stocks up on the day versus down)
- % new highs versus new lows
- % stocks above their 50-day SMA and % below
- % stocks above their 200-day SMA and % below
- % bull-bear sentiment of subscribers

All of these indicators tell you much about the direction of the market and the sentiment of traders. These are often referred to as internal indicators for the overall market. As I previously discussed, it is better to be working with the market you have versus taking a trade that is not aligned with the overall market direction.

Much like paddling a boat in a river, it is easier to paddle downstream with the river's current versus paddling into the current. Strong paddlers may make headway upriver, but the average and poor paddlers are going to be swept downstream no matter which direction they are paddling. It is the same with securities; there will always be some securities in a strong trend that will defy the market and go in the opposite direction, while the majority of securities will move with the overall market. In markets that are trending very strongly in one direction, almost all of the stocks will be swept in the direction of the current.

In a market that is trending strongly in one direction, swing traders should be more inclined to find trades that are moving in the same direction as the overall market. For example, if you see these indicators showing many more stocks are declining versus advancing, and the percentage of new lows are much higher than new highs, and a greater percentage of stocks are dropping under their 50 and 200-day SMAs, then we are in a strong downtrending market. The size of that downtrend will be reflected in the actual numbers for each of these measures. If stocks making new lows are at 80% compared to only 20% making new highs, then it indicates a strong bear market overall and swing traders should be looking at short opportunities more than long trades.

Figure 12.1 below shows these indicators on the Finviz site. When this image was taken the market was not strongly trending one way or the other and most of the indicators were sitting in the middle of their ranges. For example, the new highs compared to new lows were 123 versus 107 respectively, which is slightly bullish but not considered a strong uptrending market.

Swing Trading Strategies

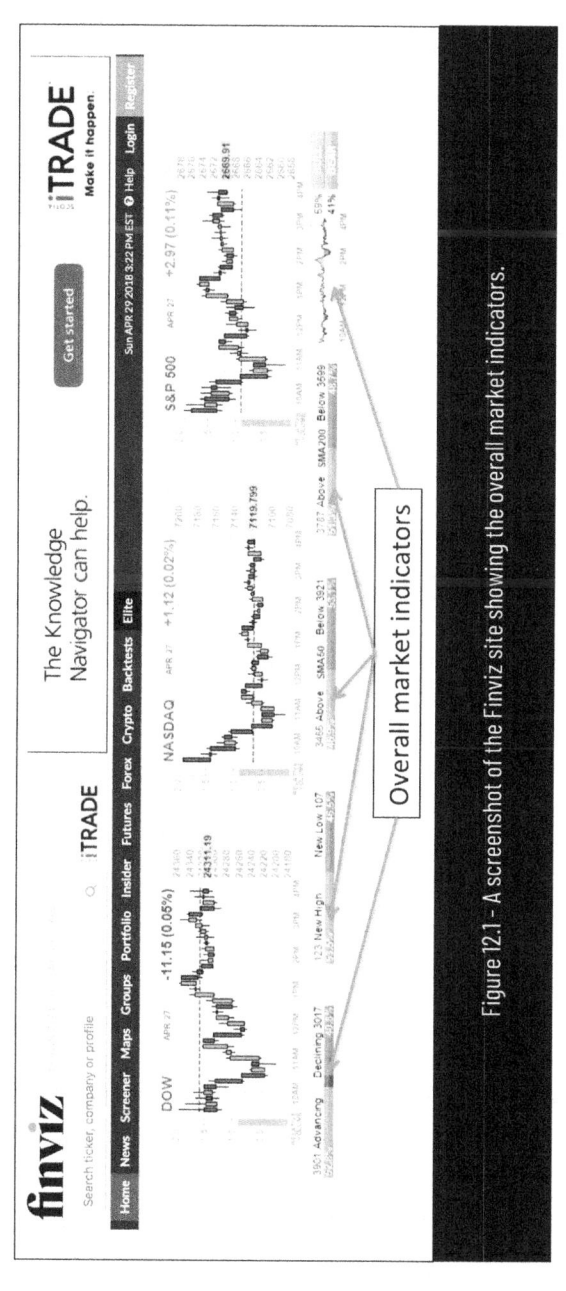

Figure 12.1 - A screenshot of the Finviz site showing the overall market indicators.

In summary, it is beneficial to be informed on how the market is performing so you can consider aligning your trades in the same direction.

Review Performance of Market Sectors

Taking this alignment concept a little further, a swing trader will also be concerned with the various sectors in the market and how they are performing. You will hear professional traders and analysts talk about "*rotation*" in the market or how a particular sector is leading the market higher. This means that traders and investors are moving capital from one sector to another or they are favoring certain sectors over other ones. Finviz offers a very good tool to determine which sectors are performing well and which are performing poorly over a number of different time frames. By selecting the Groups tab on the home page you will see some bar charts that show performance by sector for 1-day, 1-week, 1, 3 and 6-month periods. This illustration provides a quick and easy way to survey the specific sectors in the market to see which ones investors and traders currently favor and which ones are out of favor.

Figure 12.2 shows an image of the page taken at the end of April 2018. At the time this screenshot was taken, it was the utility and health care sector stocks that were showing strength over the previous 1-week and 1-month time frame. Over the previous month, basic materials had done well, but their weekly performance indicated that this sector had now slipped lower.

While it will not show in the print edition of this book, you will see on the Finviz website that the sectors which are out of favor (the bottom rows in each time frame) appear in brighter shades of red depending upon how out of favor they are. Likewise, the more in favor a sector is (the top rows in each time frame), the brighter the shade of green they are presented in.

Swing Trading Strategies

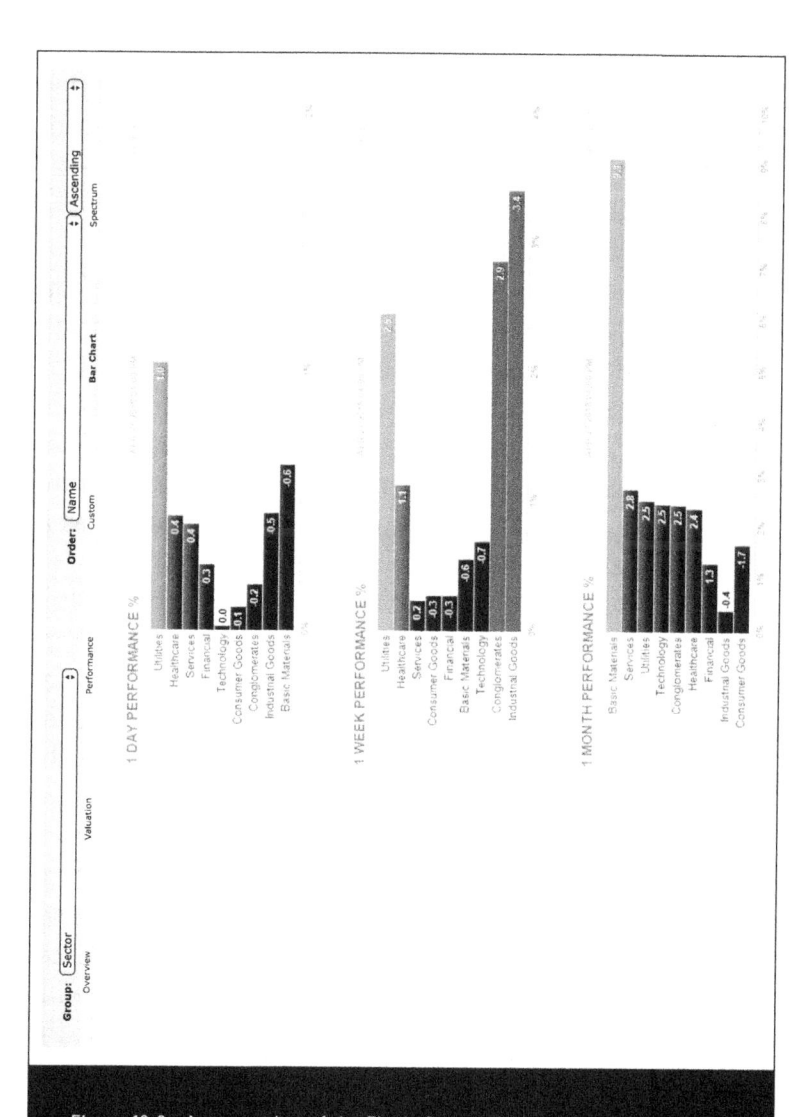

213

Figure 12.2 - A screenshot of the Finviz Groups tab showing which sectors are in favor and which are out of favor over multiple time frames.

For long and short opportunities, you should take note of the sectors at the top of the charts and which ones are at the bottom. In addition, look for the alignment of multiple time frames: for example, is the 1-week and 1-month performance of a sector aligned? Don't forget that I suggested it is better to have alignment of your swing trades on several timelines and not just one.

Being aligned in a sector can be even more beneficial compared to being only aligned with the market. Consider that the market is made up of different sectors such as: retail, banking, technology, defense; and transportation to name but a few. While some of these sectors could be making significant moves higher, other sectors may be performing poorly at the same time. To illustrate this point, let's look at the performance of the XLK Technology ETF and compare it to the performance of the Utilities ETF XLU over the same period of time. Referring to Figure 12.3, you can see from the 2 charts that a long trade in the technology sector was a much better trade compared to utilities. The XLK gained about 10% during the period while the XLU lost about the same percentage.

In summary, if you are considering an individual stock, check the sector category it is in to see how the overall sector is performing. Are you trading with an overall sector trend or against it? You should also check multiple timelines to make sure that they are aligned or at least showing signs of reversing. If you do not get confirmation that the longer-term sector trend is moving or starting to move in your expected direction, then you might just be trading a short-term correction that will turn against you. This will ensure that you are on the right side of a trend or trend change and not just looking at a short-term correction.

The next step is to start to look for specific trading opportunities. Let's look at how this is done in the following section.

Swing Trading Strategies

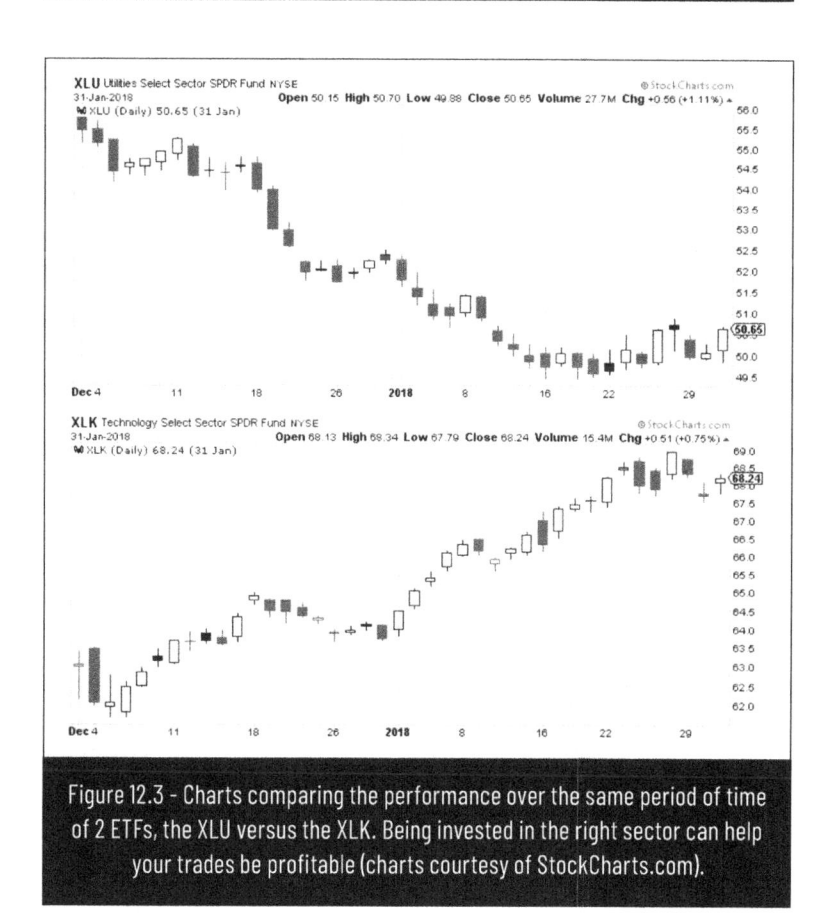

Figure 12.3 - Charts comparing the performance over the same period of time of 2 ETFs, the XLU versus the XLK. Being invested in the right sector can help your trades be profitable (charts courtesy of StockCharts.com).

Screen for Opportunities

In the next step of the scanning process on the Finviz site, you will select the Screener tab. Figure 12.4 shows what this page will look like when selected. Near the top, you will see 3 tabs called Descriptive, Technical and Fundamental. By working with these 3 tabs, you can filter out stocks that meet specific parameters. Each filter selection eliminates stocks from the total list of stocks, which will narrow down the list of opportunities for a more detailed review. With no filters in place, the total number of stocks listed on this page is an overwhelming 7,438 at the time of writing.

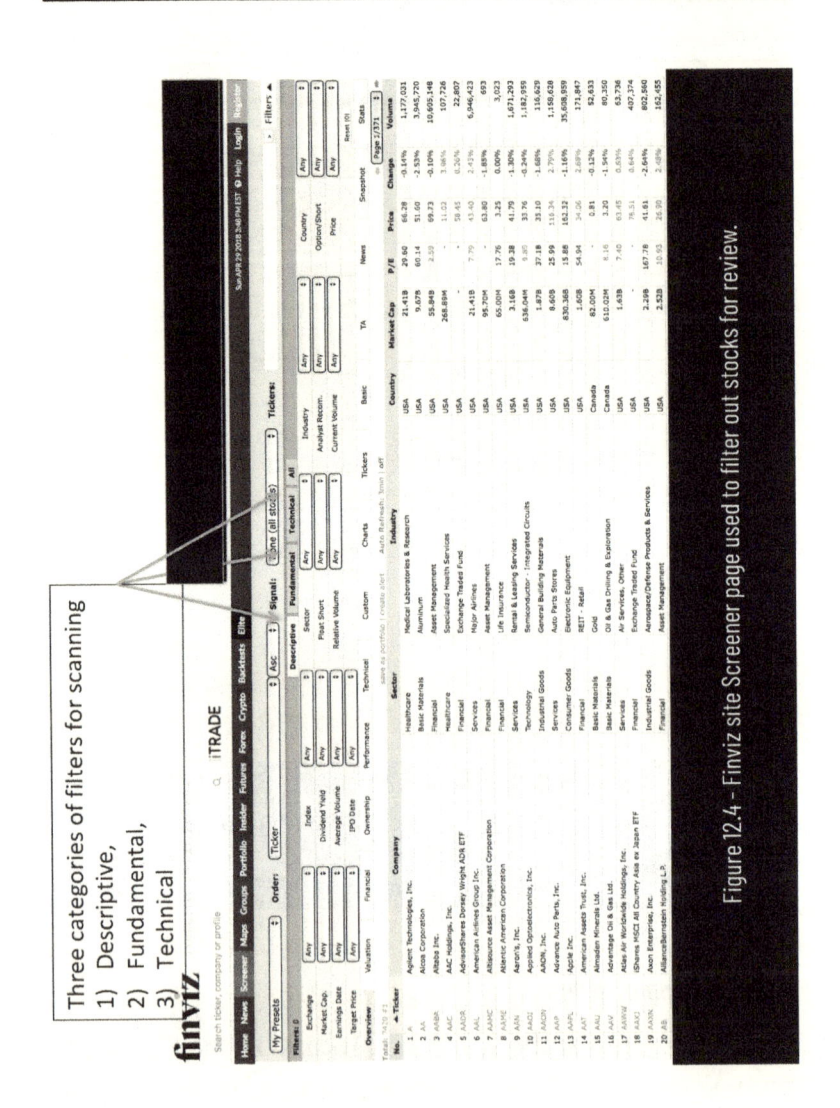

Figure 12.4 - Finviz site Screener page used to filter out stocks for review.

Descriptive Tab

Let's go through a scanning process that you could follow and see how to narrow a search from 7,438 stocks down to a manageable few that you can look at more closely for a possible trade. On the Descriptive tab you could select a few items for a scan as follows:

- Average volume: for a swing trade I like to see at least 200,000 shares per day. The fewer shares that trade during the day, the lower the liquidity and the harder it may be to get out of a position profitably. Lower volume stocks often have wider spreads (distance between the bid and ask), which puts you at an immediate disadvantage. Some people refer to this term as "average daily volume".

- Relative volume: I like to use this as an indicator of increasing interest by traders in a stock. If the recent volume is higher than average then it is likely the stock is going to move and not trade sideways. I use a setting of "Over 1.5". Some people refer to this term as "average relative volume".

- Country: "USA" is the normal setting here for most trades, but if you do want to trade a different market then you can adjust this accordingly.

- Price: the size of your account is going to impact where you set your maximum price. Be aware of how much money you have in your account and specifically how much you want to risk on a trade. Also be aware that if you buy shares that are less than $5.00 per share then they may not qualify as a marginable security and it will reduce your buying power in your account. If you are looking for opportunities to short stocks, then you will need to assess the impact on your capital requirements. I usually use a setting of "Over $2" per share to eliminate the penny stocks. A number of swing traders like the lower-priced stocks for good percentage moves while some prefer higher-priced stocks – this is a matter of personal preference.

Fundamental Tab

This is where you can filter stocks based on their numerical fundamentals, which include items such as price to earnings, earnings per share growth quarter over quarter, return on equity and percentage of shares owned by institutions. Some of these fundamental parameters were discussed in Chapter 6. Filtering based on these types of fundamentals can be challenging for traders who are not educated in accounting numbers and what these numbers mean.

However, many swing traders like to see 1 or 2 of these fundamental parameters used when they do a scan. For long opportunities, it is best to look for companies that are growing in sales and profits because investors and traders are willing to value these companies more highly. Investors and traders in stocks are essentially buying the future cash flow in a company, so if the cash flow is growing, the company is worth more in comparison to a company with flat or declining sales and profits.

Other long opportunity filters that can be used include the debt to equity ratio, which should be less than 1. The more debt a company has compared to equity, the riskier it is perceived to be by knowledgeable investors and traders. Another filter that can be used is the measure of return on equity. This measures how much the company's equity is earning each year. A good return on equity is anything over 20%.

If you are a swing trader who is more interested in shorting stocks with the expectation that they will drop in price, then you should use the opposite settings I have suggested for long setups. Search for companies that have shrinking sales and profits as well as high debt levels and a low return on equity.

To keep things simple, I recommend you start with using no filters in this section. If you complete your scan and you still have hundreds of stocks to choose from, I would come back to this section and start with the debt to equity filter of less than 1 for trading setups to take a stock long and greater than 1 for short opportunities. Return on equity would be the next box to use for further filtering.

Technical Tab

For the final filters, I move to the Technical tab where there are numerous items to select and narrow down trading opportunities. Similar to the Descriptive and Fundamental tabs, the setting you select will first be determined by whether you are looking for stocks that are moving lower or if you are looking for stocks that are expected to move higher in price. Let's look at the case for long opportunities or, in other words, for stocks that are expected to move higher in price.

A simple moving average is a basic tool that gives a clear indication of what direction the price is moving. The Technical tab allows you to look at 20-day, 50-day and 200-day SMAs with a large number of options to search for in each time frame. If a stock has been in a downtrend and is now reversing and moving up in price, the shorter-term SMA will reflect that move before the longer-term SMA. The stock price will move above the 20-day SMA while still remaining below the 50 and 200-day SMAs. This is a good set of filters to use as an indicator when looking for a reversal in a price trend from down to up.

Let's look at an example where I set the scan up for a share price greater than 5% of the 20-day SMA and the stock price is still below its 50 and 200-day SMAs. I found 6 stocks when I did the scan. As you run your mouse pointer over each stock symbol, a small chart pops up on your screen. This is a very useful feature because you can now quickly look at the chart to see if you recognize any patterns or trends.

Figure 12.5 shows how running the mouse pointer over the stock symbol brings up the chart on the screen.

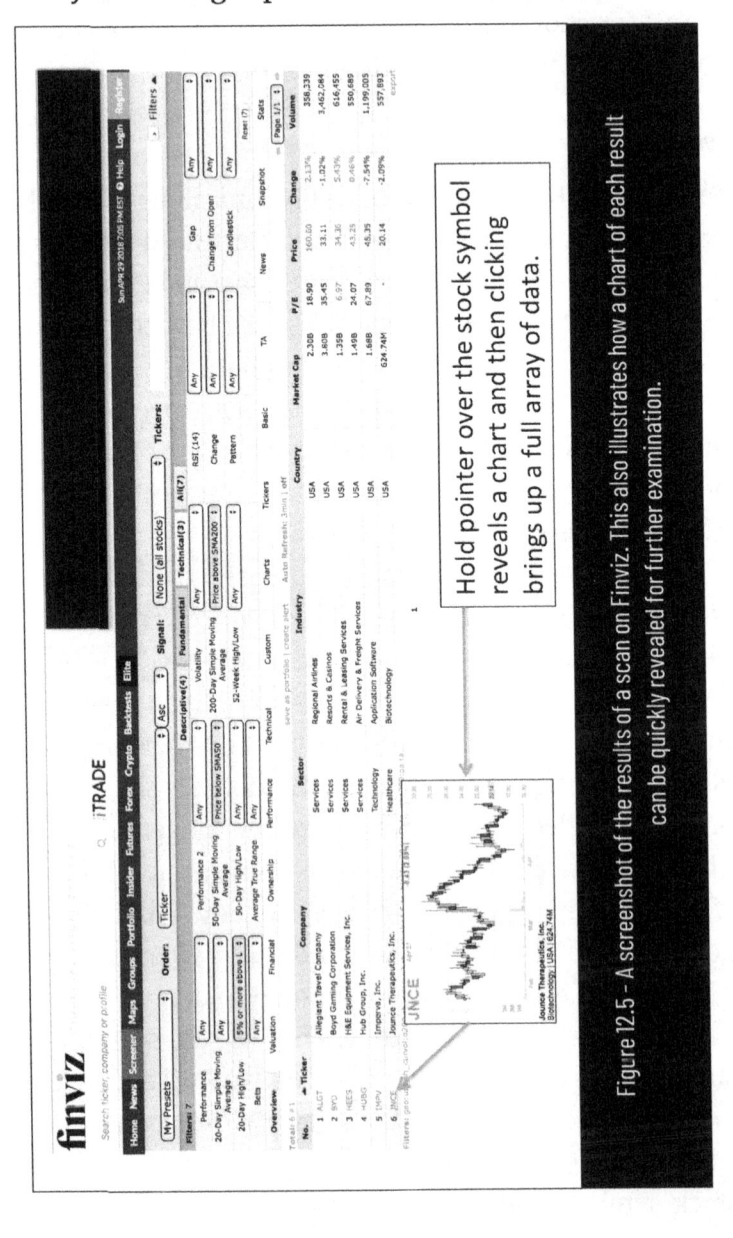

Figure 12.5 - A screenshot of the results of a scan on Finviz. This also illustrates how a chart of each result can be quickly revealed for further examination.

As you can see, you can quickly run your mouse pointer over each stock symbol and scan the charts for any of the familiar patterns that were discussed in Chapters 7, 8 and 9. In Figure 12.5 I ran my pointer over JNCE and you can clearly see the JNCE chart has traced a double bottom pattern. You can also see that it moved higher into an area of prior resistance and failed to break through. This is not a good setup for an entry but it might be a stock I could keep on watch for a break through resistance.

If I had caught this a few days earlier it might have been an interesting long opportunity. The next step would have been to click on the symbol to bring up much more detail on this stock. Figure 12.6 illustrates what this more detailed analysis looks like.

Finviz will automatically draw support and resistance lines in the chart for you, which is another useful feature. A considerable amount of fundamental and technical analyses is also presented below the chart for further review. If you are not familiar with this process, you will likely start to recognize how powerful and important these scanners are for you as a swing trader.

If you wish to look for short opportunities, then a scan would be set to look for the reverse of a long. The scan would look for a price level below a 20-day SMA but still above the 50 and 200-day SMAs. This would indicate the price of a security is just starting to move lower while the longer-term SMA has yet to reflect the change.

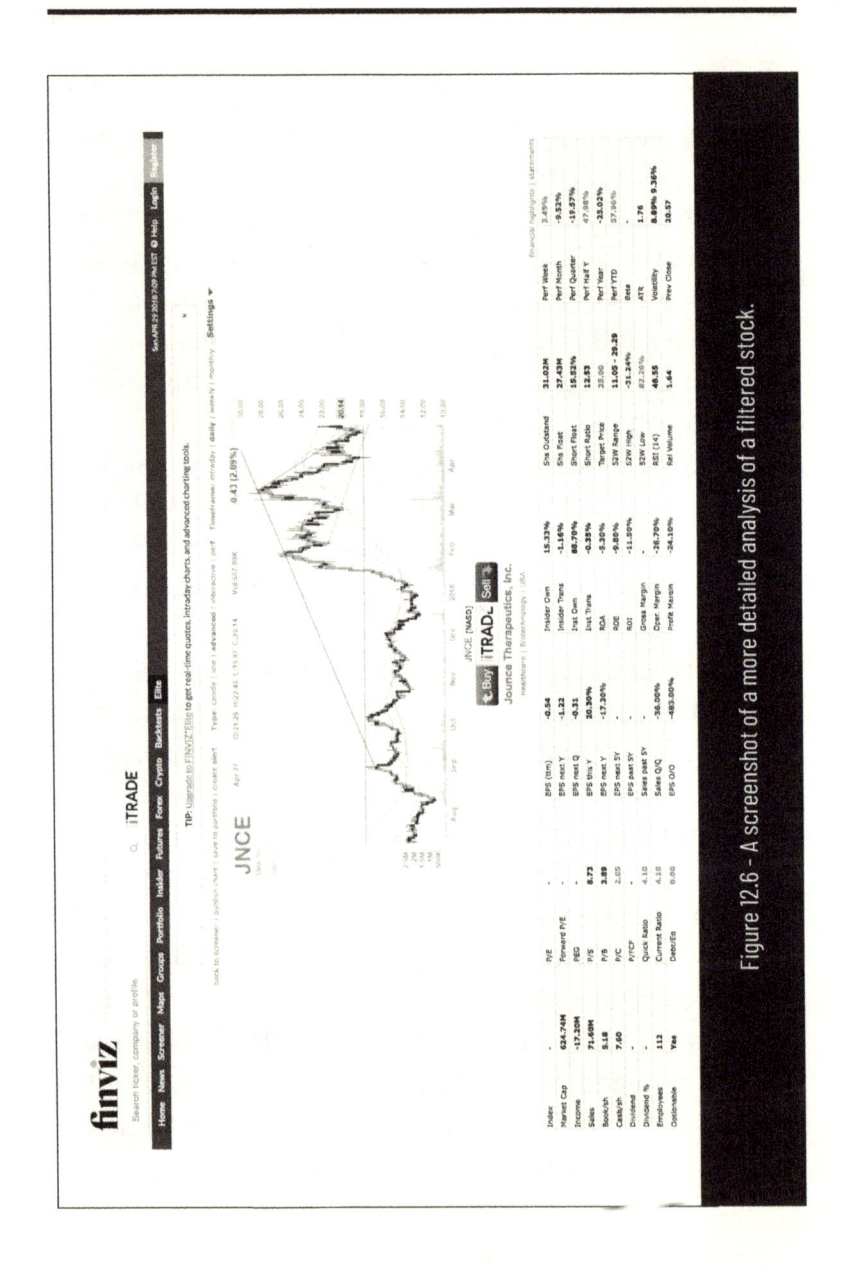

Figure 12.6 - A screenshot of a more detailed analysis of a filtered stock.

The following Table 12.1 provides a summary of some of the more useful combinations for scans that I have used in the past. If you are new to this process, you can experiment with the Finviz scanner or another scanner of your choosing to develop filters that work for you. As markets shift and change, you will likely need to update and revise your scanning filters to suit existing market conditions.

Search type	Filters	Other potential filters
Strong uptrending stock	Stock price above 20-day, 50-day and 200-day SMAs	EPS greater than 20%, increasing RSI not over 70 (overbought)
Strong downtrending stock	Stock price below 20-day, 50-day and 200-day SMAs	EPS negative and decreasing RSI not under 30 (oversold)
Reversal trend down to up	Stock price above 20-day, below 50-day and 200-day SMAs	Float short greater than 20% Dragonfly candle pattern
Reversal trend up to down	Stock price below 20-day, above 50-day and 200-day SMAs	Gravestone candle pattern Float short less than 5%
Reversal trend down to up*	Double bottom, engulfing candle up, or dragonfly doji	RSI under 30
Reversal trend up to down*	Double top, engulfing candle down, gravestone doji	RSI over 70

Table 12.1 - A table of options for scanning the market for trading setups.
Note *: some scanning tools have the ability to look for a variety of patterns. Finviz has several pattern scans with more available if you subscribe.

The Descriptive scanning settings I would usually use in combination with the Table 12.1 settings were previously discussed and include the following:

1. volume over 200,000 shares to ensure liquidity
2. country selected as the USA because I focus on US markets
3. price over $2.00 per share, which is my personal preference to avoid low-priced stocks (some traders will use greater than $5.00 per share)
4. relative volume greater than 1.5 to pick up unusual activity (optional)

The process of scanning is what a swing trader should do on a regular basis to find potential trades. You can see the power of a good scanning tool to filter down over 7,400 stocks to a few that may be setting up for a solid trade. The filters that you decide to use will depend on whether you are looking for long or short opportunities and on your own personal preferences.

Review the Short List of Opportunities

After the scanning process is complete, it is up to you to review the charts of the stocks and look for those familiar patterns that indicate a good trade setup. As you become more comfortable and familiar recognizing patterns and setups in the charts, the faster this secondary screening process will happen. You will look at lines of support and resistance, determine a good entry price and then calculate out the risk to reward ratio.

Prior to entering an order to buy, you will also want to do some quick research on whether the stock is in a sector that is performing well, what the analysts' ratings are, the earnings dates, the RSI value, the MACD and any pending news that you might not want to hold through (you'll recall that I do not like holding stocks that have pending events like the outcome of a drug trial or an earnings report). Alignment with more of these indicators would further confirm a decision to enter a long or short position.

I have presented a Finviz scan, however, as previously mentioned, this is not the only option for doing scans. Your broker may offer scanning tools or you could choose another free online platform such as ChartMill.com to do your scans. ChartMill offers a similar setup as well as some customized scans that already have filter criteria for particular trading setups. These predesigned scans can be helpful for a new trader but you should also be aware of what criteria is being used in the scan so you understand what the specific search is looking for.

You can use the same types of filters on ChartMill and end up with a similar list of stocks and corresponding charts to review for trade setups. The Stock Screener page for ChartMill is shown below in Figure 12.7.

ChartMill also has a rating feature under the More Technical tab. This rating feature provides a score of the overall technical health of a stock and another score provides an indication of the setup quality for a breakout pattern. The "Analyzer" page is an additional feature that uses their proprietary algorithms to come up with possible trade setups as well as an analysis of a stock that you may be considering for a trade.

The choice of which market scanner to use is completely up to the individual swing trader. The 2 I have covered are both excellent in my opinion and will give you many ideas for swing trading setups. However, these scanning tools only provide you with a list of possible trades based on the criteria entered. It is up to you to review the information presented and to then decide whether there is a good trading opportunity. The entry price on the trade and the reward compared to the risk needs to be at the top of your mind before your capital is put at risk with a decision to buy or sell.

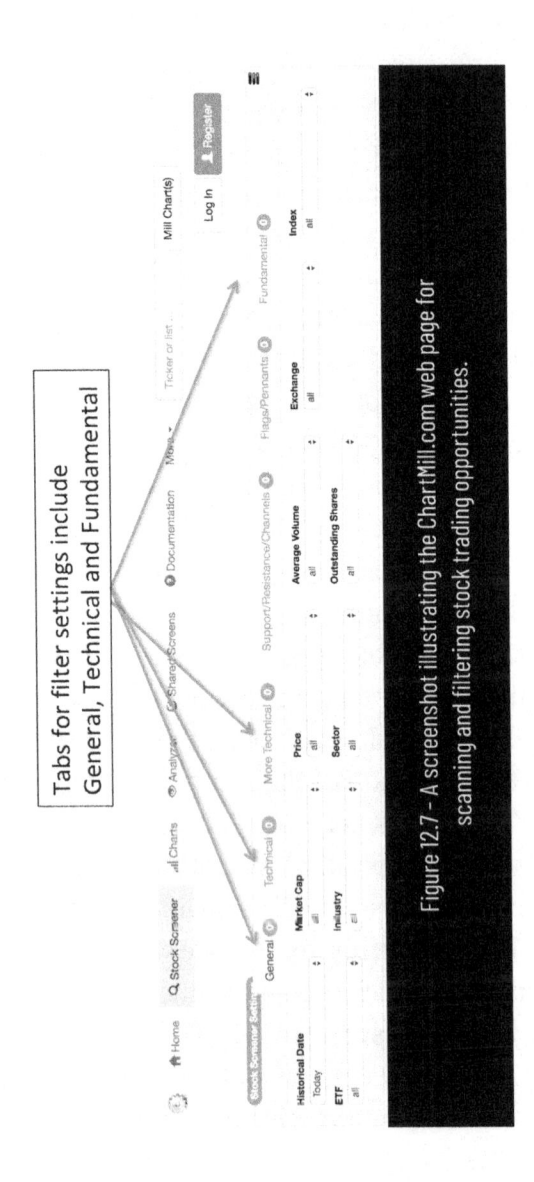

Figure 12.7 - A screenshot illustrating the ChartMill.com web page for scanning and filtering stock trading opportunities.

Short-term Gap Trades

The "gap trade" is another swing strategy that can be used in different scenarios. In this strategy, you are hoping to take advantage of a multiday run in a stock based usually on some good or bad news. When news comes out about a particular stock or sector, investors and traders will generally take a few days to digest the news before a new valuation is determined.

I discussed the principle of the price gap in Chapter 7, Technical Analysis – Charting Basics. A gap is defined as a price range in a chart where no trading has occurred. A gap in a daily chart happens when the stock closes the day at one price and then opens the following day at a different price. In fact, these gaps happen on a large majority of stocks every day. In the absence of any news or significant events, the price difference between the close and the next day's opening price will be relatively small and insignificant. However, with significant news in a company or in volatile markets, the gap between a previous close and the following open can be very large. In addition, these gaps can of course be either up above or down below the previous close. Referring to Figure 12.8 below, you can see several examples of a gap up and gap down on Walmart Inc. (WMT) from November 2017 to April 2018.

A swing trader would be in Nirvana if they could consistently buy a stock at the close of the trading day and sell it the next morning for a profit. Unfortunately, doing this consistently is not possible but you can assess how a stock trades during the day and into the close to improve your odds if you do decide to take a short-term or an overnight gap trade.

Why do these price gaps happen every morning when the market opens? Markets usually close with a heightened flurry of activity. Some say that the last hour of trading is the most important hour of the day. Day traders are getting out of their long and short positions while the short-term traders and investors are deciding what to sell or hold as well as what stocks to add to their positions.

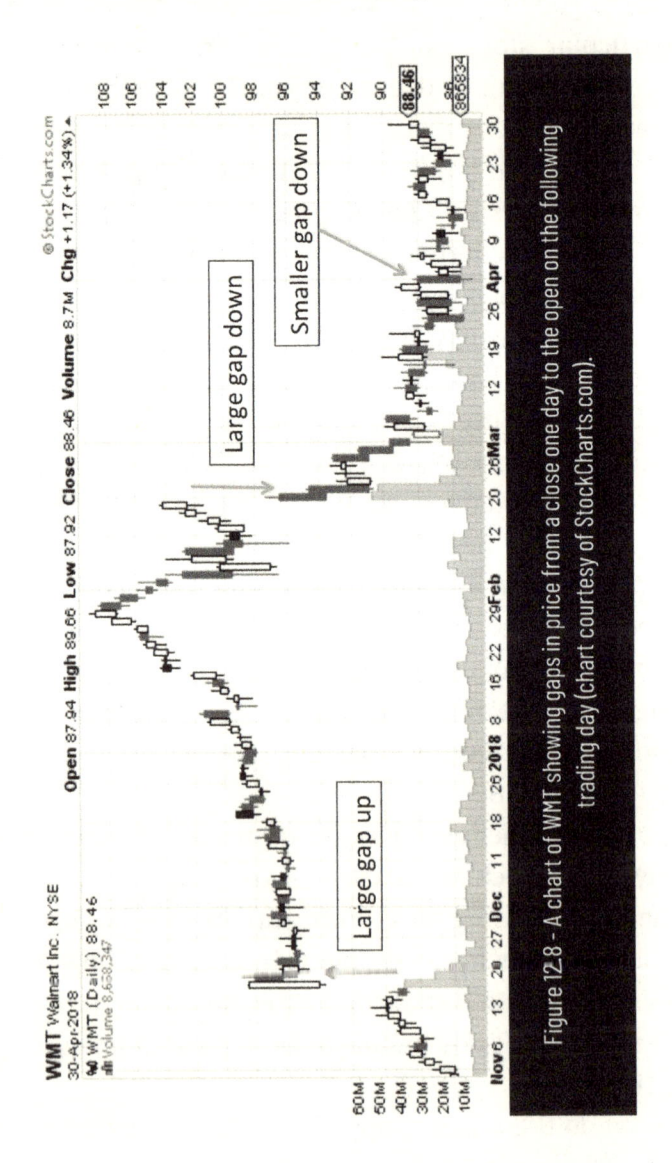

Figure 12.8 – A chart of WMT showing gaps in price from a close one day to the open on the following trading day (chart courtesy of StockCharts.com).

Once the market closes, investors and traders reassess their positions. In the morning, market players look at the latest news headlines, reassess market risks, pour over new economic numbers, and then decide what positions they want to build or reduce. Based on this analysis, buy or sell orders are placed before the open that cause the price to open higher, lower or at the previous day's close.

As a day trader, I will focus on the stocks that are making significant price gaps up or down in the morning. These gaps are often the result of some news that has been released after the market close of the previous day and traders are now revaluing these companies that are gapping based on the news. While a day trader is in cash at the end of every trading day, a swing trader can take advantage of these gaps by holding shares in a stock that they think will gap up or down the following day.

The obvious risk in using this strategy is the potential for loss. With the gap strategy, the security holder loses control of their ability to mitigate risk in their trade because the markets are closed. This is always a risk with any swing trade because every night when the market closes, a swing trader is vulnerable to the risk that some news will come out that will affect their position and cause a gap above or below the stop-loss that they have in their trading plan. As a swing trader, you need to be prepared for this event to occur and know how you will react.

In Chapter 5 (Risk and Account Management) and Chapter 11 (Swing Trading Rules), I discussed how to mitigate some of the risks involved when holding a trade, whether for just overnight or for as long as several weeks. Let's review again 2 of the company events you will want to avoid:

- Earnings reports: I avoid holding securities through their earnings reports because share price reactions can be unpredictable and create a significant risk of capital loss. Earnings report dates are readily available at no cost on sites such as Estimize or Zacks earnings calendar.

- Pending news events: I also avoid holding securities for companies that are expected to make a significant announcement that would impact their valuation. These events might include the results of a drug trial or the closing of a big merger deal. News with these events will move share prices significantly and if you're positioned in a security on the wrong side of the news, it can result in a very big loss. Remember, preserving your capital is one of the most important jobs of a trader, therefore in my opinion the potential gain is not worth the risk of a major loss. Various sites like Yahoo Finance offer insights on pending events where the outcome could be either very positive or very negative.

All of your other risk mitigation strategies should also be employed with each trade you make. These include controlling the size of your position and only entering trades that provide a good reward compared to the risk you are taking. This will ensure you do not lose too much of your capital in the event of bad news and that your good trades will return more than you could potentially lose.

So what do you do in the event that a security gaps below your stop-loss if you are long or gaps above your stop-loss if you are short? There is not a lot you can do in this case except be prepared to immediately exit your trade and prevent any further losses.

I am almost always online before the market opens in the morning so I know where my swing positions are going to open at. If I am in a long trade that gapped down below my stop, I will watch it at the open of the market. After some initial volatility (the first 5 minutes), sometimes a stock will start to trade higher and move "into the gap". If this happens, then my new stop is the low of the day for my long position. I will continue to hold through the day if the price does not cross my new daily stop. As the day ends, I will also watch the price action of the stock. If I am still long the stock and it looks like it will close the day below my original trade plan stop-loss, I will likely stick to my plan and sell the position. If my long stock appears to be closing above my trade plan stop-loss, then I will likely continue to hold but only after reassessing my plan to see if something significant has changed that resulted in an increase in the downside risk.

There is a small chance that the stock will return to the previous day's closing price and save my position. More often than not though, a stock that gaps down will move up briefly and then the selling will resume as traders see the opportunity to exit long positions and short traders add to the selling. The stock price will then drop below the opening range and head lower from there. This is a chart pattern that day traders focus on at the open and is referred to as an "opening range breakdown".

If you are short a stock and it gaps up in the morning against you, then your options are the same. You can hope for a sell-off which sometimes will occur. At other times, a stock will drop for a short period of time on some initial profit-taking at the open and then head higher as more buyers come into the trade. Covering the position for a loss on a break to a new high of the day is your best option to prevent further losses from accumulating.

Alternatively, if you do not want to monitor the stock and continue to hold, then you will just sell the position for a loss and move on. It's important to remember that having a losing trade does not mean that you are a failure; it is all part of being a successful trader and having the discipline to follow your trading plan with a consistent risk to reward strategy.

It is also important to recognize that the gap trade strategy may not be a technique that many swing traders can use due to the timing required and their availability during the trading day. This strategy requires you to monitor the market during the day for stocks that are trending as well as for possible news that might be moving the market or a sector in the market. You should also have access to the market action as the trading day is ending to see how specific stocks and sectors are closing. If you cannot at least occasionally monitor these factors during the trading session and be online to see the close of the day, then the gap trading strategy will be difficult to utilize.

Trading for an Overnight Gap Up or Down

One swing trading strategy that I have used successfully is the overnight gap trade. In this case, I might buy a stock that has been very strong (or short a stock that has been weak) during the day and hold a position overnight. The expectation is that there will be follow through on the next trading day as whatever news that is moving the stock is further digested by investors in the market.

I am expecting a follow through because during the day other swing traders and investors have probably been building positions in expectation that the price will move higher. In the evening, traders and investors look at their holdings and go over the news of the day as well as do scans and look at charts. Stocks that have been strong during the day show up on their scans, which the following morning will bring in more interest and ultimately buying.

Many professional traders have a rule of thumb called the "3-day rule". This rule is based on the belief that if some event has moved a stock price, the effects will be felt for about 3 days before the volatility returns to normal and the price finds a new equilibrium between the buyers and the sellers. If you get in on a first-day move, then there is a greater chance you will catch a follow through on the second day based on this rule of thumb. If a stock's price is already up several days in a row, then you should move on to find other opportunities with a better entry and risk to reward ratio.

Listed below are the attributes in a stock that make for a good overnight long swing trade:

1. Recent good news is released in the market. It is important that it is recent news and not days old or news that has already been anticipated by the market. An announcement of a successful drug approval just prior to the market open is new and probably tradable news.

2. Strong price action throughout the day. Stocks that start strong and stay strong all trading day are obviously popular among traders and investors likely due to some news release or other event. There is a good chance that their popularity will continue into the following 1 or 2 days.

3. A strong close in the last 30 minutes of trading is also a good indication that a gap up will occur in the following morning open. New investors

are getting in and current holders are not selling because they are expecting the share price to move higher. Be aware that at the close there may be more volatility with prices moving up and down more violently.

4. If the stock in play is part of a sector that is performing well, then this is also a positive sign. For example, if the stock you are considering for an overnight gap trade is a technology stock and the entire technology sector is leading the market higher, then all the better.

5. A market that is generally trending higher is also good for an overnight long gap trade. Market and trader sentiment is positive so they are more likely to buy into strength. In a weak market, traders will often take any pop up in price as an opportunity to sell.

6. The overnight gap strategy is not very reliable in markets that are not trending up or down. Markets that lack direction will fluctuate sideways and a follow through on a stock's price action is not as likely to happen.

7. For long trades, stocks with a low float (less than about 10 million shares, however this number is somewhat subjective) can be good overnight gap trades because of the limited number of shares available to trade. The principle of supply and demand applies where a big demand and small supply will drive a price higher.

8. Companies with their shares heavily shorted also make for good long trades. Traders with short

positions in a stock need to cover at some point and if they get nervous on good news and upward share price action, then the short traders add to the buying pressure.

9. Check StockTwits to see if the company is trending. It is a good indication that people are chatting and posting about the company, but do avoid getting drawn into the stupid comments and wild price predictions that are made by people posting on this site.

10. Mania stock plays that will be discussed next in this chapter make for very good overnight gap trades. In this case, you can do a partial position sale on the big gap as it moves up at the open and hold some for a long-term run. But remember my rule, never let a winner turn into a loser – move your stop up above your original entry price and sell if it hits there.

When you have some or most of these aforementioned factors working for you, taking a long overnight swing trade has a good chance of success. But remember, you are still at risk and the market is always full of surprises. What might have looked like a great trade with many factors aligned, may not work out as you had expected.

Here are some ways to mitigate the risk you are taking:

1. Keep your overnight gap trade position small. Again, never risk more than 2% of your portfolio. You should assume that your long position might open at a price that gave back half of yesterday's gains. How much will you lose? For example, imagine that the stock you are looking at was

trading around $10.00 and it gapped up to open at $12.00 in the morning. It then ran from $12.00 to $14.00 throughout the day to close on that high. How much will you be down if your stock gapped down to open at $13.00? If you had 500 shares and your entry price was right at the high of $14.00, then you are down $500.00. That $500.00 loss should be less than 2% of your portfolio.

2. Have a trading plan before the market opens the following morning. What will you do on a gap down if you're in a losing position? Will you sell and cut your losses or do you have time to wait and watch as I outlined above? What will you do on a gap up? Will you sell some and set a stop and trail the rest higher or will you sell it all and book your profits? Have a plan – do not make these decisions on the fly.

3. Try to get in early on trades that look like good overnight gap plays. Check the markets at lunchtime Eastern Time to see if you can find a good candidate for this play. Scanners and StockTwits are good sources of information for trending stocks. If you find a stock that looks good and is trending higher, take a small entry position up to about half of what you would consider holding. Getting in earlier on a trending stock will lower your average price when you take your final position near the close. Therefore, if your stock does gap down against you unexpectedly in the morning, your loss is not as great as it would have been if you had taken the entire position at the close.

Under the right conditions, overnight gap trades can be a profitable trading strategy. They can be employed at most any time but they do work much better in markets that are trending either higher or lower. In times of volatility and no market leadership or direction, the following day's gap direction can be less predictable and therefore it may be better to avoid the added risk of holding overnight.

Hot Sector Manias

In Chapter 6, I discussed these fundamental analysis-based trade opportunities. These trades will also pop up on scans when you do technical analysis but they start out as being "story-driven" trades. This is probably one of the best opportunities for a swing trader to make a great profit. The unfortunate aspect of this strategy is that it does not occur that often. You may get 1 or 2 of these opportunities in a year and then go a year or 2 without any hot sector mania stories.

Let's look at few that have occurred during my trading career.

The 1990s Gold Rush

Yes, there was a gold rush in the 1990s but it did not happen in the Yukon or California, it happened in the stock markets. I was trading stocks back in that era and caught gold fever, which resulted in some very profitable years.

The gold sector really took off during the Bre-X era. For those of you not familiar with the Bre-X story, it involved a Canadian publicly listed company that bought an Indonesian property in March 1993, and then in October 1995 announced significant amounts of gold had been discovered, sending its stock price soaring higher. The stock price started out at well under $1.00 and reached a peak of $286.50 (*split adjusted*) in

May 1996 on the Toronto Stock Exchange (TSE). That share price gave a total capitalization of over $6 billion Canadian.

After much drama and rumors of fraud, Bre-X Minerals Ltd.'s stock collapsed in 1997 after the gold sample results were discovered to be a fabrication and that in reality there was very little gold on the property. What a ride for investors.

Some smart swing traders made millions. Others lost big as some investors bought late in the cycle and held on, hoping for a bounce or price rebound higher. Some investors and traders actually doubled down and bought more as the stock price dropped when the initial rumors started to surface that it was a massive fraud. There were also people who saw the story unwinding and took short positions as the stock dropped precipitously. The bottom line of the story is that there was lots of money to be made here if you were watching this unfold and were in early and smart about getting out when the story started to change. Rumors of fraud are never a good sign for any security.

I never owned a single share of Bre-X during its entire run up and subsequent crash back to Earth. However, Bre-X was one of the catalysts that really got things heated up in the gold sector. Investor money came pouring into the gold mining sector in the hopes of finding the next Bre-X. Greed is a great driver and following the money often works if you're in early. Many junior gold companies saw their stock prices run higher with the money pouring into the gold sector.

One example of a stock that rocketed higher was a company called Gold Rush Casino Mining Corp. Starting out at under $1.00, it eventually topped out at over $20.00 Canadian. I caught this one very early and scaled out all of the way up, selling some shares for as high as around $18.00.

The gold rush that occurred in the 1990s was a great example of how a sector can take stock prices to unreasonable valuations. An alert swing trader will watch for these opportunities and get in early to ride the wave.

Dot-com Bubble

Most people have at least heard of the dot-com bubble and some older traders actually lived through it. The dot-com bubble started around 1995 and ran until 2000. It offered a great opportunity for swing trades or just sticking with trading an index. This bubble was characterized by a parabolic move in the equity markets (particularly the Nasdaq) due to money flowing into Internet-based companies. During this period, the technology-dominated Nasdaq index rose from under 1,000 to more than 5,000.

The dot-com bubble was the result of speculative hot sector investing – nothing particularly new here – just follow the money. Investors threw their money into Internet startups during the late 1990s. Anything whatsoever that had something to do with this new thing called the Internet attracted funds. A lot of investors and venture capital funds did not seem to worry about how these companies were ever going to find a path to being profitable. As long as the company had some idea about using the Internet, that was good enough for them.

The bubble gradually formed over those years from 1995 to 2000, fueled by cheap money, easy capital, speculation and greed. Remember, if you're a swing trader, a greed-fueled market is very good, but you need to recognize it for what it is and ride the wave. Venture capitalists were tripping over each other to find the next big deal, which meant they were willing to invest in any company with a "dot-com" after its name. Sound familiar – i.e., add "blockchain" to your company's name.

The traditional methods of valuation that I discussed earlier, like revenue and earnings, would not occur for several years, assuming that these new business models would actually work, but investors were more than willing to overlook these traditional fundamentals. Many companies that had not generated any revenue, let alone shown a profit or a finished product, went to market. Many of these initial public offerings saw their stock prices triple and quadruple on their first day of trading. This added to the feeding frenzy that was occurring during this period.

The Nasdaq index peaked in March 2000 at 5,048. All parabolic movements have to come to an end at some point. In this case, several of the leading high-tech companies, such as Dell and Cisco, placed huge sell orders on their stocks. Investors heard of the selling and started to sell as well, and that led to some panic. A few weeks later, the stock market had lost 10% of its value. The loss of confidence that the market would keep going higher put the brakes on the flow of investment capital, which was essentially the lifeblood of these cash-strapped dot-com companies. Dot-com companies that were, in some cases, previously valued at hundreds of millions of dollars became worthless within months. By early 2002, a very large number of dot-com companies had gone bankrupt. Trillions of dollars of investment capital disappeared with these incredible stock price declines and bankruptcies.

This is another great example of how a swing trader could have made a significant profit by recognizing a hot sector mania play early in the game. It also illustrates how you need to recognize when the play is done and the money has stopped flowing. Too many investors and traders get so caught up in the story that they refuse to recognize and accept that it is over. Others are latecomers who get stuck with losses almost immediately and hesitate to sell because they do not want to take a loss. Vigilance pays off for traders who get in early and recognize when it is time to get out.

Marijuana Mania

Since the 1970s, marijuana has been classified as illegal under the US federal *Controlled Substances Act*. In fact, it is listed as a Schedule I drug, which means that in the eyes of US federal law, marijuana has no accepted use for medicinal purposes. Being classified as Schedule I also means it has a high potential for abuse—just like heroin and LSD.

At that same time in the 1970s, marijuana was also illegal under the laws of every state in the US. However, over the last 20 plus years, many state marijuana laws have transformed and changed significantly. The change began in 1996 when California became the first state to legalize marijuana for medical purposes. One by one other states started to follow California by allowing marijuana use for medicinal purposes.

At the time President Barack Obama was first sworn into office in January 2009, 13 states had already legalized the use of marijuana for medical purposes but none allowed its recreational use. Fast forward to the inauguration of Donald Trump, and 28 states, including Washington, DC, had legalized the use of medical marijuana, and 8 of those states also permitted its recreational use. Today, while it is still a federal crime to possess marijuana, there is no shortage of stores in these states permitted to sell this drug to the public.

In Canada, like in a number of other countries, the federal government recognizes medicinal uses of this drug and has permitted facilities to grow pot for this purpose. At the writing of this book, the Canadian federal government has announced that as of October 17th, 2018, the recreational use of the drug will be legalized, as it is in 8 states in the US.

So what does this all have to do with making money? Lots as it turns out. The illicit drug trade has generated countless billions, which is probably why many governments are legalizing the sale and use of marijuana. Of course, this interest also attracts entrepreneurs (legitimate and not-so-much) along with the venture capital investment crowd, all eager to get in on the perceived bonanza of money generation. Follow the money as they say.

Marijuana stocks started sprouting up like tulips in spring, particularly in Canada because of the more favorable legal environment and the support of the Canadian federal government, in comparison to the US. Old publicly traded mining companies that were dormant got renamed, becoming marijuana companies, and the money started to flow. Like most mania investing, nobody cared that the management had no experience or knowledge or even a legitimate Business Plan to become profitable. The important thing was that they were in the marijuana business. It was the start of another hot sector and investors were throwing money into it. Let's look at a few businesses that I made swing trades in with a large degree of success.

One swing trade I was in and out of was in a company called Canopy Growth Corp. (CGC), formerly called Tweed Marijuana Inc. It is a company that is in the medical marijuana business. CGC was the first Canadian federally regulated, publicly traded cannabis producer in North America. The equity began trading on the Toronto Stock Exchange under the appropriate symbol of WEED. The company was given much credibility when it was described by a prominent newspaper as "one of the world's ... premier exporters of marijuana".

Looking at the chart of WEED in Figure 12.9 below, you can see the phenomenal price run this stock had. One can only imagine how much money early investors made.

Swing Trading Strategies

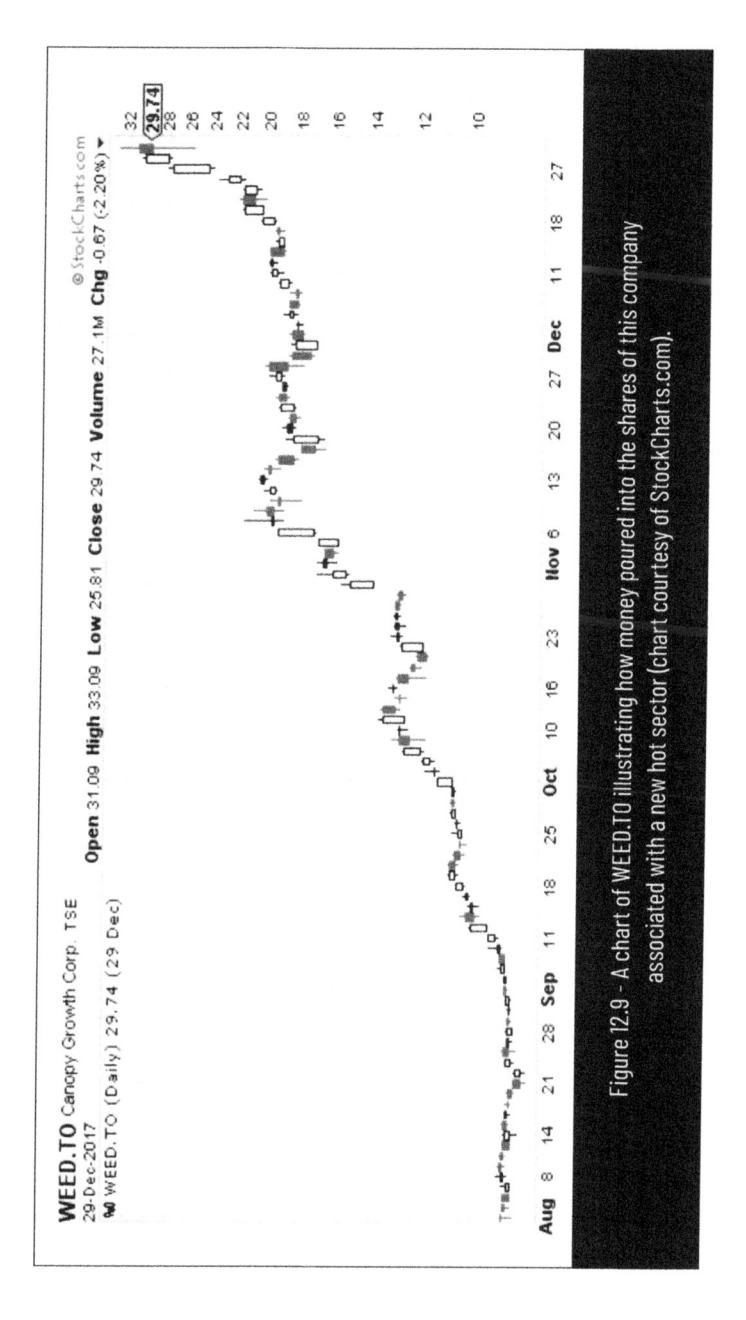

Figure 12.9 - A chart of WEED.TO illustrating how money poured into the shares of this company associated with a new hot sector (chart courtesy of StockCharts.com).

Canopy Growth Corp. is just one example of how investing in a hot sector can be very profitable. Figure 12.10 illustrates the stock price action of another marijuana company called

Aurora Cannabis Inc.

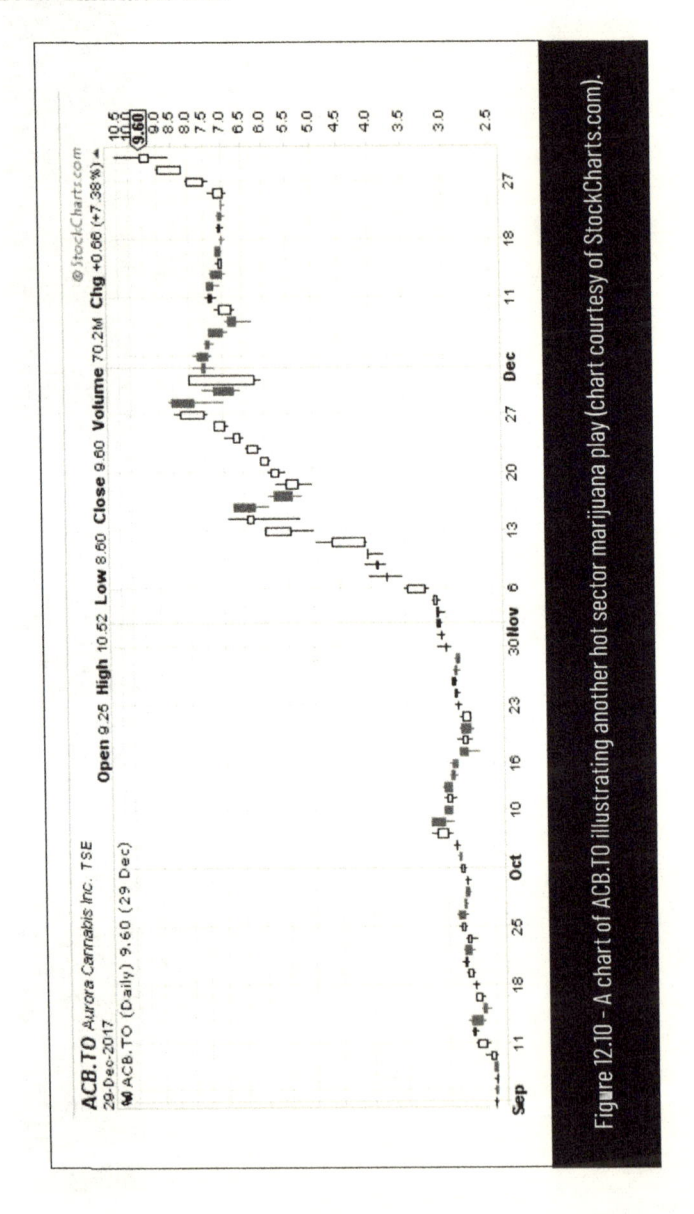

Figure 12.10 - A chart of ACB.TO illustrating another hot sector marijuana play (chart courtesy of StockCharts.com).

Equity offerings in Canadian weed companies went from about $300 million in 2016 to almost $1 billion in 2017 as reported by Thomson Reuters. Small independent brokers are great at seeing these trends and jumping on board to take advantage of underwriting fees and making sure they get *warrants* that take advantage of any stock price appreciation with no risk of initial investment.

The marijuana sector is a recent example of a hot sector mania play that swing traders were able to capitalize on in a big way.

Bitcoin and Blockchain Revolution

I discussed in Chapter 6, Fundamental Analysis, the bitcoin and blockchain mania as the latest example of a hot sector mania play. There have been more such plays in recent years that I have not discussed, and as long as human nature does not change, there will be more in the future.

Strategies for Trading Hot Sector Mania Stories

The first rule for taking advantage of these market opportunities is to have patience. As I mentioned, these hot sector manias do not happen often. These are not weekly or even monthly events. Sometimes a year or 2 will pass with no hot sector stories but you should remain vigilant. The key to taking advantage of these opportunities is being in early and, more importantly, not being one of the last out.

If you are getting your news on a hot sector play from an Uber driver or the barista who is making your lattes, then you are probably too late on the trend. In fact, I sold a significant amount of my bitcoin holding after a barista at a coffee shop told me he was buying as much bitcoin as he could afford. It had been going parabolic in price so there were other signs a top was near – that discussion with the barista was just another confirmation that the bitcoin party was about to end or at least have a significant correction.

So how do you find these trends at an early stage? Below are several suggestions for finding new hot sector trends.

1. Business articles: a swing trader should be in the habit of scanning business articles on popular websites like Yahoo Finance and CNBC. They are often a little late to pick these trends up, but they are still a good source of information on what the pros are watching and investing in. You should also read business news regularly on sites like Benzinga. This site has a good pre-market and after-market summary every day. You are a professional money manager so you need to be an informed trader and in touch with your business.

2. Social media sites: you should be watching social media sites like StockTwits. Unfortunately, there are a lot of *"twits"* on StockTwits, so you need to separate out the noise from the intelligent posts and conversations. Find a few people to follow on StockTwits and focus on their posts. The people you want to follow will usually have a large number of people following them already because they have good quality posts with information that can be helpful in identifying opportunities. You can also just look for securities that are trending on this social media.

3. Stock market connections: most traders never talk to a broker because everything they need to trade with is available online. However, the venture capital groups and some of these brokers are the ones that are in at the beginning on a lot of these hot sector mania plays. They are either

involved funding them or see them coming first. If you have a professional or non-professional connection to this industry, then you need to use it to find out if anything new is developing. This is not implying that you should look for insider information or information that is not already in the public domain. You are looking for information that is public but not widely circulated. You want information that a large percentage of investors have not yet caught wind of.

4. Technical scans: I discussed scanning for potential swing trades in the first section of this chapter. Often these scans will also reveal hot sector manias, and you should therefore be watching for this type of trade as you utilize this other strategy.

5. Chatrooms: chatrooms with a community of traders can also be a good source of early information on a hot sector play. For example, at BearBullTraders.com, we share information about day trading opportunities and have a discussion forum on the site that covers swing trading ideas.

In summary, become a well-informed trader. If you are involved in the investment business, you need to know what is going on in that business. You are looking for a sector where money is flowing. Is it a new product or service or is it an old product that is gaining popularity again? It might be a sector like technology or a specific story like blockchain.

The best phrase that applies to this swing trading strategy is "FOLLOW THE MONEY".

Chapter Summary

In this chapter, I discussed 3 different strategies for finding and entering swing trades. Each of these strategies is based on very different techniques that can allow a trader to potentially make profits by holding securities from as short as overnight to as long as several weeks. The 3 different strategies are summarized below.

1. **Regularly Scanning for Trades**

- Regularly scanning the market is one way to find opportunities for swing trades.

- The regular scanning process involves using a scanning tool to look for particular events happening with a stock. A number of good scanning tools are available for free on the Internet including but not limited to Finviz and ChartMill. The broker you use may also have a scanning tool as part of their platform.

- Whatever scanning tool you decide to use will likely yield the same results as the others do. Stick with one and get used to using it.

- The scanning tool will produce a list of "swing trade candidates" depending on the filtering parameters that you decide to use. With this list, you review each chart in the list and look for the familiar setup patterns I discussed in Chapters 7, 8 and 9 regarding technical analysis.

- From the review of the charts, perhaps a few setups will look promising. You should then go through a process of determining a possible entry point on each trade and calculate the risk to reward to ensure that the ratio is at least 2 times the reward for the risk being taken.

- Checking the market sentiment and specific sector performance is a good step to take before entering a swing trade in an individual stock. It is usually better to take trades where the stock and sector are both moving in the same direction. Ideally, a swing trader wants alignment in sentiment.
- Prior to entering a position in a stock, look for pending events that you might not want to hold your position through, such as an earnings report or a drug trial result. I do not recommend holding positions during these events.

2. **Short-term Gap Trades**

- Overnight gap trades are opportunities you can take advantage of under specific market conditions. These gap trades rely on the opening market price of a stock being different from the previous day's closing price. This will often happen because traders and investors have had a period of time to digest new information that has come forward or because the price momentum has continued as more traders have entered the trade.
- These gap trades work best in markets that are trending and when you are trading a stock that is aligned with the movements of the sector the stock is in as well as the overall market.
- In choppy or non-trending markets, gap trades are generally less reliable.
- A good gap trade starts with strong or weak price movements during the trading day. Price movements that remain strong in the last 30 minutes of trading are also a good sign that the momentum will continue into the following trading day.

- Always use good risk management strategies and never take large positions that might result in losing a significant amount of capital if the trade does not go as planned.
- Always have exit plans, regardless of whether the trade is profitable or not. If your stock is profitable, it may be wise to take some of the profit and let the rest go higher with a stop to ensure your winner does not turn into a loser. If you are down, take your loss and move on or set a stop and see if it comes back to a break-even trade.

3. **Hot Sector Manias**
- Hot sector mania plays are a good example of the type of trade to take overnight or to hold for a longer period of time as market players and investors rush to get into a specific sector or stocks.
- Greed takes over and the normal fundamentals of stock and company valuation are mostly ignored.
- Hot mania sector plays do not occur very often. You might have to wait 6 months to a year or more for one to occur.
- Patience and diligence is the key to making money using the hot sector mania strategy.
- Monitoring news feeds, chat rooms, social media sites, scanning the market with tools and using any connections you might have in the brokerage or venture capital industry are all ways to keep up to date on where the hot money is flowing.
- Follow the money.

CHAPTER 13

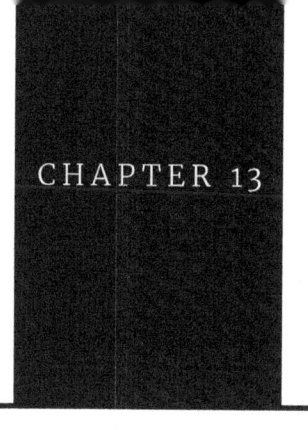

The Entry and the Exit

Now that I have presented 3 different strategies that a swing trader can use to profitably trade, let's review in more detail the entry and the exit in a trade. You will likely do a significant amount of work up front looking for trades and analyzing them before you decide whether they are worth entering, best taking a pass on, or worth monitoring for a potential entry in the near future. Once you have done this work and decide to take a position, your actual entry and exit will become the next important steps to ensure that you have the best chance of making a profit. Let's discuss both aspects of the trade in the 2 following sections.

The Entry

After doing your analysis and deciding to make a trade, the next important step is getting a good entry. Your risk to reward analysis will have been done on an assumed entry price that in many situations will be the price that the security traded on at the close of the trading day. Unfortunately, there is no way to know if this price is where the stock will open on the following day. It may gap the next morning and start the move you were expecting without you getting an entry. Therefore, your trading plan should include the most extreme price you are willing to pay to maintain that important risk to reward ratio.

For example, you have planned out a long trade based on a $10.00 per share entry. Your downside is at the $9.00 level before you get stopped out and resistance is at $13.00, which is your targeted exit price. You have a good risk to reward ratio of 3 times, assuming you can get in at $10.00. Unfortunately, when the market opens the next day, the stock price gaps up to $11.00 per share and you are left with a challenge. If you take an entry at $11.00, then your risk to reward is now only 1 to 1 with the downside being $2.00 (entry at $11.00, stop-loss at $9.00) and the upside being $2.00 (entry at $11.00, exit at $13.00). Therefore this is no longer a good trade.

As a disciplined trader, you would not take this trade with an entry at $11.00. Instead, you would determine the entry you need to get a 2 times reward, which in this case would be about $10.30 per share. You are now risking $1.30 (entry at $10.30, stop-loss at $9.00) to make $2.70 (entry at $10.30, exit at $13.00) per share, thus giving the appropriate risk to reward ratio. If you still wanted to proceed with the trade, you would therefore enter a buy at or below the $10.30 price level and hope to get a fill on the buy order at that level.

In our example, if the stock price opens lower than the $10.00 previous close, then the disciplined trader would take the trade unless some significant news happened overnight to radically change the outlook for the stock. The trader can consider themselves lucky because now the risk to reward ratio is even better if they can get in at under the $10.00 level.

In summary, chasing a stock price higher will likely end up giving you a bad entry with a bad risk to reward ratio. As a disciplined trader, you should continue to monitor the price action for a good opportunity to enter a trade or move on and look for other opportunities.

Limit Order or Immediate Fill

The other decision you will need to make when entering a long trade is whether to go for an immediate fill by entering an order to buy at the ask price or to place a bid lower and hope to get your entry filled later in the trading day. If you are going short, your option is to go for an immediate fill by selling at the bid price, or to place an order higher with a hope to be filled at some point during the trading day. There are pros and cons for entering the trade using these 2 different approaches.

If you try to get an entry by bidding at a lower price for a long position, you might get a better price but you may also miss the trade completely if the price starts moving higher and you do not have a position. The stock could quickly move to a point where your risk to reward ratio is no longer a winning trade. The same situation applies if you are trying to enter a short position and the stock price starts to drop quickly, leaving you out of the trade opportunity.

Each trade will be different, and if you believe that you can get an entry at a lower price on a long, then you can set a *"limit order"* at a specific price and hope to get a position during a normal day's volatility in price. You can refer to the ATR value to see if your limit price is reasonable and within a price range that you could expect to see on any one day.

Another option is to take half of a position at the market price and set the other half of the order at a limit price in the hope that you will get a better average entry price. This increases your commission costs but also ensures that you do not get completely left out of a good trade with half of the position taken immediately.

I feel that, in most cases, if you have an opportunity to take an entry at or below your targeted entry price in your trading plan, then it is better to take the entry immediately. This is my preference but you may decide another entry strategy works better based on your personal preferences and trading style.

The Exit

Once you have entered a trade, 1 of 2 things will usually happen. If a trade does not work out as planned, then you will be stopped out for a loss. This is pretty straightforward and an unfortunate outcome of a trade that did not go your way. This will happen because not a single swing trader on Earth has a 100% success record. As I have said a number of times throughout this book, a good trader will accept a loss as part of their business, not take it personally or emotionally, and move on to another trade.

If the trade does work out as planned, then you will be exiting the trade with a profit. Remember though, you have not made any money on a trade until you exit the position and the cash is in your account.

In the following section I will discuss the 2 outcomes where you exit the trade at a profit or you take a loss.

Exiting for a Profit

If the trade goes as hoped, then the security price will hit the targeted exit price and you will exit the position for a profit. However, some swing traders will not exit their entire position if they feel that there is more profit to be made in the trade. They may hold a portion for further gains. This is called "*scaling out*" and is an acceptable practice as long as the minimum risk to reward ratio of 2 times is maintained.

For example, you have identified a trade that will give you 3 times the reward to the risk that you are taking. That is obviously a good trade and you take a position. The trade works and the target exit price is hit. Now you have a choice of selling the entire position or selling a fraction for a profit in anticipation of making further gains down the road. The obvious advantage of scaling out is that you can make more gains compared to selling the entire position. The downside is that the stock might reverse direction against you and you will get stopped out, giving back some of the gains that you made on the trade.

In the case mentioned in the previous paragraph with the possibility of a 3 times reward, you could scale out at the target price and move your stop price up so that the reward on the remainder does not fall below a 2 times reward level. By selling half at the target and getting stopped out at the lower level, you will still receive an acceptable 2.5 times reward on the trade (3 times on half and 2 times on the other half gives an average of 2.5).

Let's look at how scaling out would have worked in a chart of TTD shown in Figure 13.1 below.

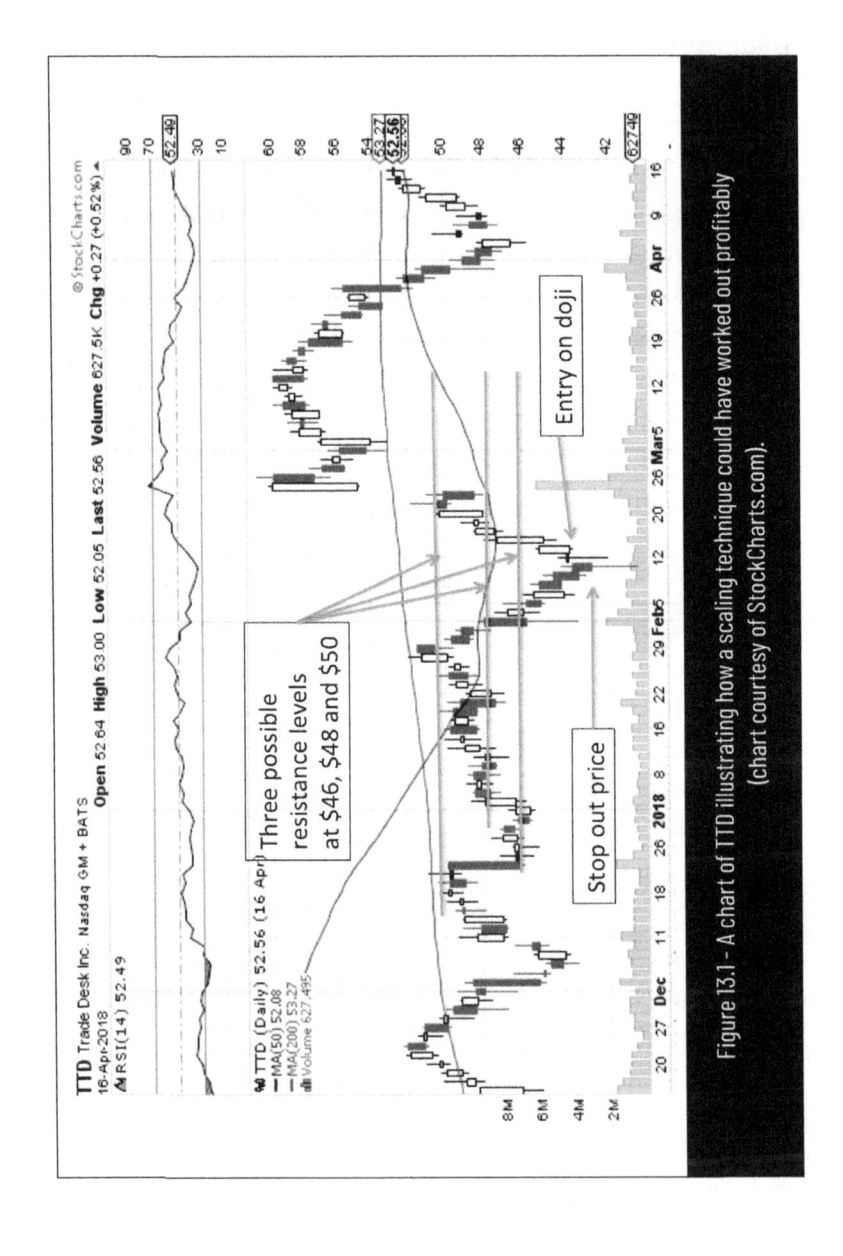

Figure 13.1 - A chart of TTD illustrating how a scaling technique could have worked out profitably (chart courtesy of StockCharts.com).

The Entry and the Exit

TTD gave a reversal signal around February 12th, 2018 with a dragonfly doji pattern. You could have taken an entry just under $44.00 with a stop out price level of around $43.00 on the low of the pattern. Three levels of prior resistance of about $46.00, $48.00 and $50.00 can be seen through December 2017 and January 2018. The first level of $46.00 gives the minimum risk to reward of 2 times and the stock ended up aggressively moving through this area. Knowing that the older resistance level was likely going to be weaker than the other 2 resistance levels of $48.00 and $50.00, you could have taken half of the position off and held the remainder for more gains into these next levels of resistance.

The trade could have played out as follows:

- buy at $44.00
- sell half above the $46.00 level and move the stop out price up to just under $46.00
- sell another quarter at $48.00 and move the stop up to $47.50 to trail the stop
- sell the remainder at $50.00

In this case, the trade was much more profitable compared to selling 100% at the $46.00 price level.

As illustrated in Figure 13.1, if the stock position moves aggressively through your exit price, then you can continue to hold some of the position, but you should move your stop price to the planned exit price of $46.00. This now ensures that you will keep your risk to reward ratio while you profit from further price movement in your favor. Never allow the process of scaling out turn your winning trade into a loser. To be clear, a losing trade may still be profitable, but if you barely broke even by not taking profits and did not maintain the risk to reward ratio of at least 2, then you had an unacceptable trade.

In summary, below are some final thoughts on selling out of a position versus scaling out:

- Scaling out works well on the hot sector mania strategy. These price moves can take a long time to play out and you want to be in them for the long run higher. Refer back to Figures 12.9 and 12.10 in the previous chapter to see the longer-term performance of the marijuana stocks. Scaling out of a position that keeps trending higher is a good strategy to get more profits out of a trade.

- You will usually have a solid reason to base your target exit on, such as having identified an area of resistance or support. If a security price gets to that area, there is a good chance it will respect the level and the price action will reverse. It may be a temporary reversal like a flag and resume the trend or it may be a switch to a new trend that will go against you. You will need to decide whether to scale out or sell 100% of the position. You can reference market conditions, sector conditions as well as the strength of the level and the other indicators that I have discussed (such as the RSI and MACD) to determine if scaling is a better option.

- At a target price based on areas of resistance or support, generally speaking at least half of the position should be taken off and the stop moved up on the remainder. On hot sector mania plays, scaling out should be done more gradually.

- As a disciplined swing trader, you should never let a trade fall back into a situation where you do not get a 2 times reward for the risk that you took. When scaling out, a stop on the remainder should be moved up so that a reward of 2 times is respected if the trade gets closed on a reversal.

- A *"trailing stop"* can be used on the remainder of the position if you have chosen to scale out. If the trend continues, you can continue to monitor the position and move your price stops up or down (depending on if you are long or short) to follow the trend. You want to be prepared to lock in the additional profit once the trend does change. You can use the ATR as a guide to how far away the stop should be set from the current price to avoid being stopped out on a normal price variation during a trading day.

- Indicators like a 20-day SMA and other tools that I have discussed can be used to keep you in the position as the trend continues in your favor.

- Once you have taken a position in a stock or security, enter another trade to exit your position at your first target price regardless of whether you decide to scale out or exit your entire position. That way you will lock in profits if your target is hit while you are away from your trading platform. Alternatively, you could decide to set an alert and get a notification by email or text from your broker, but I usually prefer to get a fill immediately when my target is hit.

Selling for a Loss

Every time you take a position, there is a chance that the trade will not work as hoped and you will be stopped out. In order to protect you, all trading platforms have a feature that allows you to enter a stop. In other words, once you have a position in a stock, your platform will allow you to enter 2 conditional trades that will only be executed if a certain price is hit. This *"either or"* trade allows you to set 2 different trades on a position and 1 trade is cancelled when the other is executed.

Let's assume you have a long position in a stock at $10.00, your target price is $13.00 and your stop out price is $9.00. You can enter a sell order at $13.00 and another sell order that will be executed when the price hits the $9.00 price level. If your stock position moves against you, the position will be sold at $9.00 and the sell order at $13.00 will be cancelled. Alternatively, if the stock price moves to $13.00, you will sell at a profit and the $9.00 sell order will be cancelled. This feature protects you from any downside risk while allowing you to lock in profits at the same time.

Setting stops for a swing trader is more important compared to a day trader who is sitting in front of their screen constantly monitoring their positions. As a swing trader, you will not be monitoring your positions every moment of the day. Therefore, the stop order will ensure your loss does not exceed what you planned on risking and you will lock in profits when your target is hit.

Another option you have is to use the alert feature that your broker likely offers. Instead of entering a stop price, you may opt to get an alert that will allow you to quickly look at the position and the current day's price action. Some traders opt to stop out only if the closing price is below their stop target, however, I personally do not like this strategy.

If the price action has started to move against you, then it will likely continue.

Setting stops to protect from further losses is an important tool for you to use on your broker's platform. You will also use this tool to sell at target prices for a profit. The "either or" stop tool helps you honor your risk to reward ratio and ensures you lock in profits and minimize losses.

Chapter Summary

In this chapter, I discussed the importance of getting a good entry on a position that you intend to take as well as the different points to consider when entering a trade. I also presented various scenarios when exiting a position for a profit or loss. An overview of the chapter's contents follows.

- A good entry on a trade is the key to maintaining the risk to reward ratio that you assumed. Do not chase a price to get into a trade that has started to move without you. Chasing a price will likely cause you to break the 2 times risk to reward ratio you assumed in your analysis.

- When taking an entry short or long, you have an option to either get an immediate fill by hitting the bid or ask, or you can set a limit price and hope to get a fill at a better price during the trading session. I feel if you can get your entry price or better as per your trading plan, then you should take the sure thing or at least take half of the position immediately.

- When exiting a trade, you have an option to sell the whole position or sell a fraction and hold the remainder for more profit. This works well for mania plays that could have lots of room to run.

- Scaling should be based on an analysis of the current market and stock indicators to determine if the stock has more potential to move in a profitable direction.

- Never let a winning trade with a minimum 2 times risk to reward ratio turn into an unacceptable trade by giving back some of the gains and ending up with an overall less than 2 times risk to reward ratio.

- Use a trailing stop up or down (depending upon whether you are long or short) on a winning trade that is continuing to trend in a profitable direction to ensure you keep additional profits in case of a reversal.

- Once you are in a position, you can enter an "either or" order. These are 2 orders that are linked together so that when 1 is executed, the other order is cancelled. This type of order can be used to protect your capital by honoring your stop-loss price while locking in profits if the stock moves in your favor.

CHAPTER 14

The Routine of a Swing Trader

In the previous chapters of this book, I have explained all of the basics that you need to know about swing trading. I have explained how trading works, the tools and platform you will need to trade, risk and account management, as well as how to do some simple analysis of companies from a fundamental perspective. I dedicated 3 chapters to discuss the technical analysis that is commonly used in swing trading to find good trades and give you the ability to assess the risk and potential rewards of entering a trade. In addition, in Chapter 12 I covered 3 specific strategies that you can use under the right market conditions to find and execute potentially profitable trades.

In this chapter, I will discuss the following 2 steps that you should take to start your swing trading business. The 2 steps are as follows:

1. setting goals, objectives and strategies

2. defining and building a routine to run your business

Each of these steps will be discussed in the following sections.

Setting Goals, Objectives and Strategies

Before I go into the details of how to develop a routine, you should give some thought to the bigger picture regarding your trading business. I encourage you to reflect upon and then write down your responses to the following items:

1. Why am I swing trading? What is my objective or ultimate goal? Is it to build a living around trading or to just manage my money actively so I can save for retirement or for some other purpose? Perhaps it is to build enough income to have a monthly payout that supplements your existing income. Another possibility is that you are already doing some day trading and you believe swing trading will be a way to improve your trading knowledge, experience and psychology. Decide on your objective or goal for your business and write it down. Post it somewhere that you can easily see it so that it is a constant reminder of your goal. You should also feel free to revisit and modify your goal if your situation, abilities or circumstances change.

2. What markets and securities will I focus on in my business? There are many different investment and trading vehicles that a swing trader can play from cryptocurrencies to individual stocks. All of

these options have varying degrees of risk and with this risk comes both reward and the potential for losses. If you are a swing trading beginner, then you should probably start with individual stocks or non-leveraged ETF. If you are a more sophisticated trader, then you may expand on the trading vehicles you are open to working with. Deciding upon what vehicles and markets you will trade will help you to focus your scans on specific opportunities.

3. Decide on a strategy or set of strategies to use. This decision will be based on personal preferences. Do you want to focus on only long trades, short trades or both? Do you want to focus on only one type of setup such as a double bottom or are you open to more than one of the trading patterns that I discussed in Chapter 9, Technical Analysis – Patterns. These decisions will impact the types of market scans that you perform when searching for trading setups. Once you decide on patterns or trade setups that you intend to use, I recommend new traders write them down and keep them easily accessible for reference. Until you become familiar with your trading strategy, this will help to ensure you are getting the process right.

4. Decide on a stock price range for your trades. If you are starting with a smaller account of $5,000.00 or less you will likely want to focus your trades on lower-priced stocks so you can take a big enough position to make your trade worthwhile. If you buy 10 shares of a

higher-priced stock, it will have to move a lot just to cover the commissions on your trade. Some traders actually focus their attention on trading stocks or securities that are priced under $5.00 per share because they feel that these lower-priced shares give the best potential for gains. The downside of trading stocks under $5.00 per share is that they may not qualify for use as margin in an account, which will limit your borrowing ability and purchasing power. My feeling is that most of the swing trading techniques work on stocks in all price ranges.

5. **What time frames are you open to trading?** Swing traders normally have some thoughts about how long they want to hold a position. Ultimately, this hold time will depend on how each trade works out and how fast your position hits its target or you get stopped out. Some traders might decide to sell half of a position at a target, move their stop up to stay profitable and keep another half for more gains. This would extend the hold time on your position. A swing trader may also need to modify their hold time expectations based on the current market conditions. Remember that you can only work with the market you have, you will never win if you try to work with a market that you wish you had.

Once you have the answers to the aforementioned questions and goals, you can start to build a trading routine that you should follow as consistently as possible. In the next section, I will discuss how to go about building that routine.

Defining and Building a Routine

I am now going to cover the routine of a swing trader. To have consistent results as a swing trader, you need to operate like you would with any type of business that you own and manage. As a business owner, it is important to have and maintain a routine for the following reasons:

1. If you have existing positions, you need to be monitoring them daily. You may have an open position in a stock that is nearing your target price, which means you should be entering an exit order to ensure you follow your trading plan. If a position is not moving in the direction you had hoped, then you need to set stops to prevent your small loss from becoming a big loss.

2. You should be monitoring overall market conditions for shifts in sentiment or new events that might impact your position, such as politicians starting to attack drug companies for overpricing. If you held a position in that sector, it would likely be the time to modify your plan and exit.

3. A swing trader should be constantly on the watch for new trends in sectors and hot sector mania plays. This requires a bit of patience but can result in a big payoff if you catch one of these hot sector plays early in the cycle.

4. If you are actively working as a swing trader, you should be routinely looking for new opportunities or setups for a trade, either long or short depending upon market conditions and your personal preferences.

5. If you are not consistently following a routine of scanning and monitoring, then your performance results will likely be inconsistent as well. You will not be able to develop your skills as a trader because it will be hard to determine what works and what does not work for your trading style.

In the following sections, I will discuss several important aspects of your routine as a swing trader. These aspects include the following:

- time schedule
- record and review process (trade journal)

Each aspect of your routine is discussed separately below.

Time Schedule

In the development of your routine as a swing trader, you have to a large degree the luxury of setting your own schedule. Unlike a day trader, you are not tied to working only during market hours, however, if you have time, you will likely want to check in with the markets once or twice during the day. This will allow you to check in on any open positions you have. You should also dedicate some time every day to do your investigative homework and monitor your positions. The time you do this is up to you and your own personal schedule.

I do a review of the markets in the evenings from Sunday to Thursday. This does not have to be a time-consuming process and as you develop your business, you can decide what activities are worth doing and when. For example, I like to stay physically active, go to the gym, ride a bike, etc. Often I will listen to podcasts instead of listening to music while I do my workouts. This allows me to stay in touch with what is going on with my business (the markets) while maintaining my physical health, which is equally important.

Some screen time in the evening also works well. This is when I review trading activities for the day and look for opportunities and setups for the following morning. This activity includes monitoring active trade positions and the review process that takes place after a trade is closed. Again, it will be up to you and your schedule to determine what waking time of the day or evening works best for you.

In the following section, I will provide suggestions for this review process and a corresponding method of recordkeeping. These are only suggestions and it is up to you to decide if this system and process of recordkeeping will work for you. Over time, you can customize and modify this system to meet your own specific needs and preferences.

Record and Review Process

You should first decide if you want to use a conventional paper-based system or an electronic system. Either recordkeeping system will work, but in the long run an electronic system will be more flexible and will be able to handle larger amounts of data. The following is a suggestion for a daily review process, which starts by reviewing the market day and overall market conditions. Some things that you should note include:

- % of stocks advancing versus % declining
- % of new highs versus % of new lows
- % of stocks above 50-day and 200-day SMAs versus those below these SMAs

This information is available on Finviz, ChartMill or other platforms and it gives you an overall read on the market for that day. You should be looking at these numbers to determine if the market is trending up, trending down or churning sideways. The indexes like the Dow Jones Industrial Index, S&P 500 and Russell 2000 will tell you how the market did on any particular day but the numbers listed above are a reflection of what is going on with the internal market parameters. Looking at market internals is similar to what you would do when purchasing a used car; a prospective buyer should be looking under the hood at the engine and not just at the exterior. These internal numbers can be thought of as the engine of the market, giving a broader overview versus a 1-day result offered by the index moves.

Market sentiment can also be evaluated from evening news reports, podcasts as well as commentary from various websites such as StockTwits, Benzinga and others you may choose to review. Watching and reading these news sources is a good way to identify possible trends in the market and where traders' and investors' money is flowing. Remember that you always want to follow the money, getting in as early as possible so you are not the last one in before the rally ends.

The next step is to review your existing positions or securities that you are currently monitoring for a possible entry. I do this by using a spreadsheet or form where I have recorded important information about my trades. This is my trade journal that I have made reference to numerous times throughout the book.

Your journal should contain the following information:

- date
- market internals (bullish, bearish or neutral market condition based on your review of market internals outlined above)

- stock symbol
- source of idea
- reason for consideration of trade (double bottom, dragonfly doji, bear flag, etc.)
- sector performance confirmation
- RSI confirmation
- MACD confirmation
- check for coming events like earnings reports
- entry price (desired)
- stop out price
- target price
- reward/risk
- actual entry price
- actual exit price
- profit/loss
- comments (scan used, what did and didn't work, improvements for future)

A simple spreadsheet can be used to journal your watchlist and trades such as the one shown below in Figure 14.1.

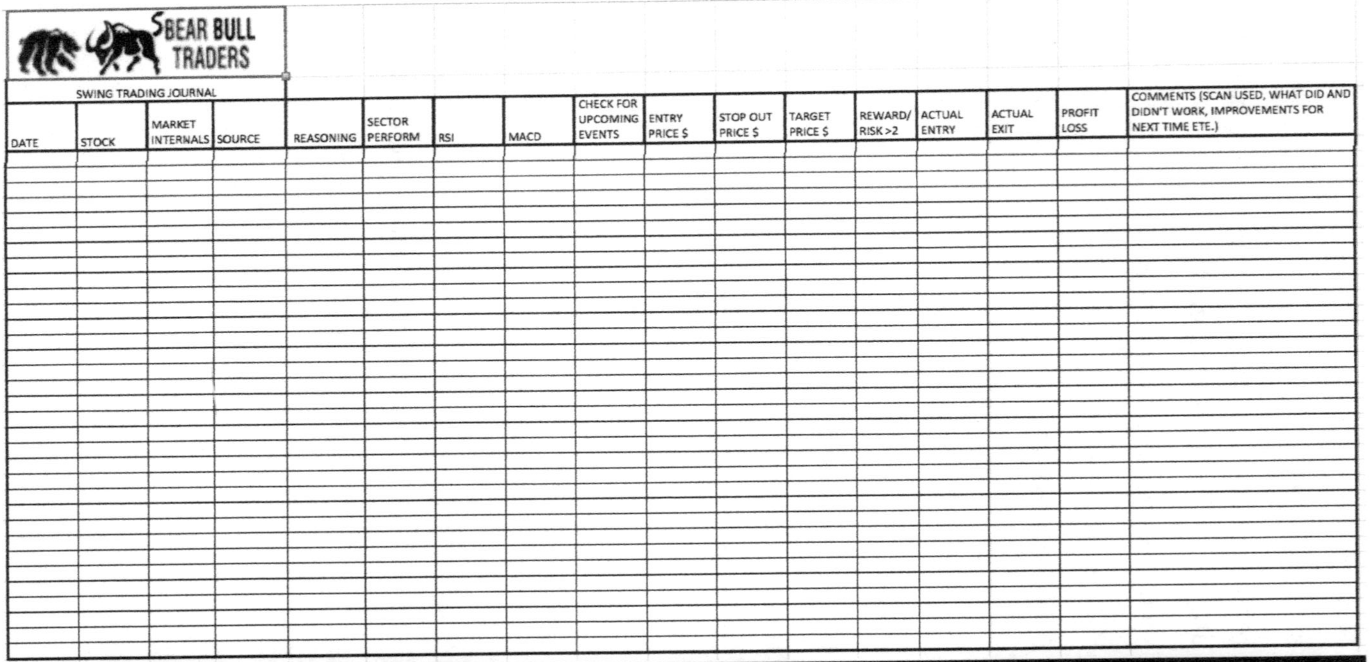

Figure 14.1 - An example of a spreadsheet based trade journal that you can use to record and review trades.

The trade journal shown above can be easily generated by anyone with basic spreadsheet skills. It is a suggested starting point and can be modified to suit your preferences and trading style.

Using this journaling tool should be relatively easy to figure out. As you do scans and develop trade ideas, you will start to complete a row entering the date, the stock symbol and the source of the idea. You then continue to do your investigative work on the security, such as checking the market internals, the performance of the sector your security is in and other indicators including the RSI and MACD to see if there is positive alignment with the trade you are considering. You also should check for coming events to make sure you're not buying, for example, just before an earnings release.

As you build a list of trading opportunities to monitor, you may want to consider doing this on a separate sheet and record your actual trades on another sheet. This will keep your active trade sheet less cluttered and enable you to see clearly what trades you are currently in versus ones that are "on watch". Most trading platforms have an alert feature that will also provide you with notification (email or text) that a price level has been hit in a stock you are monitoring for a possible entry or exit.

The next step in the process is to look at your potential entry, the downside risk and the target for your reward. With this information, you can determine the reward to risk ratio and see if it is equal to or more than 2. If the trade looks good, then you would try to get an entry on the security at around the price where you did the reward to risk calculation. If you do not get a fill close to that price and you have to chase the price up (in the case of a long) to get into the position, then it may negatively affect the reward to risk ratio. The number of shares you will purchase will depend on how much capital you decide to put at risk. I have recommended no more than a 2% capital risk on each trade.

Once you have a position, you should record your actual entry price and then monitor the position each day until your stop out price is hit and you have to sell for a loss, or your target is hit and you sell some or all for a profit. If you decide to hold some, then you would set your new stop for the remainder at or near your targeted selling price. Never let a winner turn into a loser and keep your rewards at least 2 times the risk that you take on a trade.

Your final step to close out the process is to complete the row by adding in the exit price, whether the trade was a profit or loss, and any thoughts you might have about how the trade went. What did you like about the trade? Are there things you would have done differently? Remember to stay positive. Hindsight is 20:20 and you can only make decisions based on the information you had at the time. Not all trades will work in your favor and some will work better than planned.

Developing a consistent routine of checking in with the markets, scanning for new opportunities and staying in touch with trends is the final step in the process of becoming a swing trader. Throughout this book, I have provided you with a roadmap on how to set up your trading business and have given you some ideas on possible strategies that could be used to find profitable trading opportunities. With the information and tools you now have at your disposal, this chapter serves to provide you with some insight and recommendations on how you should operate your business venture if you do decide to try swing trading.

Only you can decide if this type of trading is right for you and your personal situation. In the next chapter, I will provide you with some final thoughts to consider before you decide to take the next steps and try swing trading for yourself.

Chapter Summary

In chapter 14, I discussed setting goals and objectives for your swing trading business and developing a routine that you will use to find trading opportunities on an ongoing basis. It is also very important to continually review and monitor existing positions.

The section on setting of goals, objectives and strategies you may use in your business included the following points.

- Objectives or goals in your business are important to spell out so you know why you are trading and what specifically you hope to achieve.
- You should decide what markets and securities you will initially focus on. This will depend on your existing skill level, market conditions and your personal preferences.
- Another decision you need to make is in regard to the trading strategies and setups that you will use to enter and exit trades.
- When you are looking for trading opportunities you may also be constrained by the price of stock. Traders with smaller accounts will likely focus on lower-priced securities so they can take a large enough position to make a profitable trade after commission costs.
- You may also want to consider the time frames of a trade. Do you want to be in a trade for days or for weeks?

Once you have the answers to these questions and goals, you can start to build a trading routine that you should follow as consistently as possible. To build a routine you will need to consider the following.

- You will need to decide on how much time you want to dedicate to your business and when you are going to fit it into your day.
- You can consider combining some activities that you normally do, like exercising at a gym, with reviewing business information instead of listening to music.
- Constantly staying in touch with market conditions and trends in various sectors and industries is an important activity that needs to be done on an ongoing basis.
- It is important to have and maintain a routine as much as is possible so you can have consistent results.

Reviewing and recording is another process that a swing trader should do on a consistent basis. In this section, I introduced the trade journal and how to use it in your routine. Always stay in touch with market conditions by reviewing the internals, such as the percentage of new highs versus new lows and the percentage of stocks above the 50 and 200-day SMAs versus stocks below those SMAs.

- Market sentiment can also be gauged through the use of market websites, social media and just paying attention to the news flow.
- When you use one or more of the strategies I discussed to find a potential trade, use a trade journal like the one I presented to do a review process. This will help confirm if it is a trade worth acting on.
- Ensure you calculate the reward to risk ratio to confirm it is greater than or equal to 2.

- Your reward to risk ratio will be based on an assumed entry price. Be careful not to chase your desired entry price too far away from the target entry in an effort to get into the trade. Chasing the price will affect your reward to risk ratio.
- Once your trade is completed, finish the journal entries, including any thoughts you might have on what went well and what you might do differently next time.
- Stay positive even when trades do not work as planned. Hindsight is 20:20 and you can only make decisions based on the information that you had at the time.

CHAPTER 15

Final Thoughts

If you are new to trading, I suggest that you start out practicing the process first to see if it will work for you and your situation. You do not need a brokerage account in order to practice, and everything that you require to start swing trading is available for free on the Internet. As a new trader, you can do what is called "paper trading", where you go through the process of scanning for trades, identify opportunities and pretend to enter the trade. Start with an imaginary account size that is the same as you intend to begin with if you do take the next step and trade with real money. Try to keep your simulation as realistic as possible in every respect.

Journal your trades as you would with a real trade and see how they work out. If you find you enjoy the process and think it will work for you, then you can consider opening a brokerage account and putting your real capital at risk. Be aware that many traders say that it becomes a little more difficult when they switch from simulated or pretend accounts to trading with real money. This is because you are not as emotionally attached to your play money compared to your real money. Once emotions get added to the mix, trading can become more difficult.

For the more experienced traders, you will likely already know many of the concepts and principles set forth in this book. I hope that there was still enough new information to help you find and make more profitable swing trades.

Regardless of your level of experience, a swing trader gets to slow everything down, and that is an advantage, especially for new traders. You do not get caught up in a process where you need to make a decision in a matter of seconds. This type of pressure situation is where many day traders lose out and let their emotions get the better of them. Swing traders have the luxury of time to make their decisions and are less likely to make an impulsive trade move in the heat of the moment. Regardless, all of us have mental weaknesses that we must overcome as traders.

As a disciplined trader, you will do your scans of the charts, recognize patterns and develop trading strategies. You will make a plan and stick with it unless something fundamentally changes with the reasons you entered the trade. And that can happen. You should stay in tune with the market and be aware that you might need to adjust your trading strategies as the market sentiment changes. You must also accept that there is no shame in losing on a trade. Not all trades will go in your favor. You need to accept that and move on.

If you do not follow your trading plan when the trade does not work out, then you will likely pay the price in your account. Some traders are unwilling to accept a loss and exit stocks that trade against them. Others will take small profits early instead of waiting for their planned profit target. These are the actions of a trader who will struggle to make gains.

Last but not least, if you enjoyed reading this book and found it useful, I would very much appreciate if you took a few minutes to write a review on the Amazon website. The success of a book like this is based on honest reviews, and I will consider your comments in making revisions. If you have any feedback, feel free to send us an email.

Please remember that the author is NOT an investment advisory service, a registered investment advisor or a broker-dealer and I do not undertake to advise clients on which securities they should buy or sell for themselves. The information contained in this book is only a suggested starting point for doing additional independent research in order to allow you to form your own opinions regarding trading and investments. Investors and traders should always consult with their licensed financial advisors and tax advisors to determine the suitability of any investment.

Thank you for reading, and happy trading!

Glossary

A

Alert: brokerage trading platforms offer an alert feature that can be set up to advise a client by text or email that an event, such as a stock hitting a specific level, has occurred. You may be watching this stock and wanting to enter a trade once the specific event has occurred.

Algorithm: a proprietary computer program that executes trades based on programed inputs. The inputs could be technical indicators such as moving averages or they could be newswire feeds where computers will trade off of key words or phrases.

Ask: the price sellers are demanding in order to sell their stock. It's always higher than the bid price.

Average daily volume: the average number of shares traded each day in a particular stock. I don't trade stocks with an average daily volume of less than 200,000 shares. As a swing trader, you will want sufficient liquidity to be able to get in and out of the stock without difficulty. At times this term will also be referenced as "average volume".

Average relative volume: this is the number of shares traded in a stock compared to its average daily volume. I like to see stocks with an average relative volume greater than 1.5, which means the stock is trading more than 1.5 times its normal daily volume. This would likely be due to heightened interest by traders and investors in the stock. At times this term will also be referenced as "relative volume".

Average True Range/ATR: how large of a range in price a particular stock has on average each day, taking into account gaps that occur between market sessions.

Averaging down: a technique that some traders employ which involves adding more shares to a losing position in order to lower the average cost of that position. They hope the stock will eventually move back in their favor enough so that they can sell and break-even. I do not average down because this may magnify losses. I stick with my trading plan and sell when I hit my stop out price.

B

Bear: a seller or short seller of stock. If you hear the market is bear, it means the entire stock market is losing value because the sellers or short sellers are selling their stocks. In other words, the sellers are in control.

Bearish candlestick: a candlestick with a big filled body demonstrating that the open was at a high and the close was at a low. It tells you that the sellers are in control of the price for the period represented by the candlestick and it is not likely a good time to buy. Figure 7.4 illustrates 2 bearish candlesticks.

Beta: the amount an individual stock will move in relation to the market or underlying asset. High beta stocks or ETFs will move more on a percentage basis than the market or underlying asset.

Bid: the price that traders and/or investors are willing to pay to purchase a stock at a particular time. It's always lower than the ask price.

Bid-ask spread: the difference between what traders are willing to pay to purchase a particular stock and what other traders are demanding in order to sell that stock at any given moment. It will change throughout the trading day. Traders will refer to a "wide spread" when the bid and ask are far apart. This spread is partly a function of the stock price. For example, a $300.00 per share stock might have a bid-ask spread of $1.00 versus a highly traded $20.00 per share stock where the bid-ask spread would be $0.02.

Broker: the licensed company that buys and sells stocks on various stock exchanges based on instructions taken from investors and traders. These instructions can be placed online and directed to the exchanges or taken by an employee at the company which executes the trade. Having an employee place a trade is much less common today versus 30 years ago when it was the only way to buy and sell stocks. Using an employee is also a much slower process compared to trading online.

Bull: a buyer of stock. If you hear the market is bull, it means the entire stock market is gaining value because the buyers are purchasing stocks. In other words, the buyers are in control.

Bull flag: a type of candlestick pattern that resembles a flag on a pole. You will see several large candles going up (like a pole) and a series of small candles moving sideways (like a flag). After consolidation, the price will break higher.

Bullish candlestick: a candlestick with a large body toward the upside. It tells you that the buyers are in control of the price and will likely keep pushing the price up. Figure 7.3 illustrates 2 bullish candlesticks.

Buying long: buying a stock with the expectation that its price will go higher.

Buying power: this represents the capital in a trader's brokerage account. Buying power will vary depending on the type of account you have, the broker's rules on lending if you have a margin account and what you hold in the account such as cash, shares etcetera.

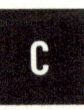

C

Candlestick: a very common way to chart the price movement of stocks. It allows you to easily see the opening price, the highest price, the lowest price and the closing price value for each time period you wish to display.

Chasing the stock: chasing happens when you try to enter a position and the price keeps moving away from your desired entry. For example, you want to go long on a stock at $4.50 per share and the share price keeps moving higher above your bid. As the share price moves higher, you keep entering a higher and higher bid hoping to get filled. This will negatively affect your reward to risk ratio if you chase the price up too far from your desired entry price.

Chatroom: a community of traders. Many can be found on the Internet. As a reader of this book, you are welcome to join the BearBullTraders.com chatroom.

Choppy price action: occurs when the price of a stock cycles up and down in a range with relatively small movements of price within the cycles. You should try to avoid stocks with choppy price movements and wait for signals that the stock price is ready to move outside of the trading price range.

Churning: this refers to a specific type of price movement where a security will not be trending in any direction. Instead, there are small waves of erratic buying and selling with no significant price movement in one direction or the other.

Close ("the close"): this refers to the last hour the stock market is open: 3:00 to 4:00 PM ET. Higher levels of volatility or price movements can occur in the last hour of trading.

Consolidation period: consolidation usually happens after a sharp move up or down in the price of a stock. Some traders are getting out of their positions while others that missed the move are entering.

This fight between the buyers and sellers causes the stock price to pause before resuming the original trend or reversing.

D

Day trading: the business of trading stocks based on very short-term technical signals. Time frames of 1 minute and 5 minutes are commonly used to find trades. Day traders do not hold any stocks overnight; any stocks they purchase during the day are sold by the end of the trading day. At the close of every trading day, a day trader holds all cash in their accounts.

Death cross: occurs when an uptrending stock changes to a downtrend. The death cross event occurs when the faster moving 50-day simple moving average (SMA) crosses the slower reacting 200-day SMA. The 50-day moves from above the 200-day to below it when the cross is made.

Doji: an important candlestick pattern that comes in various shapes or forms but are all characterized by having either no body or a very small body. A doji indicates indecision and means that a fight is underway between the buyers and the sellers.

Double bottom: a "W" pattern that occurs in a chart when a stock price drops to a low, bounces higher temporarily, and then drops again back to the previous low. On the second dip lower, the buyers take control again, thus moving the price higher. This creates a strong level of support and is an indication that the stock price will likely continue to move higher.

Double top: an "M" pattern that occurs in a chart when a stock price rises to a high and then drops back temporarily. The price pushes higher again but fails to make a new high on the second run higher. The sellers then take control again, moving the price lower. This creates a strong level of resistance and is an indication that the stock price trend will likely continue to move lower.

E

"Either or" order: this is 2 orders that are entered by a trader. The orders are linked so that as soon as 1 of the orders is filled, the other order is cancelled. This allows you to both set a stop-loss to protect from excessive losses and also enter an order at a profit-taking price.

Entry point: when you recognize a pattern developing in your charts, your entry point is where you enter the trade.

Exchange-Traded Fund/ETF: an investment fund traded on exchanges and composed of assets such as stocks, bonds, currencies and indexes to name just a few. There is a huge variety of ETFs that are available today where you can play almost any sector or tradable asset.

Exit point: this is the price where you plan to dispose of all or part of your position in a security. It can be the profit target price or it could be the stop-loss price. You make a plan before taking an entry and you stick to your plan unless there is a good fundamental reason to change the plan.

Exponential moving average/EMA: a form of moving average where more weight is given to the closer dates in the moving average period. The EMA will respond more quickly compared to the simple moving average where all prices over the period are given an equal weight.

F

Flag pattern: a chart pattern that resembles a flagpole and flag. Flag patterns can be bullish or bearish and represent a strong move, followed by a period of consolidation (which forms the flag part of the pattern) and then there is a continuation in the trend.

Float: the number of shares in a particular company available for trading.

Forex: the global foreign currency exchange market where currencies are traded. All currencies are traded in pairs, such as the US dollar against the Euro.

Forward guidance: refers to comments made by a company's management that is related to how they see business prospects in the future. The companies may provide earnings projections for coming quarters. These remarks are usually made during an earnings report conference call and can have a significant impact on the stock's future price movement.

Fundamental catalyst: some positive or negative news associated with a stock or a sector, such as a US Food and Drug Administration approval or disapproval of a medicine, or a series of hurricanes in the Gulf affecting oil and building supply prices.

Futures: futures are a contract that requires the buyer to purchase an asset at a specific price and future date (such as oil, lumber, wheat, currencies). A seller of the futures contract is contracted to deliver that asset at a specific date and price. These financial instruments are highly risky, only used by sophisticated traders and big companies, and often as part of hedging strategies.

G

Gap down: occurs when a stock closes the previous day at 1 price and opens the next morning at a lower price, leaving a gap between the 2 prices. Small gaps will often happen between trading days and large gaps will happen if there has been some negative news regarding the stock, associated sector or market.

Gap up: occurs when a stock closes the previous day at 1 price and opens the next morning at a higher price, leaving a gap between the 2 prices. Small gaps will often happen between trading days and large gaps will happen if there has been some positive news regarding the stock, associated sector or market.

Golden cross: occurs when a downtrending stock changes to an uptrend. The golden cross event occurs when the faster moving 50-day simple moving average (SMA) crosses the slower reacting 200-day SMA. The 50-day moves from below the 200-day to above it when the cross is made.

H

High-Frequency Trades/HFT: a type of trading done by the computers on the various exchanges. These trades are being executed at a very high frequency and often to make tiny gains on price movements in stocks. There's no need for swing traders to be concerned about this activity because swing trades take place over days, weeks or even longer periods of time.

I

Illiquid stock: a stock that has a very low volume of shares traded during the day. These stocks can be more difficult to sell and buy and therefore you may not get the price you had hoped to get on entry or exit. The bid-ask spread can also be wider in the absence of higher daily trading volume.

Indecision candlestick: a type of candlestick that has a small body and similarly sized high tails and low tails. They are referred to as spinning tops and they usually indicate a fight for control of the price between the buyers and sellers. It's important to recognize an indecision candlestick because they often indicate a pending price change.

Indicator: an indicator is a numeric value produced from a mathematical calculation. The calculation can be based on a stock's price or it can be based on both price and volume. These numeric values can be used as a gauge of trader and investor sentiment toward a stock or security and are often used to scan the market for trading opportunities. Understanding these indicators can help you find and execute trades.

Institutional trader: a trader who works for an investment bank, brokerage firm, mutual fund or hedge fund.

Intraday: trading all within the same day, between 9:30 AM and 4:00 PM ET.

Investing: investing involves purchasing some asset and expecting it to grow in value in the short term or the long term.

Investment account: a regular brokerage account that allows you to trade stocks up to the maximum value of the cash in your account.

L

Lagging indicator: lagging indicators are indicators that provide you with information based on activity that has already taken place, but they do not provide any guidance for a future event.

Leading indicator: leading indicators are indicators that provide some information about what the future could hold. For example, an increase in building permits filed likely indicates higher levels of construction activity.

Level 2: a tool commonly used in day trading that will show you buying interest and selling interest (bid and ask) at various price levels. It is not applicable to swing trading.

Leverage: the margin your broker provides you based on the capital in your account. The leverage varies between brokers, what you are holding in the account (cash and securities) and share price.

Limit order: an instruction you give to your broker to buy or sell a stock at a specific price versus a market order which is filled at the best possible price at that time. There is a chance the limit order will never be filled if the stock price moves away from your order.

Liquidity: liquidity means there is sufficient trading volume in a stock for you to be able to enter and exit a trade around where you target. You always want to ensure you can easily get in and out of a trade.

Long: being long or "going long" means you have purchased stock in the hope that it will increase in price. For example, "long 100 shares Tesla" means you have purchased 100 shares of Tesla in anticipation of their price increasing.

Low float stock: this is a stock with a low supply of tradable shares. Usually, this means less than 10 million shares available for trading. When there is a large demand for shares in low float stocks, their price will rise dramatically due to the shortage of shares available to own and trade. These stocks are typically lower-priced shares and can represent good trading opportunities.

M

Margin: the leverage or borrowing power your broker gives you to trade with based on the assets (money and stock) that you hold in your account.

Margin account: an account that allows you to buy and sell using margin or leverage based on assets held in the account.

Margin call: a notification you receive from your broker that the assets in your account no longer meet their lending requirements. This will happen when you have trades that are going against you and the account value is decreasing. Immediate action needs to be taken by adding more cash to the account or exiting some current stock positions.

Marketable limit order: an instruction you give to your broker to immediately buy or sell a specific stock within a range of prices that you specify. This helps you to get a fill but not to overpay for an entry.

Market cap/market capitalization: a company's market capitalization is the total dollar value that investors consider a company to be worth. It is calculated by multiplying the share float by the price of the shares. A company with a float of 50 million shares that trades at $10.00 per share is considered to have a market cap of $500 million.

Market maker: a broker-dealer who offers shares for sale or purchase on a stock exchange. The firm holds a certain number of shares of a particular stock in order to facilitate the trading of that stock at the exchange.

Market order: an instruction you give to your broker to immediately buy or sell a specific stock at the current price offered on the bid or the ask. You get an immediate fill on your order but the price could be subject to volatility and there is a small chance you may not get the entry price that was expected.

Medium float stock: a stock with a medium-sized float of between 10 million and 500 million shares.

Mega cap stock: a stock with a very large number of shares. For example, Apple Inc. has over 5 billion shares available for trading.

Micro-cap stock: a stock with a low supply of shares available to trade at a relatively low price. The market capitalization of the micro-cap stock (also called small cap) ranges between $50 million and up to about $300 million.

Mid-day: 11:00 AM to 2:00 PM ET. During this time the market trading volume often drops off a little and then picks up again into the close.

Moving average/MA: this is a widely used trading indicator that is calculated by taking past closing stock prices for a certain period and then averaging them over that time. Two commonly used MAs are the simple moving average (SMA), and the exponential moving average (EMA), which gives more weight to more recent prices and therefore reacts more quickly to changes in sentiment.

O

Open ("the open"): the first one hour the stock market is open: 9:30 to 10:30 AM ET. Trading volume is often higher during this period.

Options: a specific type of vehicle for trading. Options are a contract that gives a purchaser a right to buy or sell a security at a certain price by a specific date. They can be used in a number of different trading strategies and are considered to be a more sophisticated trading vehicle.

Over-the-counter (OTC) market: the OTC is another venue or way to trade different securities such as less regulated stocks.

P

Paper trading: this is a technique that can be used by new traders to develop and test their skills before risking their money. You start with an imaginary account and go through the process of scanning and finding stocks for trading. You record the trades that you would take on paper with a plan for an exit (profit or loss). You then monitor the stock and record the profit or loss on the trade after one of your exit points are hit.

Penny stock: the shares of companies that trade at lower prices. The share prices are typically under $1.00 per share.

Position sizing: refers to how many shares you buy or sell per trade. Recall that you should not risk more than 2% of your account in any one trade.

Pre-market trading: regular trading on the stock markets starts at 9:30 AM ET and ends at 4:00 PM ET. Some brokerages will allow traders to trade before the official open and after the close. This is called pre-market and after-market trading. During this period, liquidity is often lower and volatility is much higher. This is not a good time for swing traders to trade.

Previous day's close: this is the closing price of a stock on the previous day. If a stock closes on or near the high of the day, then it may be an indicator that the stock price will continue higher on the following day.

Price action: a term that is used by traders to describe the movement in price of a stock. For example, if a stock price is dropping, price action is considered poor and likely a good short opportunity.

Profit target: this is the expected exit price of a profitable trade opportunity identified by a swing trader. It is based on reviewing your charts and identifying the reward and risk in each trade.

R

Real-time market data: real-time market data allows you to see current bid and ask prices as well as last trade price and volume of shares. You need to ensure that you are using real-time data as some sources offer data that can be delayed 15 minutes or longer.

Relative Strength Index/RSI: a technical indicator that compares the magnitude of recent gains and losses in the price of stocks over a period of time to measure the speed and change of price movement. Your scanner software or platform will automatically calculate the RSI for you. RSI values range from 0 to 100, with an extreme RSI below 20 or above 80 definitely catching my interest.

Retail trader: individual traders who do not work for a brokerage firm or manage other people's money.

Risk management: this is one of the most important skills that a successful swing trader must master. This is done by only entering trades with a good reward to risk ratio, risking 2% or less of your capital on any trade and following your trading plan with stop-losses and targeted profit gains.

Risk to reward ratio: this ratio is determined by assessing how much you expect to profit in a trade versus the most that you would be prepared to lose before exiting the position. Good trades offer at least 2 times the reward compared to the risk. For example, if you expect to make a $2.50 per share gain and are prepared to stop out if you lose more than $1.00 per share, then the reward is 2.5 times the risk and it is a good trade from a risk to reward perspective.

Rotation: refers to a process where investors and traders move their money from one sector to another. One sector may fall out of favor with investors and they will move their money to another sector that they consider to have a better opportunity for a return on their investment.

S

Scaling out: a process you use to take advantage of a longer-term trend in a security. Instead of selling all of a profitable position at a target price, you will sell a portion of the position at the first target and hold the remainder for more gains. You should move the stop out price up to a level that is close to the first targeted sell price so gains are not given back.

Scanner: software that you program with various criteria in order to find stocks that could be setting up for a profitable trade. Scanners are available on the Internet and are also supplied by some brokerage firms as part of their trading platform.

Sector: a sector is considered to be a group of stocks that are all in the same business. For example, the financial sector refers to banks and other financial institutions, with companies such as Wells Fargo, Toronto-Dominion Bank and JPMorgan Chase in that sector.

Short: an abbreviated form of "short selling". It occurs when you borrow shares from your broker and sell them. You are expecting the price of the shares to drop and you are hoping to return the shares by buying them back at a lower price. If you say that you are short IBM, for example, it means you have borrowed and sold IBM shares and are hoping their price goes lower.

Short interest: this is the number of shares in a stock that have been reported to be sold short by the brokers.

Brokerages are required to report to the exchanges how many shares they have loaned out for short positions. A very high short interest (greater than 20%) is an indication that a lot of investors and traders hold a very negative sentiment toward a stock and the consensus is that the share price is going to go lower. It can also cause a "short squeeze".

Short selling: this occurs when you borrow shares from a broker and sell them with the expectation that the price will go lower and can be bought back at a lower price. You return the borrowed shares to your broker and keep the profit.

Short selling restriction/SSR: a restriction placed on a stock when it is down 10% or more from the previous day's closing price. Regulators at the exchanges place a restriction on short selling of a stock to prevent short sellers from continuing to drive the price down. The restriction only allows a short entry when the price of the stock is going higher.

Short squeeze: occurs in a stock where there is a significant short interest. If some positive news comes out about the company, the price may move aggressively higher. Traders who are short get very worried and start buying shares to cover their positions. Combined with the investors and traders buying on the good news, this can create a frenzy of buying which will drive the stock price higher and higher. Short squeezes are bad to be caught in and good to ride higher.

Simple moving average/SMA: a form of moving average that is calculated by adding up the closing price of a stock for a number of time periods and then dividing that figure by the number of time periods. As the time period moves forward, the oldest price is dropped and the newest period price is entered to calculate a new value.

Simulator: some brokerages offer simulator accounts that start with a set amount of "fictitious funds" or "imaginary money". You can use the simulator to trade with the imaginary money, allowing you to develop your skills and build experience in trading. This is similar to "paper trading".

Size: the bid-ask information on a stock order page will also likely display the "size" or number of shares being bid for (wanting to buy) and the number of shares being offered for sale. This will change often throughout the trading day on an actively traded stock.

Spinning top: a type of candlestick that has similarly sized high wicks and low wicks that are usually larger than the body. They can be called indecision candlesticks and they indicate that the buyers and sellers have equal power and are fighting between themselves. It's important to recognize a spinning top because it may very well indicate a pending price change.

Split adjusted: after a stock split the price will drop in relation to how many new shares were given to current shareholders. A stock may be split more than once if it keeps going higher over time and, with each split, the price will drop. A split-adjusted price is the price a stock would have been before the split or splits.

Standard lot: a standard trading size is 100 shares. The "size" column on the stock order page will indicate how many standard lots of shares are being offered for sale or purchase. For example, a bid size of "4" means there are buyers waiting at the bid to purchase 400 shares at the bid price.

Stock in play: stocks in play are shares of a company that are being actively traded by traders and investors. They are characterized by higher than normal trading volumes in the shares being traded and by more price movement than previously experienced.

Stock split: on occasion a company will want their share price lower to allow more potential investors to buy and own their stock. For example, a stock that trades at $300.00 per share may be too expensive for many investors to own. To address this issue, a company will split the stock so all of the existing shareholders own more shares. In order to do this, they could perhaps offer another share for every one a shareholder currently owns. With twice as many shares in the market, for the value of the company to remain the same the stock price will drop by half. In our example, the share price would drop to $150.00.

Stock ticker: short abbreviations of usually 1 to 5 letters that represent the stock at the exchange. All stocks have ticker symbols. Apple Inc.'s ticker, for example, is AAPL.

Stop-loss: prior to entering a stock position, you must determine what is the maximum you are prepared to lose on a trade. This level could be based on an indicator or pattern. You enter a position hoping for a profitable trade but if this does not occur then the stop-loss is used as an exit point to protect your capital from greater losses.

Support or resistance level: these are areas in a chart where share prices often reverse or pause. There can be areas where resistance to further price increases occur and there are areas where the downward price pressure ends and the share price pauses or moves higher. These areas often repeat, as if the share price has a memory.

Swing trading: the serious business of trading stocks that you hold for a period of time, generally from 1 day to a few weeks. Swing trading is a completely different business than day trading is.

T

Technical analysis: this is an analysis method that is used to forecast the future direction of prices by studying past market data. The data used is primarily price and volume.

Trade management: this is what you will do once you enter a trade. You will monitor your position and be prepared to take a profit or get stopped out and take a loss.

Trade plan/trading plan: the plan you develop before entering a trade. The plan includes determining an entry price and an exit strategy with a profit target price and stop-loss price. The plan concludes by closing the position and then recording and reviewing the result.

Trading platform: this is the software that you use for sending orders to the exchange. All brokers will offer a trading platform.

Trailing stop: this is a technique used to stay in a position as it continues to move in your favor. As the trend continues, you move your stop price to trail the move so that when the trend does finally change, you capture most of the profit in the trend.

V

Volume: the number of shares that are traded during a period of time. The period could be daily, weekly, monthly, etc., or the current volume during the trading day.

W

Warrant: a right to purchase shares in a company at a specific price. Warrants have an expiry date so they can expire worthless if the actual share price does not move above the purchase price on the warrant.

Watchlist: you may build a list of stocks that you are interested in taking a position in. You may very well not be ready to enter at the time the stock first catches your interest and, instead, you are waiting for a confirming event like a bounce off of a double bottom. In this case, you build and maintain a watchlist of potential future trades. The brokerage may also offer an alert feature on their platform so you will be advised when the confirming event occurs.

Made in the USA
Monee, IL
29 July 2021